LIBERTY OVER LONDON BRIDGE

# LIBERTY OVER LONDON BRIDGE

## A HISTORY OF THE PEOPLE OF SOUTHWARK

MARGARET WILLES

YALE UNIVERSITY PRESS
NEW HAVEN AND LONDON

Published with assistance from the foundation established in memory of Oliver Baty Cunningham of the Class of 1917, Yale College.

For information about this and other Yale University Press publications, please contact:
U.S. Office:    sales.press@yale.edu    yalebooks.com
Europe Office:    sales@yaleup.co.uk    yalebooks.co.uk

Set in Adobe Caslon Pro by IDSUK (DataConnection) Ltd
Printed in Great Britain by TJ Books Limited, Padstow, Cornwall

Library of Congress Control Number: 2023947206

ISBN 978-0-300-27220-8

A catalogue record for this book is available from the British Library.

10 9 8 7 6 5 4 3 2 1

# CONTENTS

# CONTENTS

# ILLUSTRATIONS

## Plates

I. Claude de Jongh, *View of Old London Bridge from the West*, 1650. © Victoria and Albert Museum, London.

II. The north bank of the Thames, viewed from Southwark, c.1630. Digital Image Library / Alamy.

III. The high altar screen in Southwark Cathedral. © Angelo Hornak.

IV. Nuns and a ferryman from a stained-glass window in Southwark Cathedral's retrochoir. © Angelo Hornak.

V. Tomb of John Gower. Photograph by Adrian Pingstone.

VI. Monument of the Humble family. © Angelo Hornak.

VII. Tomb effigy of Lancelot Andrewes. © Angelo Hornak.

VIII. A street performance of Charles Dickens' *Oliver Twist*, photograph by E. Bacon, 1928. E. Bacon / Hulton Archive via Getty Images.

IX. William Hogarth, *Southwark Fair*, 1733. incamerastock / Alamy.

X. The Lions part leading a parade through Borough Market. Photograph by Issy Croker for *The Borough Market Cookbook*. © Hodder & Stoughton 2018.

### In the text

### Maps

# ACKNOWLEDGEMENTS

I am very grateful to a whole range of people who have helped me to discover the rich facets of Southwark. From the cathedral, thanks to Dean Andrew Nunn, Jon Dollin and Jessica Kingsley. Thank you to Martha Carlin for helping me to avoid, I hope, the pitfalls of interpretations of medieval writings. To Bishop Stephen Platten for circumnavigating the pitfalls of Tudor and Jacobean religious non-conformity. To Alderman Tim McNally and Chris Wilson for guiding me on Southwark in the twenty-first century. To Gary Maygold for showing me the delights of the Biscuit Museum, and to Caroline Swan for introducing me to Southwark's burial grounds. To Kate Howell for information on Borough Market. To Robin Reynolds for help on the complexities of the historical perspectives of London, and for allowing me to reproduce his drawing. My lack of technological skills has been nullified in part by the help of Mike Patterson and Nina Sophia Miralles. Lastly, thank you to Julian Loose at Yale University Press for taking on the book, and to Rachael Lonsdale and Frazer Martin for their wise editorial support.

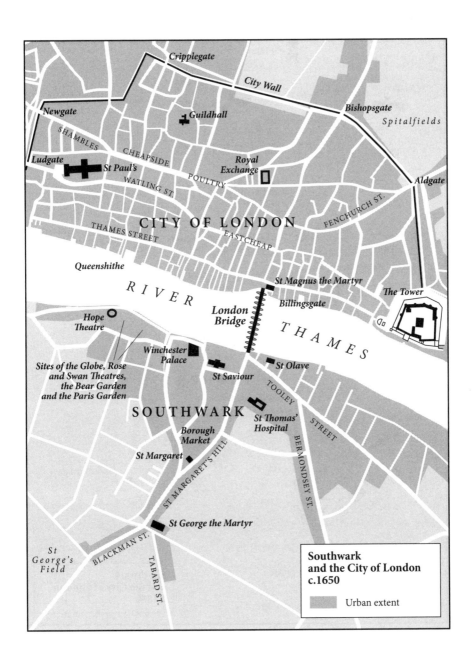

Southwark
and the City of London
c.1650

▨ Urban extent

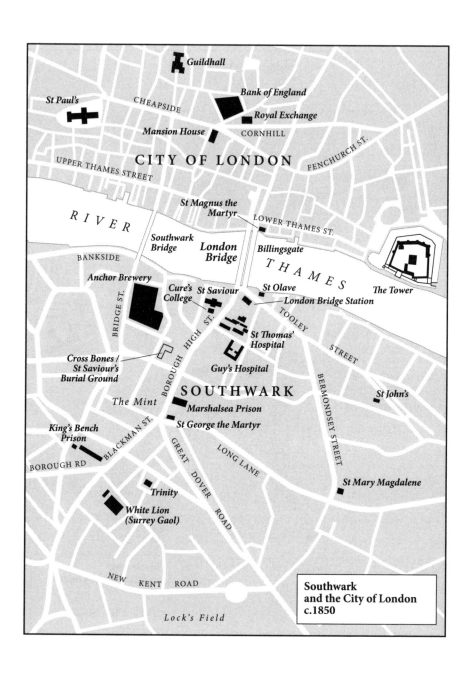

Guildhall

St Paul's

CHEAPSIDE

Bank of England

Royal Exchange

Mansion House

CORNHILL

CITY OF LONDON

FENCHURCH ST.

UPPER THAMES STREET

RIVER

St Magnus the
Martyr

LOWER THAMES ST.

Southwark
Bridge

London
Bridge

Billingsgate

BANKSIDE

THAMES

Anchor Brewery

BRIDGE ST.

Cure's
College

St Saviour

St Olave

London Bridge Station

The Tower

TOOLEY

BOROUGH HIGH ST.

St Thomas'
Hospital

Cross Bones /
St Saviour's
Burial Ground

Guy's Hospital

SOUTHWARK

STREET

BERMONDSEY STREET

St John's

The Mint

Marshalsea Prison

BLACKMAN ST.

St George the Martyr

King's Bench
Prison

BOROUGH RD

GREAT DOVER ROAD

LONG LANE

St Mary Magdalene

Trinity

White Lion
(Surrey Gaol)

NEW KENT ROAD

Lock's Field

Southwark
and the City of London
c.1850

# Introduction

One of the most striking things about Southwark is that, although it is one of the oldest parts of London, it is so often overlooked, or scarcely considered, in histories of the city. Royal London, the stuff of great occasion and pomp; civic London, with the Lord Mayor and his aldermen in fine procession every autumn: these are the images that are so often presented as historic London. Yet Southwark is rich in history, and the community that has lived here over the centuries has been equally rich in character.

My focus is what is described as 'Old Southwark', an area that resembles the delta of the Nile, roughly triangular in shape, with Bankside stretching along to the west to Lambeth and Tooley Street to the east to Bermondsey, while southwards runs Borough High Street. Southwark has long held the alternative name of Borough, because here in Anglo-Saxon times a *burh* was created as part of Alfred the Great's system of fortifications to protect his kingdom from the Vikings. It was vital that the southern approach to the City via London Bridge should be defended as the one link across the Thames until the eighteenth century.

'Liberty' appears in the title of the book for various reasons. The first relates to the particular land ownership in medieval Southwark, which was based on a group of manors, some of which were known as liberties as they lay outside the jurisdiction of the Crown and the City. As a result, certain activities could take place here that were not allowed north of the river. The writer V.S. Pritchett, who was brought up in Southwark, wryly points out in *London Perceived*: 'There is usually money at the bottom of the London liberties: there has been nothing abstract in the London view of the desirable life.'

In the liberty of the Clink belonging to the Bishops of Winchester, for example, brothels in the Middle Ages were licensed. The prostitutes, known as the Bishop of Winchester's Geese, represented a valuable source of episcopal income. The Clink was also the bishops' private gaol, and it has come down in the English language as an alternative name for a prison. Here is a paradox, for the liberty of one person is bondage for another. In the troubled years of the sixteenth and early seventeenth centuries, religious dissidents were imprisoned in the Clink. Some suffered death for their faith; many were able to find liberty by making the perilous journey to the early colonies across the Atlantic Ocean, including John Harvard, whose name is enshrined in American academe.

One man who suffered the terrible death by burning at the stake during the reign of Mary Tudor was Prebendary John Rogers, following his trial for heresy in what is now the retrochoir of Southwark Cathedral. The cathedral, dedicated to St Saviour and St Mary Overie, lying 'over the river' as its name suggests, sits like a bird on its nest, amid soaring buildings such as the Shard, currently the city's tallest structure. This is in marked contrast to London's other cathedral, St Paul's, which has dominated the skyline north of the Thames ever since the Normans created a monumental symbol of Christianity a thousand years ago. Although cathedral status for Southwark was only achieved in 1905, the building was a priory in the Middle Ages, becoming a parish church during the Reformation. Indeed, legend has it that originally, in AD 606, there was a house of nuns founded here. If this is true, then the foundation of both churches dates from almost exactly the same time: St Paul's in 604, and St Mary Overie two years later.

My story of Southwark is thematic rather than chronological, though it does proceed down the centuries from the rather exclusive Roman settlement through to the current day. The cultural aspects of Southwark life are rich, with three of our greatest writers particularly associated with the Borough: Geoffrey Chaucer, William Shakespeare and Charles Dickens. They, along with other commentators, provide a treasure house of stories, featuring not just the great and the good, but ordinary members of the community, many of them nameless.

This richness, not of wealth but of association, was very evident when the parish church of St Saviour was transformed into Southwark Cathedral at the beginning of the twentieth century. The niches of an early-sixteenth-century screen behind the high altar were accordingly filled with two rows of figures, reflecting the early ecclesiastical history, the saints of the original parish churches, prominent bishops of Winchester and, as mentioned above, John Rogers, martyred for his religious views but also playing a significant role in the publication of the Bible in English.

Stained-glass windows have been installed in the church depicting figures from Shakespeare's plays, and Chaucer's pilgrims setting out from the Tabard Inn on the High Street in his *Canterbury Tales*. Literary figures such as Samuel Johnson and Oliver Goldsmith figure in other windows, although Johnson's contribution to Southwark was to help his friend Hester Thrale run the huge Anchor Brewery, and Goldsmith's was to practise as an apothecary. The mercantile community is recalled by the monuments to be found in the cathedral, some of them made by local artists and craftsmen, often religious refugees from mainland Europe who formed an important element of Borough's population.

Several of the themes on which I have focused stem from the location and topography of Southwark. As long as there was just one bridge across the Thames, all the land traffic had to come through the Borough to gain access to the City. To cater for this traffic, a series of inns lined Borough High Street, or Long Southwark, as it was often called. These inns were considerable in their size, providing accommodation both for travellers and for their horses. The footfall of these establishments can still be seen, although only one survives: the George Inn, now looked after by the National Trust. Traffic of course moved in the other direction too, avoiding the great bottle-neck that was Old London Bridge. Thus, Geoffrey Chaucer's pilgrims set off from the Tabard to make their way down to Canterbury, and Harry Bailly, the host of the inn, is based on a real Southwark figure.

Much of Old Southwark runs along the south bank of the Thames, so water transport is an enduring theme right through to the end of the nineteenth century. Not only did boats that were unloading goods dock along the bank, but it was also the home of thousands of ferrymen, making up a substantial proportion of the Southwark community. The most famous of these was John Taylor, the 'Water Poet', who produced not only verses but also long commentaries on early-seventeenth-century life, some of them composed in his fight against the construction of more bridges across the river. We know a lot about Taylor because of his writing, but evidence shows that ferrymen in general were forthright in their views both on Thames life and on the religious debates of the sixteenth and seventeenth centuries.

At this time Bankside became the centre of entertainment for London, free from the regulations that prohibited theatres in the City. John Taylor and his fellow ferrymen would bring theatregoers across to Bankside, where they could also enjoy the spectacle of animal baiting and pay a visit to one of the many brothels. So many of the prostitutes remain anonymous, but one stands out: Bess Broughton, a high-class courtesan residing in a brothel known as Holland's Leaguer. This was an appropriate description of the building, for it was like a military encampment, located in the watery area to the south of Bankside. A play was written about her and Holland's Leaguer in 1631, at the time when the Southwark playhouses were closing down and the West End was becoming the theatrical heartland of London.

However, dramatic performances continued to be enjoyed in Southwark at the annual fair. This began in medieval times and became one of the great fairs of England. We have pen portraits of it from the two diarists Pepys and Evelyn, and, from a century later, a great painting by William Hogarth showing many of the acts and characters. The presence of this important fair underlines how Southwark has long been a centre of commerce and a flourishing town in its own right. The fair only took place on a few days in the year, but there was also a market on Borough High Street, again dating back to medieval times. Both the fair and the market were closed down in the mid-eighteenth century, but the parishioners of St Saviour's were able to secure a fixed market close to their church: this is now the world-famous Borough Market.

Southwark has also long been a centre for medicine. The Augustinian canons of the priory church established a hospital dedicated to St Thomas Becket on the east side of Borough High Street. During the Reformation the dedication was switched to St Thomas the Apostle thanks to the visceral animosity of Henry VIII to the opposition that Becket had offered to his king. St Thomas' became one of the great hospitals of London, joined in the eighteenth century by an establishment founded by the wealthy bookseller Thomas Guy. Although the writer Oliver Goldsmith is depicted in a window in the cathedral for his Southwark connection, his role as an apothecary was not a successful one. Another literary figure, John Keats, proved an able medical assistant until he abandoned the rough and tumble of early-nineteenth-century hospital life to devote himself to poetry. St Thomas' moved to Lambeth in the nineteenth century, selling out to the railways on the receipt of an offer that could not be refused, but Guy's Hospital remains on its original site.

The railways came early to Southwark, with London Bridge station opening in 1836. It was set high, with passengers climbing up to reach the platforms, and the tracks were laid over on arches running south and east down to Surrey and Kent. The railway companies were able to buy land comparatively cheaply and to undertake widespread demolition of housing. Not only was the community of Southwark affected, but the coming of the railways resulted in the end of the raison d'être of the great inns that lined Borough High Street. The original line stopped at London Bridge, with passengers required to travel to the City and West End by road, but soon developers set their sights on constructing bridges across the river. The purchase of the site of St Thomas' Hospital was the result of one such development, and the skyline of Southwark is still dominated by trains.

Southwark has always been a place of factories and workshops, but the coming of the Industrial Revolution was particularly felt here, with many businesses of a noxious nature, such as tanning and hat-making, which the City was only too happy to keep at a distance, on the other side of the Thames. The novels of Charles Dickens and the reports of social reformers such as Henry Mayhew and John Hollinghurst provide vivid descriptions of this part of Southwark in the Victorian period. Matters did not improve with the arrival of the twentieth century, with the borough seeing particularly heavy bombardment during the Second World War. It was the closure of the docks and the redevelopment of the riverside from the 1970s that was to transform this area of deprivation.

Today, 'Old Southwark' contains resonances of the past and of the people who lived here, and I have brought in many of these. Just as the herb garret overlooking the former operating theatre of St Thomas' Hospital is a reminder of Southwark as a medical centre, so the Globe Theatre, the brainchild of the American actor and director Sam Wanamaker, takes us back to Tudor and Jacobean times, when Bankside entertained all of London. Next door, the Bankside Power Station, now the home of the modern art collection of the Tate Gallery, recalls how the Industrial Revolution hung heavy upon Southwark. However, flourishing Borough Market, the heir to the fair and the markets along Long Southwark, is a reminder of the enduring characteristic of both the area and the people who live and work here, making it one of the most vibrant areas of London.

# 1

## Setting the Scene

The settlement of London, or Londinium, as it was called by the Romans, was established at a point where the River Thames could be crossed with comparative ease. In his history of the Gallic Wars, Julius Caesar wrote that the river was fordable at only one point, and even then, with difficulty. Southwark, or 'the South Work', was developed at the southern end of this crossing. There has been debate about the origin of the name Londinium. Geoffrey of Monmouth, writing in the 1140s, maintained that it was named after a British warrior king, Lud. Over the centuries various attempts have been made to solve the etymological mystery. One modern suggestion is that the name derives from 'Plowonida', meaning 'swim' or 'boat' river. As the Celts could not pronounce 'p', it became 'Lownida', and for the Romans when they arrived in Britain, Londinium.[1]

The one certainty is that the river played a major part in shaping London. Two hills on the north bank, now known as Ludgate Hill and Cornhill, with their gravel tops rose some 15 metres above the marshy ground of the Thames Valley, and thus offered a good site for urban buildings. Archaeological explorations have shown that a bridge, erected on iron-tipped wooden piles, was located slightly downstream from the present London Bridge. A box-like structure dating from around AD 90 has been uncovered on the north bank, next to a later Roman quayside, and it is thought that twenty such piers may have formed the bridge, with a central drawbridge that could be opened for sailing ships.

Londinium had streets laid out in a formal pattern, with public buildings such as a forum, and was fortified by walls, including one running along the bank. In contrast, the community on the south bank, which was to become Southwark, had the character of a suburb. The land was marshy, with tidal islands intersected by small rivers and streams. One such river was the Neckinger, which flowed into the Thames by twisting north at three points: one of these can be seen today emerging at St Saviour's Quay in Bermondsey. The islands were linked by draining the water and laying foundations of timber logs to take a firm road surface. Two roads from the south, Stane Street from Novius Ragnensium, Chichester, and Watling Street from Portus Dubrae, Dover, met at the site of what is now the church of St George the Martyr and combined to run up to the bridge crossing. A third road may have led westwards towards a crossing upstream at modern Westminster.

Given the susceptibility of the tides, some houses in this southern suburb would have been built on stilts, with flat-bottomed boats used to ferry goods along the rivers. This would appear to have been a comfortable place to live, with archaeological evidence of under-floor heating and household objects such as statuettes of gods, as well as industries, such as leather tanning, metalwork and the manufac-ture of glass. Bones uncovered suggest that bear-baiting might have taken place here, and there is some evidence of the presence of 'night moths', or prostitutes, associated with the worship of Isis at a temple.

Archaeologists from the Museum of London Archaeology (MOLA) in 2022 uncovered a spectacular find in the course of the construction of the Liberty of Southwark close by the Shard: the largest area of Roman mosaic found in the capital for over half a century. It includes two highly decorated panels set within a red tessellated floor. Large, colourful flowers, surrounded by guilloche decoration, have been attributed by the archaeologists to the 'Acanthus group', a team of mosaicists thought to be from Trier in Germany, who travelled to Britain and worked in their own individual style.

The mosaic had been set in a large room, probably a *triclinium*, or dining room where diners would recline on couches. It has been dated to the late second or early third century AD, but traces of an earlier mosaic underneath suggest that the room had been refurbished over the years. It might have been part of a Roman *mansio*, a luxury 'motel' with accommodation, dining facilities and stabling for state couriers and officials travelling to and from Londinium. It is thought that this was a considerable complex, with many rooms and corridors surrounding a central courtyard. As the site is near the main road that for centuries has connected London with other urban centres and the coast of south-east England, this building can be considered the forerunner to the famous inns that lined Borough High Street from the medieval period onwards.

At the time of writing, another significant find has been made close by: a mausoleum with its walls and mosaic flooring. This has been pronounced exceptional because it shows more than the usual footprint of such a building.[2] While the *mansio* was being used around the year AD 300, the mausoleum appears to date from a century later, reflecting the move of the living in Southwark to nearer the Thames, leaving the site for the burial of the dead. It is planned that the Roman remains should be put on display in a modern setting on the site.

The wooden bridge over the Thames is thought to have been swept away before the year AD 330 and not reconstructed at the time, so that Southwark as a settlement could also have been abandoned even before the Romans withdrew their legions and administration from Britain in the first years of the following century. When the Anglo-Saxons arrived, they colonised the north bank but at first stayed beyond the Roman walls in the area to the west, which is now Covent Garden, referred to in records as Lundenwic. In 604 a cathedral dedicated to St Paul was built on the western hill, Ludgate, in the former city of Londinium, though it may originally have stood in isolation, as the Anglo-Saxons only gradually moved back into what they described as Lundenburh.

According to a legend related by the Tudor chronicler John Stow, a convent was founded just two years after the founding of St Paul's, in 606, on the south bank of the Thames. He wrote of 'a fayre church called saint Mary over the Rie, or Overie, that is over the water. This Church, or some other in place thereof, was of old time long before the conquest a house of sisters, founded by a mayden named Mary; unto the which house and sisters she left (as was left to her by her parents) the oversight and profits of a cross ferry, or traverse ferry over the Thames, there kept before any bridge was builded'.[3]

In the seventeenth century this legend had been expanded into a dramatic tale published as 'The True History of the Life and Sudden Death of Old John Overs, the Rich Ferry-Man of London'.[4] This characterised John the ferryman as a miser, who faked his own death to save the expense of a day's food, then appeared at his funeral feast, only to be knocked on the head with an oar by one of his watermen and killed. His daughter, Mary, in flight from her many suitors attracted to the wealth that had accrued from the ferry service, resolved to retire from the world and founded a holy house. This watery tale reflects the importance of the ferrying of people and goods as a vital part of Southwark life that lasts through the centuries.

Stow continued his tale to describe the foundation of the priory church in Southwark: 'this house of sisters was after by Swithen, a noble lady, converted unto a colledge of Priests, who in place of the ferrie builded a bridge of timber.'[5] The 'noble lady' was in fact St Swithun, the Bishop of Winchester, who had close links to the royal house of Wessex and who in 862, shortly before his death, founded a college of priests of the order of St Augustine of Hippo in Southwark, which was part of his diocese. Swithun is perhaps best known today because the translation of his body from its original burial site into the Old Minster at Winchester was made in pouring rain on 15 July 971, giving rise to the belief that rain on St Swithun's Day will be followed by forty more days of rain.

The first firm written evidence for a church comes in the Domesday Book, compiled for William the Conqueror in 1085, stating that a monastery had existed here during the reign of his English predecessor, Edward the Confessor. We do not know what form the original priory church took, as a stone building was subsequently erected at the very beginning of the twelfth century by two Norman knights, William Pont de l'Arche and William Dauncy, and dedicated to St Mary. The Bishop of Winchester at that time, William Giffard, decided to found a priory of Augustinian 'Black' canons to administer it. A few remains of the twelfth-century church are still extant, behind a door in the north aisle of the present cathedral.

After a major fire in 1212, the church and the monastic buildings were rebuilt by Bishop Peter des Roches of Winchester. This new priory church of St Mary Overie was built in the fashionable Gothic style, based on a cruciform with a nave and choir flanked by side aisles, with transepts at the tower crossing and a retrochoir at the eastern end, behind the sanctuary. Although almost the whole building, apart from the retrochoir, has been reconstructed at various times, the style of the building would be familiar to those thirteenth-century canons. Between the church and the Thames various buildings of a monastery were added, including a refectory, infirmary and cloisters.

To the west of the priory the Bishops of Winchester built themselves a fine palace amidst an extensive park. The land here was particularly marshy, so an embankment was created to keep back the tides of the Thames and to provide a base for people and goods to land. This is still known as Bankside. To the east a causeway was built, now marked by Tooley Street, leading to the Cluniac priory of Bermondsey, founded in 1082 and dedicated to St Saviour. The monks began the development of this area by embanking the riverside, cultivating the land around the inlet of the River Neckinger and building St Saviour's Quay.

As John Stow had noted in his survey of London, a bridge of timber was built in Anglo-Saxon times, and 'lastly the same bridge was built of stone', leading onto a main road heading south which was to become Borough High Street. By the tenth century the key point of the southern bridge foot was known as Suthringa geweorche, which can be translated as 'the Surrey folk's defence work', hence Southwark. Four parish churches were to be established: St Olave's on Tooley Street, St Mary Magdalene, which was attached to the priory church, and, on Borough High Street, St Margaret's and St George the Martyr.

Historians have found it difficult to define exactly what was medieval Southwark. Martha Carlin described it as 'less than a formally delimited town, [yet] it was more than a coincidence of parishes and manors, and its periphery formed part of its extended community'.[6] It was never like other London suburbs, for it was vitally important in terms of defence, as it provided the gateway from southern England, and at the same time it was the largest and wealthiest town in Surrey.

Land ownership in medieval Southwark was based on five manors: alongside the river moving from west to east were Paris Garden, Clink, Guildable and Great Liberty, with the fifth, King's, lying to the south. Paris Garden belonged first to the Templars, and then to the Hospitallers; the Clink to the Bishops of Winchester; the bridgehead manor of Guildable to the Crown; the King's Manor to the Prior of Bermondsey; and the Great Liberty Manor to the Archbishops of Canterbury. These manors were not coterminous with the parishes.

The desire of the Corporation of the City of London to have some kind of control over the community 'over the river' was frustrated by this complexity of land ownership, and in particular by the status of the liberties. However, a political crisis in 1327 offered the opportunity to control at least some part of Southwark, the Guildable. The king, Edward II, had contrived through his favour of the Despensers, father and son, to alienate both the citizens of London and his Queen, Isabelle, 'the she-wolf of France'. Returning from France with her lover, the Marcher Lord Roger Mortimer, she secured baronial support and took control of London. A royal charter was granted to the City with rights over Southwark. This was the first of a series of several charters, with the aim of investing the City with greater control; Southwark, however, for the most part, 'pursued its accustomed way, unruly and unruled'.[7]

In 1550 a significant move appeared to have been made when the ward of The Bridge Without was created, and the government of Southwark was entrusted by Edward VI and his ministers to the Lord Mayor and Corporation. In fact, again, this royal charter meant that only three of the five manors came under the control of the City. Unruliness continued in the other two, and the anomalous survival of the manorial structure often made it difficult for the alderman to maintain his authority.

This, then, was the administrative setting, along with the basic topography, of what we now think of as Old Southwark when the Bohemian artist and engraver Wenceslaus Hollar undertook his preparatory sketches for his famous *Long View of London* that was to be published in Antwerp in 1648. He almost certainly climbed up the tower of the former priory church that became St Saviour's parish church with the dissolution of the monasteries. He may well have drawn for reference on a perspective known as Visscher's view, published by the Dutch printer Hondius in Amsterdam in 1616, and also have used a device called a topographical glass to note the details.[8]

In the printed prospect, Hollar moved himself, like a bird, higher to give us a more extensive overview of the city. Across the river is the City of London on the north bank, dominated by the tower of Old St Paul's Cathedral, and the spires of the many churches. Creating a

1. *Wenceslaus Hollar's Long View of London, published in 1648.*

link between the City and Southwark is London Bridge, so packed with houses and shops that it constitutes a town by itself, with the heads of traitors stuck on poles on its southern gate.

In the foreground, to the left is the parkland of the Bishop of Winchester's palace, by the 1640s the site of theatres and a baiting ring for animals, so similar in form that Hollar confused the Globe Theatre with a ring. The river itself has boats of every size, from ferrymen's wherries to merchants' ships. To the right a glimpse is provided of Borough High Street, often known as Long Southwark.

He is providing us with not just a perspective of London but also a view of everyday life in Southwark. When he came to make the etching in 1647, the kingdom was gripped by political turmoil. The first phase of the English Civil War had just ended with the defeat of the king, Charles I, and his imprisonment. The establishment of the Commonwealth was making an uncertain future for all kinds of institutions, including the system of bishoprics in the Church of England. Hollar depicts people promenading in the park of Winchester House, no longer the residence of the bishop, with others walking along the built-up path of Bankside. A tide mill is shown near London Bridge, with sacks of grain and a bed of chaff. A ferrymen's landing stage has oars laid out on the shore. A large inn is populated by figures in the courtyard, including a man on horseback preparing to leave. Nearby is another berthing place for the ferrymen.

In the chapters that follow, the stories of some of the men and women who populated this landscape, not only in Hollar's day but over the centuries before and after, will be told.

# 2

# London Bridge is Falling Down

Historians now avoid the term 'Dark Ages', but very little is known for certain about Southwark during the centuries that followed the withdrawal of the Romans at the beginning of the fourth century and the arrival of the Anglo-Saxons. What is clear is that when the various Anglo-Saxon kingdoms were developed, London stood on the edge first of Kent, then of the East Saxons, then of Mercia, before finally it became part of Wessex.

Although Winchester became the capital of 'all the English', London was developing as the commercial centre. In the words of the Venerable Bede, written in the eighth century, London, on the banks of the Thames, was a 'trading centre for many nations who visit by land and sea'.[1] Some of those visitors were not so welcome. From the last years of the century, covetous eyes were cast across the North Sea by both the Danes and the Norwegians, drawn to the city's prosperity. Frequent attacks were suffered over the years that followed.

In 878 the King of Wessex, Alfred, known to posterity as 'the Great', was almost overwhelmed by a Viking invasion but managed to defeat Guthrun the Dane and to establish a peaceful arrangement with him: the Danelaw ran north of the line of the rivers Thames and Lea while Alfred retained the south, including London, under his rule. He proceeded to organise the defence of this kingdom. The walls around London were strengthened, with its citizens made responsible for its defence. Across the country earth forts known as *burhs*, based on a Viking design, had been thrown up and garrisoned in the years preceding Alfred's reign, but he added several more. In essence these were fortified towns created from scratch, some with streets laid out as grids, and combining both urban and military functions.

Two such *burhs* were built on either bank of the River Lea to the north-east of London to prevent the Danes escaping down the river and into the Thames. Alfred added one at Southwark, or Suthringa geweorche, 'the defensive work of the men of Surrey', to protect the southern end of the crossing over the Thames. According to the document known as the Burghal Hidage, drawn up some time after 924, the Southwark *burh* was allocated 1,800 hides of land, assessed on food rent, to support it. Hidage varies from 150 for Southampton to 2,400 for Winchester, so Southwark was comparatively near the top of the list. To ensure that the fortresses were fully manned, a number of hides was allocated, with one man required to defend just four feet of wall. Southwark, therefore, in theory had 2,400 yards of fortification, although the measurement varied according to the value and resources of the land.[2]

When the bridge across the Thames was rebuilt is not known, but fortifications were probably added to it to prevent further incursions after a successful Viking attack on London in September 993. Timbers of this bridge have been found and, through dendro-chronological tests, they have been shown to have been from trees felled around this time.

In 1013 the Danish king, Swein Forkbeard, invaded southern England, capturing London and forcing the English king, Ethelred II, to flee. Ethelred has gained the soubriquet 'the Unready', not because he was habitually unprepared, but because he was poorly counselled: it is a play on his name, for Ethelred means 'noble counsel'. One historian has compared him to the Plantagenet King

John, who was dubbed by the authors of *1066 and All That* as the 'Awful King'.[3] The times were exceedingly perilous, with constant threats from Scandinavia, but made truly awful by Ethelred, considered heavy-handed and unjust in his rule.

The king's flight in 1013 may have been regarded with mixed feelings by his subjects. However, Swein died the following year, and Ethelred resolved to retake London with the mercenary support of the Norwegian prince, Olaf Haroldsson. Olaf, aged around eighteen, was acting rather like the *condottieri* of Renaissance Italy, lending his warrior followers to various rulers in the bitter and ferocious disputes that were a feature of northern Europe in this period.

Enshrined in Nordic folklore is Olaf's scheme in 1014 to pull down the bridge over the Thames and to split the Danish forces. A detailed account is given by the Icelandic *skaid*, or poet, Snorre Sturlason, in the thirteenth century: 'On the other side of the river there was a great market town, called Southwark, and there the Danes had a great host fitted out; they had dug dikes and within they set up a wall of trees and stones and turf, and they had a great army.' Sturlason described the bridge over the Thames as 'so broad that two wagons could be driven past each other over it. On the bridge there were built strong-holds, both castles and bulwarks, down towards the stream as deep as waist-high, but under the bridge there were piles which stood down in the bed of the river.'[4]

Using wattle and daub walling from nearby houses to shield his longboats, Olaf ordered the crews to row up to the bridge, attach ropes to its timber piles and then row downriver on the ebb-tide to bring the bridge down. The Danish soldiers who survived the fall of the bridge were soon rounded up and their fellow countrymen then surrendered to Ethelred. Intriguingly, during redevelopment around the site of the medieval London Bridge, spearheads, battle axes and a grappling iron from the Anglo-Saxon period have been uncovered.[5]

No mention of this incident is recorded in the *Anglo-Saxon Chronicles*, which has led to scepticism among historians. However, in the eleventh century, an Icelandic poet, Ottar Svarte, referred in his skaldic verses to how Olaf had destroyed a bridge over the Thames in London. This duly was rendered in verse in the nineteenth century as:

> London Bridge is broken down,
> Gold is won and bright renown
> Shields resounding
> War horns sounding,
> Hildur shouting in the din!
> Arrows singing,
> Mailcoats ringing –
> Odin makes our Olaf win![6]

These lines are instantly reminiscent of the nursery rhyme 'London Bridge is falling down', which is thought to be seventeenth-century in origin. There are various versions, one of which begins:

> London Bridge is broken down,
> Broken down, broken down.
> London Bridge is broken down,
> My fair lady.

By the seventeenth century the medieval stone bridge was showing considerable signs of dilapidation, and attempts were being made to repair it. The nineteenth-century rendering of Ottar Svarte's words is significant in that they bring in figures from Norse pagan mythology with a touch of Richard Wagner. The clamorous Hildur was a Valkyrie, with power to revive the dead on battlefields, sometimes taking on the personification of battle. Odin was the father of the gods, and of wisdom and of poets. The pagan Prince Olaf, however, was about to embrace the Christian faith.

Having restored Ethelred to London and his throne, Olaf moved on to spend the winter in Normandy with Duke Richard II, a fervent

Christian. The Norwegian prince was duly baptised in Rouen Cathedral by Richard's brother, Archbishop Robert. On his return to Norway, Olaf declared himself king, gradually uniting the country through his military prowess and enforcing Christianity upon his subjects. This did not endear him to some of his leading nobles, and Olaf was killed, aged only thirty-five, at the Battle of Stiklestad in 1030.

With his cunning that is reminiscent of Homer's Odysseus, and his warlike actions, which often tipped over into brutality, he does not seem to represent the traditional attributes of saintliness, but history has been kind to Olaf's memory. In 1031 he was canonised by Bishop Grimkell at Nidaros (modern Trondheim) after miraculous cures at his burial place were recorded. In 1164 Pope Alexander III established Olaf as a saint of the Roman Catholic Church, and he was also regarded as such by the Eastern Orthodox and Lutheran churches. He became a symbol of Norwegian independence and pride, commemorated by the battle axe in the nation's coat of arms, and Olsok on 29 July is still his day of celebration.

Once converted to Christianity, the Norse were keen on establishing parish churches, founding many in London, as can be seen in their dedications. St Olaf, or Olave, was commemorated in no less than five of these in the City, of which only one survives, on Hart Street. A sixth was established in Southwark on the causeway to Bermondsey to the east of Borough High Street. This causeway is now Tooley Street, a corruption of 't'olous', the Church of St Olave.

St Olave's Church may well have begun life as the private chapel of Earl Godwin of Wessex, whose London residence stood on the bank of the Thames in Southwark. Ethelred's recovery of London from the Danes was not to endure, for he died in 1016. According to one version of the *Anglo-Saxon Chronicles*, his son, Edmund Ironside, was chosen as king by the councillors and citizens of London, but another has it that the English bishops, abbots and nobles agreed to accept that Swein Forkbeard's son, Canute, should succeed to the throne. In the event, Edmund Ironside was defeated in battle in the autumn of 1016 and died shortly afterwards, so that without dispute Canute became king.

One of Canute's first acts was to take Ethelred's Norman wife, Emma, as his queen, despite the fact that he already had a wife living. This marriage was to make the question of who might succeed him, always fraught, even more complex. On top of this, Ethelred had earlier done exactly the same, and put aside a first living wife to marry Emma. The issue of succession was laid aside for the time, however, as Canute sorted out how to govern England alongside Denmark. Suspicious of the leading Englishmen, he divided the country into four major earldoms based on the old Anglo-Saxon kingdoms. While he retained Wessex under his own control, Northumbria, East Anglia and Mercia were given to Scandinavians. However, he singled out Godwin, son of a Sussex thegn, as a valued councillor, appreciating the loyalty that he had shown to Edmund Ironside. He may well have been persuaded to this view by Edmund's stepmother, Queen Emma.

Canute came quickly also to appreciate Godwin's careful advice and military support, according to him in time the governance of Wessex, which is why Godwin's London residence was in Southwark. Godwin twice accompanied Canute to Denmark: on the second occasion, in 1022 or 1023, marrying Gytha, daughter of the chieftain Thorgil Sprakling and the king's sister-in-law. In the years that followed, Canute gave Godwin many manors spread through the southern counties, while Gytha presented him with many children – six sons and three daughters. Earl Godwin became the strong man of England, in time sharing power with his sons.

After Canute's death in 1035 the question of the succession developed into a maelstrom, with the throne eventually offered to Edward Aetheling, son of Emma from her marriage to Ethelred, who had spent his life in exile in Normandy, the home of his mother. He is known as Edward the Confessor for his piety. When he succeeded to the throne in 1042, Edward married Edith of Wessex, the eldest daughter of Godwin and Gytha, and no doubt Godwin hoped a grandchild would inherit the crown. However, according to a chronicle of the life of Edward the Confessor, both the king and Edith maintained a life of celibacy.[7] Although Godwin died in 1053, his sons continued to exercise power. When the Confessor in turn died in January 1066, the question of the succession once more raised its head, and Harold, Godwin and Gytha's eldest surviving son, succeeded to the throne as Harold II.

Having male heirs has long been regarded as a vital asset for the maintenance of the line. Henry VIII in his increasingly frantic mission to acquire a legitimate male heir broke with Rome and executed his second queen. However, the reverse can also pertain: Henry II found in the final bitter years of his reign that his sons quarrelled both with him and among themselves; and the many sons of Edward III brought about the civil wars of the fifteenth century known as the Wars of the Roses.

The devastating fall of the House of Godwin came in the autumn of 1066, sparked by fraternal conflict. Tostig, who had been exiled after a revolt in Northumbria, returned to challenge his brother, Harold Godwinson. He was accompanied by the Norwegian king, Harold Hardrada, half-brother of St Olaf, supported by a considerable army. After an epic march northwards, the English king defeated and killed them both on 25 September at the Battle of Stamford Bridge in what is now Yorkshire. He then marched his victorious troops back to London, only to be told that William, Duke of Normandy, who claimed that he had been chosen by Edward the Confessor as his successor, was making his way across the Channel. Harold confronted the Normans in Sussex, but his forces were reduced and wearied by their efforts in the earlier battle. Despite a brave stand at Senlac, Harold was killed at the Battle of Hastings, famously said to have been struck in the eye by a Norman arrow. His brothers Gyrth and Leofwine also perished that day. The triumphant duke duly became King of England as William the Conqueror.

Gytha received news of the deaths of four of her sons at her estate in Exeter. There she had founded a 'house chapel', the Saxon equivalent of a medieval chantry, dedicated in 1053 to St Olaf, where prayers could be said for Earl Godwin. Now she must have added those for her lost sons. In the year following the Battle of Hastings, she raised a revolt against William the Conqueror, and when this failed she fled to the Continent.

With her royal connections in Denmark, Gytha may well have known Olaf personally, hence the dedications both in Devon and in Southwark. In time what was probably her private London chapel became a parish church in Southwark. An early miracle recorded at St Olave's in the 1090s told of the cure of a cripple who had come from France on his knees and knuckles.

The parish church of St Olave's in Southwark was demolished in 1826 but is remembered by St Olaf House, now part of London

*2. Early twentieth-century mosaic of St Olaf by Frank Dobson in black and gold, on the south-west corner of St Olaf House in Tooley Street.*

Bridge Hospital, designed by H.S. Goodhart-Rendel in 1931. On the landward side of the building is a striking mosaic in black and gold of St Olaf. He also takes his place among the figures in the screen that was erected behind the high altar in 1905 when the church became Southwark Cathedral (plate III). The statue there shows a young man with flowing locks, holding a shield in one hand and a battle axe in the other. This reflects the fact that Olaf was a military figure, representing the tradition of Christian knights such as the Templars and the Hospitallers. An archaeological investigation carried out on a riverside site in Barking in Essex in the 1920s recovered an eleventh-century Viking battle axe with a finely ornamented socket, looking very like the weapon shown on the altar screen.[8]

Across London Bridge on the north side of the Thames stands the church of St Magnus the Martyr. Originally dedicated to a Latin saint, it was later rededicated to St Magnus Erlendsson, the Earl of Orkney, executed around the year 1116 during a power struggle with his cousin. Magnus, unlike St Olaf, enjoyed a reputation for piety and gentleness, and he was canonised twenty years after his death.

The two men may have been very different, but their presence in the dedications of the two churches facing each other across the Thames serves as a reminder of the fierce chapter in London's history during the Viking period. The churches appear like guardians of the river in perspectives such as the one engraved by Wenceslaus Hollar in the seventeenth century. The image is rendered into words by Charles Dickens in his novel *Oliver Twist*, published in 1837–38. Rather than St Olave's Church, he talks of St Saviour's, now the cathedral: 'A mist hung over the river, deepening the red glare of the fires that burnt upon the small craft off the different wharfs and rendering darker and more indistinct the mirky [sic] buildings on the bank . . . . The tower of old Saint Saviour's Church, and the spire of Saint Magnus, so long the giant-warders of the ancient bridge, were visible in the gloom.'[9]

# 3

# Mansions of Southwark

The Norman Conquest in 1066 comprehensively put paid to the Godwinson family and their Southwark residence, but the house of another very powerful family was soon to be built close by, just off Borough High Street. This was the inn or townhouse of the de Warenne family. William de Warenne, who fought alongside Duke William at the Battle of Hastings, was eventually made Earl of Surrey and given the Guildable Manor in Southwark.

Initially the manor had been given by William the Conqueror to his half-brother, Odo, Bishop of Bayeux. Odo is remembered as the man who commissioned the Bayeux Tapestry, the wonderful needlework story of how Duke William gained the English throne. However, he was also apparently a disputatious character, quarrelling both with the papacy and with his half-brother. In the case of Southwark, his dispute was about the amount of increment that he derived from tolls known as 'dues of the stream'. When he fell from grace in 1088, imprisoned by the Conqueror's son, William II, his holdings passed to the de Warennes.[1] They shared governance and profits of the Guildable Manor with the Crown, dividing jurisdiction of the manor geographically. A vaulted undercroft close to the foot of London Bridge that survived until the early nineteenth century may have been part of their residence, which would have been described as an inn.

An inn in this context signifies a London residence, of comparatively modest size, used by the family when attending the royal court and, later, sessions of Parliament. That of the de Warennes was just one of an enclave of residences in Southwark, many of which were for clerical households, also arriving in the capital on church and state business. One was the lodgings of the Prior of Lewes, head of the major Cluniac monastery in East Sussex, founded by the de Warenne family at the end of the eleventh century. The Cluniac order had been established a century earlier in Burgundy with the aim of restoring traditional monastic life and care for the poor. It is said that William, the second earl, and his brother Ralph secured the foundation of the priory by having locks of their hair cut by Henry of Blois, Bishop of Winchester, in front of the high altar of the priory church of St Mary Overie. In the church, now the cathedral of Southwark, is a beautiful wooden figure of a knight, dressed in chain armour, holding a sword and with his knees crossed. Dating from the thirteenth century, it is thought to represent a later member of the de Warenne family.

The clerical and gentry inns along Borough Street and Tooley Street, with easy access to London Bridge and the City, were usually set back from the thoroughfares and entered by a porter's gate. Behind would have been the hall and chapel or oratory, living quarters, stables and a garden, like some of the older colleges at Oxford and Cambridge. Sometimes shops were installed against the walls of the inns, and the Prior of Christchurch in Canterbury, for example, arranged for his gardener to sell surplus produce outside his London residence.

Although these inns have all long disappeared, some of them are recalled in the topography of Southwark. That of the Bishop of Rochester is recalled by Rochester Walk, now part of Borough Market. Memory of the Abbot of Battle Abbey in Sussex is retained by Battlebridge Lane, close to the river between Mill Lane and London Bridge. The Abbot of Hyde, a monastery lying within the walls of medieval Winchester, had his inn on Borough High Street. In time, this was to become a different kind of inn, a hostelry, the famous Tabard Inn of Chaucer's *Canterbury Tales*. The inn of a Kent family, the Cobhams, became the Green Dragon, still remembered by Green Dragon Court.

In addition, there were mansions of considerable size. One such was Winchester House, the London home of the Bishops of Winchester, which stood just to the west of the priory church, in the manor of the Liberty of the Clink. It was built for Bishop William Gifford in the opening decade of the twelfth century and enlarged by his successor, Henry of Blois. Henry was the grandson of William the Conqueror and brother of King Stephen, helping him to succeed to the English throne against the claim of their cousin, the Empress Matilda. Although a bishop rather than an archbishop, the incumbent of Winchester enjoyed great wealth from the landholdings scattered around southern England. Indeed, by the fourteenth century, it was said that 'Canterbury hath the finer stable, but Winchester the deeper manger'.[2]

Henry of Blois used his wealth on many building schemes, and at Southwark he enlarged the palace and created a park of around 70 acres running west to east along the river frontage. At other residences he not only had lakes dug but also exotic birds and animals introduced: history does not relate whether he did so at Southwark. The terrain of the park was marshy in places, sometimes known as the Wilds from the willow trees that flourished here. This land was liable to flooding, even after the building of Bankside, so that it was easy to create ponds to accommodate fish for the bishop's table. These fishponds, or stews, were to take on a particular significance for Londoners.

Henry was very much the diplomat and sought to heal the bitter rift that developed between King Henry II and his Archbishop of Canterbury, Thomas Becket, over royal and ecclesiastical powers. In

1170, on his last visit to London, Becket came to Southwark. According to his biographer, William Fitzstephen, 3,000 people gathered to watch as the canons of the priory greeted him at the church door, singing *Benedictus dominus deus Israel*. Becket preached in the church on 11 December, before staying overnight at Winchester House with Bishop Henry. He then set off on the road to Canterbury and, on 29 December, was brutally murdered in his cathedral by four Norman knights.

Winchester House became yet more palatial in the fourteenth century with major refurbishment taking place when William of Wykeham was Bishop of Winchester. A great administrator, he is remembered today as having established the twin foundations of the school, Winchester College and New College at Oxford. But he also supervised the royal building works during the reign of Edward III, including Windsor Castle, where his chief master mason was Henry Yevele. It is not surprising, therefore, that Yevele played a part in the refurbishment in Southwark, named as repairing and enlarging the fireplace in the bishop's *magna camera*, or grand parlour, in 1376. A rose window was installed in the new great hall: its magnificent tracery can still be seen in Clink Street (plate XI). Yevele is also credited with building one of the stages of the tower of the priory church.

Household accounts from the early fourteenth century give a picture of the splendour of Winchester House. Between fifty and sixty horses were stabled here, increasing to over a hundred on special occasions. Inventories list heraldic tapestries and hangings for benches and for the bishop's bed. For his dining table there were silver spice dishes and spoons, exotic drinking goblets known as mazers, and table and carving knives with jasper handles. It would be interesting to have similar details of the domestic arrangements of the Augustinian canons in the priory church next door. Might they present a stark contrast?

In the screen behind the high altar in Southwark Cathedral, William of Wykeham appears between Archbishop Thomas Becket and Cardinal Henry Beaufort (plate III). The cardinal, like Henry of Blois, was a member of the royal family, another reminder of how the bishopric of Winchester was one of the most senior in the English Church and that the incumbents often combined their ecclesiastical role with high office of state. Henry Beaufort was a son of John of Gaunt, Duke of Lancaster, and his mistress, Katherine Swynford, who subsequently became his third wife. A brilliant scholar, and possibly tutor to his nephew, Henry V, Beaufort was appointed Chancellor of Oxford at the age of twenty and Bishop of Lincoln at twenty-one. When William of Wykeham died in 1404, Beaufort was translated to the bishopric of Winchester, and fourteen years later was made a cardinal.

In 1424 Beaufort presided over the wedding of his niece Joan to James I, King of the Scots, held in the priory church with a grand reception in Winchester House. James's older brother, David, had been seized by his uncle, the Duke of Albany, and died in captivity. The ailing king, Robert III, fearing for his younger son's safety, sent him to France in 1406, but en route the ship was captured by pirates and James was handed over to the English king, Henry IV. He remained a prisoner, a pawn in the power game of Scottish and English politics, for eighteen years. During those years he was treated with honour at the English court, and he must have known Joan well.

The wedding in 1424 could well have been a love match rather than a political alliance. A love poem attributed to the Scottish king in the style of Chaucer and dedicated to him, 'The Kingis Quair [Song]', is regarded as evidence of this. After the wedding the couple went to Scotland, where James was determined to strengthen the power of the crown and to halt the lawless plunder perpetrated by leading nobles such as Albany. This made him many enemies, and he was assassinated in his bedchamber in 1437 by former servants of his uncle. Despite being injured in the attack as she sought to protect her husband, Queen Joan survived and orchestrated the hunting down and execution of the murderers. She also ensured that her son would base his government on his father's concept of monarchy.

An unusual mansion lay on the eastern side of the High Street. Bridge House belonged not to a household but to a civic institution. Charters investing greater power in the City of London were issued by King Richard I, both before his departure on crusade in 1189 and on his return from captivity in Germany four years later. One confirmed the right to have a mayor rather than a sheriff: at first, this was an appointed office, but it later became electable. Another gave the City the governance of the River Thames.

The construction of a stone bridge across the Thames had begun in 1176 at the instigation of Peter, the priest of St Mary Colechurch, the parish at the Poultry end of Cheapside where Thomas Becket was born and baptised. Very soon after Becket's murder in 1170, miracles were being recorded at his tomb in Canterbury Cathedral and the beginning of a hugely popular cult was established. Peter raised funds through a fraternity of five guilds, while Henry II ordered taxes on wool and sheepskins to be collected for the considerable expenses involved, so that it was said that London Bridge, over 900 feet in length, was built on wool packs.

In fact, it was built on elm piles that were driven into the bed of the river by boat at low tide, creating enclosures that were then filled with rubble to create a base. Next, planks were placed to provide a firm working surface, and then larger piles and rubble were added to create what were known as 'starlings', a term probably derived from 'straddlings'. These were vital because of the shallowness of the foundations but resulted in major obstruction of the river flow. The piers varied in width, creating irregular arches from 15 to 34 feet apart and giving the bridge its distinctive profile.

The masons who created the bridge had worked on churches, and therefore were familiar with the construction of the pointed arches in the Gothic style. The whole structure was narrow in width, probably only 28 feet, reached through impressive gateways at either end that could be shut at night. A large, two-storey chapel dedicated to St Thomas Becket was built halfway along, marking the official start of the pilgrimage to his Canterbury shrine, with an additional entrance at river level for fishermen and ferrymen. By 1209, when building was complete, the king, now John, tried to recoup some costs by licensing building plots on the bridge, and houses with shops began to line its length. Consisting at first of two storeys, they were later to reach up to dizzying heights, some of them cantilevered over the sides of the bridge.

Once the bridge was built, 'the bretheren' carried out its maintenance, from tolls levied on traffic travelling along the roadway and from boats making the journey between the piers below. This journey was very hazardous because the gaps between the starlings were so narrow, and the watermen had to use all their skill to shoot the rapids.

The very high cost of construction was supplemented by gifts and bequests from Londoners, including rents from hundreds of landholdings in the City and metropolitan area. The headquarters for the management, both practical and financial, was Bridge House: the earliest reference appears in a document dating from 1222/23 in which a *domum de Ponte* is mentioned.[3] This was probably on the site of two properties in Southwark. The first was a monastic dwelling belonging to Peter of Colechurch, who had died in 1205. The second was a house left in the will of the first Mayor of London, Henry Fitz Ailwin, who died in 1212. He was a merchant involved in shipping, so he had docks on the Thames. The two properties were located just to the east of St Olave's Church. In 1282, in exchange for loans to Edward I, the City acquired the charter for the maintenance of the bridge, taking over from the bretheren. The south end, approximately a third of the bridge, lay in the parish of St Olave, while the northern section was in that of St Magnus the Martyr, with the entire length assigned to the London Bridge ward.

Bridge House had a riverside frontage enabling goods to be landed and dispatched. It became a considerable enterprise, with staff headed by a clerk of works, reporting to two bridge wardens, chosen by the citizens of London, the members of the guilds. One of these wardens in the fourteenth century was the mason Henry Yevele, whose private residence was just across from the church of St Magnus the Martyr on the north bank. He organised the rebuilding of the chapel of St Thomas Becket on the bridge in handsome Perpendicular style at the end of the century.

Under the clerk of works at Bridge House came a legion of clerks, rent collectors and workmen such as carpenters, masons, cooks and tidesmen. In order to feed this army, a substantial garden was cultivated, and so we have a horticultural record in rare detail from the accounts maintained from 1381, although the garden was clearly well established by this time.[4]

The accounts tell us that vegetables such as beans, onions and leeks were grown in long, narrow raised beds with wooden railings, and with gravelled paths in between to enable easy access. The principal herbs cultivated would seem to be rosemary and parsley. 'Appulympes', apple-tree grafts, were purchased for an orchard, and grapevines were cultivated using stakes and willow reeds for support. Some of the Bridge House workmen may have helped with the gardening, but the accounts also refer to garden labourers and to seed and plant suppliers. There are also references to women workers as weeders, a common practice, for nimble fingers were required. For example, Mother Tubbys, along with William Hewet, was paid 5s 4d for weeding in the year 1529/30.[5] These must have been local residents, drawn from the parishes of St Mary Magdalene and St Olave, and further south along Borough High Street, St Margaret's and St George's.

Once a year London's mayor, elevated to Lord Mayor from 1354, accompanied by his aldermen, paid a formal visit to Bridge House at the time of the audit of the income and expenditure of the estate. From 1426 they were entertained in a part of the garden near the counting house, where an 'herber', or arbour, partly enclosed by a vine trellis, had been created as a summer parlour. For the visit of the Lord Mayor it was hung with tapestries. The ritual meal was sumptuous: on the menu for 1438, for example, dishes included 'beef merybones [marrow bones], chinis [chines] of pork, signets, little pigs, geese, teelis [teal ducks], snyts [snipes] and plover[i]s'.[6] In the early sixteenth century, with Renaissance ideas coming from France and Burgundy, what was known as the Masters' Garden was laid in the fashionable style with brick walls and alleys, fountains and formal beds.

In the records for 1460–61 comes the first reference to the decoration of the gatehouse of Bridge House to celebrate the festival of St John the Baptist. This took place on 24 June, at the very opposite time of the year from Christmas, the celebration of the birth of Christ. Just as boughs such as holly and ivy were brought in to decorate houses in December, so for Midsummer particular flowers and leaves were gathered. The festivities began the previous evening when plants were carried in torchlight processions through the streets of London.

These plants were known as 'Midsummer Men'. One particularly connected with the saint, unsurprisingly, was St John's wort. The stems yield a blood-red juice that was associated with the saint's beheading, and a traditional recipe was to take the flowers and stems and put them on a windowsill in water until the sun turned the liquid red, and the so-called blood of St John could then be used to treat skin complaints. On St John's Tide, the leaves were burnt to purify communities, probably a pagan practice adopted by the Church.[7]

John Stow, the chronicler of London at the very end of the sixteenth century, described one such festival: 'On the Vigil of Saint John Baptist . . . every mans door being shadowed with greene Birch, long Fennel, Saint John's wort, Orpin, white Lillies, and such like, garnished upon with Garlands of beautifull flowers, had also Lampes of glasse, with oyle burning in them all the night.' The herbalist John Parkinson, writing a few years later, recorded that the leaves of the long-lasting orpine would be intertwined with corn marigold flowers on strings and hung up in houses, on bushes and on maypoles.[8]

The Bridge House accounts record the annual payments made for the festival, with green candles and, by the 1490s, oil lamps being purchased by the Porter. The custom ended for Bridge House in 1543, suggesting that religious reformers may have considered it an out-moded tradition based on pagan as well as medieval church traditions. Stow and Parkinson were looking at it in its last days.

To the east of the Bridge House estate stood a fine mansion with a chequered history. In 1324 Edward II had built for himself a moated house known as the Rosary on Horsleydown. In this context 'rosary' is a place resembling a rose garden, pleasant and restorative, and the king visited the moated pleasure-house on several occasions. Within the moat and the house, which was built in timber and stone, there may well have been an 'herber' adorned with roses. Contemporary illustrations of gardens often show a lady, sometimes the Virgin Mary, sitting in just such a secluded arbour.

Pleasant and restorative were two qualities much needed by the king, as the Rosary was begun during a particularly difficult time in his troubled reign. The overwhelming influence of Edward's favourites, the Despensers father and son, had alienated his queen, Isabella, the 'she-wolf of France' (p. 13). Returning from the Continent with her lover, Roger Mortimer, she secured baronial support, and the City erupted into violence in the autumn of 1326, with William de Stapledon, the Bishop of Exeter, who had the misfortune to be appointed by Edward as the *Custos* of London, knocked off his horse and dragged through St Paul's Churchyard into Cheapside, where his head was hacked off with a bread knife.

The Rosary was still incomplete the following year when the king was brutally done to death in Berkeley Castle in Gloucestershire. A century later, the estate at Horsleydown was acquired by a Norfolk knight, Sir John Fastolf, who had seen military action in France during the Hundred Years War. He turned it into a large residential complex, again surrounded by a moat. The strength of these fortifications was, however, put to the test in the summer of 1450 when Jack Cade and his followers arrived in Southwark, and Cade set himself up in the White Hart Inn on Borough High Street. A traditional seasonal gathering to celebrate Whitsun in Kent had turned into a mass movement of rebellion that included minor gentry and yeomen farmers, led by Cade, a former soldier. Their common grievance was the serious dislocation of trade following the collapse of the English campaign in France, exacerbated by increased taxation imposed by the Treasurer of England, James Fiennes, Lord Saye.

Fiennes was denounced and sent to the Tower of London for his own safety by the king, Henry VI, who then departed to his castle at Kenilworth in Warwickshire, leaving the Lord Mayor in charge. When Jack Cade and the rebels crossed over London Bridge, Fiennes was handed over to them, and after a sham trial he was paraded through the streets and executed in Cheapside on 4 July. His son-in-law, the deputy sheriff of Kent, met the same fate outside the City walls. Cade, drunk with power, and no doubt with alcohol, made the two decapitated heads appear to kiss, before attaching Fiennes' body to his horse and riding around London.

After three days of looting, the mayor began to assert his authority in the City, pushing the rebels back into Southwark with a pitched battle lasting twelve hours on London Bridge. The two archbishops, John Stafford of Canterbury and Cardinal John Kemp of York, along with Bishop William Waynflete of Winchester, then met Cade at St Margaret's Church in Borough High Street. Pardons were handed to him and to 3,000 others. Almost all of these were respected, but not for Cade, who was hunted down and, mortally wounded, died on his way back to London. His decapitated and quartered body, having been identified by the landlady of the White Hart, was dragged through the streets before his head was placed on a spike on the Traitors' Gate at the southern end of the bridge, as had become the custom. Sir John Fastolf, who had taken refuge in the Tower of London just across the Thames when his residence came under attack, no doubt felt he was lucky to have survived the bloodbath. Returning to Horsleydown, he lived there until his death in 1459 when his estate was broken up amid legal disputes. Both Sir John and Jack Cade duly make their appearance in the first part of Shakespeare's play *Henry VI*.

Along with his residence at Horsleydown, Sir John Fastolf also owned what was described as a High Beer House and Garden in contemporary records. This is probably the establishment featured in a late sixteenth-century painting by the Flemish artist Joris Hoefnagel that now hangs in Hatfield House in Hertfordshire. *The Marriage Feast at Bermondsey* shows guests in procession and dancing in front of tables laid for the marriage breakfast, with a view of the Tower of London across the Thames.

Another gentry family from East Anglia enjoyed a longer, and more peaceful, sojourn in the Borough. Sir William Brandon, from Wangford in Suffolk, leased land from the estate of the Bishop of Winchester and built a house with a frontage on Borough High Street just south of the priory church. A family tragedy propelled the Brandons to the very top of English society when Sir William's son, also William, was killed in 1485 at the Battle of Bosworth Field. Legend has it that he was cut down by Richard III himself, as William carried the standard of Henry, Earl of Richmond. When Richmond took the throne as Henry VII, the Brandon family's advancement was assured. Sir Thomas, William's brother, became one of his leading courtiers. He had taken into his household in Southwark William's one-year-old son, Charles, and brought him up there. In time, Charles became the close friend and jousting companion of Prince Henry, the future Henry VIII.

When Sir Thomas Brandon died in 1510, Charles inherited his estates and succeeded him in the office of Marshal of the King's Bench. He was also appointed marshal of the royal household so that he had control of both the King's Bench Prison and of the Marshalsea in Southwark, making him an influential figure in the borough. In 1514 he was made Duke of Suffolk by Henry VIII, apparently in a secret move for him to marry the Hapsburg princess, Margaret of Austria. But in a twist of circumstances, instead he married Henry VIII's sister, Mary, when he was sent to Paris to bring her home after the death of her first husband, Louis XII. The English king was not pleased, usually a recipe for disaster, but Brandon managed to survive the crisis, keeping his dukedom and his head.

The Southwark residence, renamed Suffolk Place, was rebuilt in grand style appropriate to his station. While we have little idea of what most of the grand mansions of Southwark looked like, we do have a fleeting glimpse of Suffolk Place from a sketch by the Flemish artist Anthony van Wyngaerde.[9] It shows a tall brick gatehouse, essentially a Gothic structure, with Renaissance-style decoration of terracotta busts of Roman emperors in laurel frames. In corroboration of this, pieces of just such terracotta decoration have been unearthed in the churchyard of St George the Martyr. The entrance gatehouse of Hampton Court Palace, built at a similar time, using the same combination of materials, by Henry VIII's chief minister, Cardinal Wolsey, gives an idea of its appearance. Wolsey is recorded as borrowing terracotta decorations from Suffolk Place for use at the pageant of the Cloth of Gold held by Henry VIII at Guisnes, just outside Calais.

Suffolk Place thereafter enjoyed a rather erratic career. The duke and Princess Mary did not reside long in this new mansion. The king wanted to have a presence in Southwark so offered Brandon one of his considerable holding of residences, and an exchange was duly made with the former palace of the Bishops of Norwich, near Charing Cross. The Southwark mansion was assigned to Jane Seymour for her short time as queen, and after her death in 1537 part was turned into a Mint. It was subsequently used by another Mary Tudor, Henry's elder daughter, when she and her new husband, Philip II of Spain, stayed here before following the traditional custom of a formal state entry into the City. Only three years later, however, in 1557, it was demolished, and in time the site became a notorious rookery, retaining the name of the Mint.

This was a fate that overcame many other Southwark properties. The last former residences of prelates disappeared following the dissolution of the monasteries, while courtiers moved further out of the City or to the fashionable West End. Winchester Palace remained the London home of the Bishops of Winchester for another century: the last incumbent to occupy it was Lancelot Andrewes, and it became a prison when the episcopy was suppressed by Act of Parliament in 1642. Although it was returned to the see on the Restoration, it was in such a dilapidated state that it was decided to let it out as tenements. The fine rose window and great hall were only discovered by chance in the nineteenth century when a warehouse was damaged by fire.

The one Southwark mansion to continue to function was Bridge House, maintaining London Bridge as the only bridge across the river into the City. In the 1760s, however, Blackfriars was constructed by the Trust, with Waterloo, Southwark and Tower bridges following. The old house of Bridge House, with its outbuildings and gardens, was sold for redevelopment in 1831, but the Bridge Estates Trust continues to this day, administered by the Corporation of London.

# 4

## On the Road to Canterbury

In the north aisle of Southwark Cathedral stands the striking monument to the poet John Gower, who died in 1408. From a Kentish family, he probably held a legal office, for he referred in one of his poems to wearing a striped or 'rayed' sleeve, the dress of some serjeants-at-law. Gower is represented by a full-size recumbent figure on the tomb, a tribute at this date to one who did not come from the uppermost echelon of society. Under a canopy of three cusped arches, his form is painted in the most brilliant colours. While his feet rest on a lion, his head is supported by three books, with their titles picked out in black on gold: *Speculum Meditantis*, *Vox Clamantis* and *Confession Amantis*. Despite their titles, the three were written in different languages, French, Latin and English (plate V).

The first of these three books is a long poem in Norman French that began life as the *Mirour de l'omme* and was later revised as *Speculum Meditantis*, 'The Mirror of Meditation'. It was written c.1376, towards the end of Edward III's reign when the king was failing both physically and mentally and he was considered to have fallen under the malign influence of his mistress, Alice Perrers. Gower introduces into the poem an allusion to what happens to a kingdom when a woman dominates. Taking the form of an allegory, both religious and cosmological, he tells of Sin, the daughter of the Devil, and Death, her son. Their offspring are seven daughters, the Deadly Sins, who are sent to win over the World and destroy Man's hope of salvation. The Deadly Sins are married in turn to World, each producing five children. Pride, for example, gives birth to Hypocrisy, Vainglory, Arrogance, Boasting and Disobedience. Reason and Conscience pray to God for help, and get seven corresponding Virtues, who are married to Reason, and in turn produce five daughters.

In the second part of *Speculum Meditantis*, Gower pictures the power of sin throughout the world, with every estate full of corruption. He is particularly critical of the activities of friars, who were very much a subject of contention by the late fourteenth century. Gower points out the paradox of the mendicant orders preaching poverty but ever ready to extend their hands to receive riches. He also looks at secular society, lawyers, merchants, craftsmen and labourers, asking World where all this evil might come from. The answer he receives is Man, but that it is possible to repent. In the third and final part of the poem, the Poet calls upon the Virgin Mary, Lady of Pity, to come to his aid.[1]

Some time after the year 1381 John Gower composed the second book to appear under his head in the Southwark monument. This was a Latin satirical poem entitled *Vox Clamantis*, 'The Song of one Crying Out'. Edward III had died in 1377 and was succeeded by his ten-year-old grandson, Richard II, although political power largely lay in the hands of the king's uncle, John of Gaunt, Duke of Lancaster. The introduction of poll tax sparked off intense social discontent, and in 1381 came the Peasants' Revolt when Wat Tyler led an attack on London, passing through Southwark and crossing London Bridge on 13 June.

In the first part of the poem, Gower vividly describes the arrival of Tyler and his followers. The Poet is out picking flowers when he sees bands of peasants crossing the fields. Suddenly, in seven groups, they are transformed by the curse of God into animals. The first are transformed into asses who refuse to bear their loads, assuming instead pretensions of dress and manner. The second turn into monstrous oxen with the feet of bears and tails of dragons, who refuse to draw the plough. The third group become swine, led by 'the wild boar of Kent', thought to be Robert Cave, one of the leading rebels. The fourth group, servants who work outside, are turned by the Devil into dogs, who mingle with the fifth group, indoor servants, transformed into cats. These domestic animals are then joined by grey foxes, who break into the city and steal because nobody can stop them. This frenzied lawlessness turns them from domesticity into wild beasts, along with the sixth group, domestic fowl that became ravens and kites. The final group of peasants take the shape of frogs and flies, a reminder of the plagues of Egypt.[2]

The world has thus been turned upside down, as Wat Tyler, here in the form of the Jay, urges the peasants towards New Troy, London. Once across London Bridge, the city is attacked and the Chief Priest, in reality the Lord Chancellor, Simon Sudbury, Archbishop of Canterbury, is sought out as the man responsible for the introduction of the hated poll tax. He is found hiding in the Tower of London and murdered. Other targets are mentioned with Homeric associations, such as the burning of Savoy Palace, the home of John of Gaunt, and of the priory of St John of Jerusalem in Clerkenwell, and, close to home as far as Gower was concerned, an attack upon the Inns of Court.

The Poet seeks flight on a boat but is attacked by storms and a sea monster. Drawing upon the actual meeting between the young Richard II and the rebels at Smithfield, he tells how the Jay, Wat Tyler, is stabbed to death by the Lord Mayor, William Walworth, for apparently insulting the king. At this point the storm abates and the Poet finds himself on an island, where he hears a heavenly voice telling him to record the drama.

The subsequent parts of the poem form a satire of a more traditional kind, complaining about the state of England. As with his earlier poem *Speculum Meditantis*, Gower details the failings of the various categories of society and urges Man to repent and live virtuously. The Peasants' Revolt was considered a warning of the fearful effects of rebellion against universal order, and Gower particularly held great store by legal justice and regal responsibility, so that he was offering advice both helpful and hopeful to the young king. However, he later revised the work to make it appear more like a foreshadowing of Richard's downfall. After a turbulent reign, he was forced in 1399 to abdicate by his cousin, Henry Bolingbroke, the eldest son of John of Gaunt, and died in prison, probably in Pontefract Castle. Bolingbroke then succeeded to the throne as Henry IV. Eleven manuscript copies of *Vox Clamantis* survive, showing how Gower changed the thrust of the poem.

The third book featured on the tomb is Gower's major English poem, *Confessio Amantis*, 'The Lover's Confession', begun in the 1390s. As in the other works, he laments the depravity of rulers, clergy and commons. When the lover, Amans, is pierced by Cupid's dart, Venus tells him to confess to her priest, Genius, who instructs him on the proper use of the senses and of the deadly sins. This instruction takes the form of over a hundred tales, in the style of the Roman writer Ovid, and of other classical sources. The poem concludes with Amans healed by Venus and the dart removed.

This poem survives in no less than fifty-nine manuscript versions, which once more enable scholars to plot the revisions made by Gower. In the original prologue he described how he was rowing, or being rowed, on the Thames when he met the royal barge, and Richard II invited him to write something new. As a result, the dedication was originally made to Richard, but was later changed 'unto myn oghne lord, Which of Lancastre is named'—Henry Bolingbroke.[3]

Another passage removed during revision referred to his friend and fellow poet Geoffrey Chaucer. At the end of the poem, Gower had Venus say:

Adieu, for I mot fro the wende.
And gret well Chaucer whan ye mete,
As mi disciple and mi poete

[Farewell, for I must from thee go.
And warmly greet Chaucer when you meet,
As my disciple and my poet]

Much debate has been aired on the reason for this removal, with one theory being that he disapproved of the bawdy tales that Chaucer was reworking for *The Canterbury Tales*, but it is more likely that the lines were omitted for technical or structural considerations.

*Vox Clamantis* was witty and clever, appealing to a courtly audience, and thus proved popular, hence the number of manuscripts circulated. It was one of the first books to be published in printed form in England when William Caxton produced an edition in 1483 on his press in the almonry of Westminster Abbey. William Shakespeare took one of the tales contained within it, of Apollonius of Tyre, and included it in *Pericles, Prince of Tyre*, the play he wrote with a collaborator between 1606 and 1608. Shakespeare uses John Gower as the presenter of the play, acting throughout as the Chorus. In front of the palace at Antioch he opens the play by introducing himself:

To sing a song that old was sung
From ashes ancient Gower is come
Assuming man's infirmities
To glad your ear and please your eyes
It hath been sung at festivals,
On ember-eves and holy-ales
And lords and ladies in their lives
Have read it for restoratives.

We know little of John Gower's early life. The date of his birth is reckoned to be some time in the 1330s or 1340s, and he would appear to have spent much of his life in Southwark. At some point he moved into a house in the close of St Mary's Priory, possibly following benefactions made towards the repair of the buildings as a result of a fire in 1377. His will gives us some idea of the size of the house, for it mentions a hall, pantry and kitchen, an oratory and a bedroom. Certainly, he was in the priory, provided with a library and a scriptorium, when he married, perhaps for the second time. His wife was Agnes Groundolf, a fellow parishioner of St Mary Magdalene, and they were married in Gower's oratory by licence from the Bishop of Winchester on 2 January 1398. Some suggest that it was a matter of convenience between an ailing man and his nurse, for Gower was going blind. Even if it was a marriage of convenience, Gower nevertheless left Agnes in his will £100 in cash, rents of two manors in East Anglia, silver table plate, all the contents of the house in the priory close and a chalice and vestment from his oratory.

Agnes outlived Gower, who died in 1408. His will was generous to her, but also to the priory, leaving his library to the canons and arranging that a *martyrlogium*, a large book containing a calendar in which saints could be entered along with details of benefactors and obits, be given to them.[4] His elaborate tomb was originally placed in a chapel dedicated to St John the Baptist, now demolished, so that it is presently located in the north aisle of the church. Gower is described as 'Angolorum Poeta celeberrimus', with a brief biographical note on the wall behind him, written by Thomas Berthelet, the printer who produced an edition of *Confessio Amantis* in 1532, including a woodcut illustration of the tomb. Gower's cap is decorated with the Lancastrian red rose, and around his neck is a double 'S' collar, symbolising the patronage of Henry Bolingbroke. In 1393 Bolingbroke gave 'un esquire John Gower' just such a collar.

Perhaps the most significant detail in the Gower monument, however, is the fact that his head rests not on a conventional pillow, but on three of his books, and that those three works are in different languages: Latin, Norman French and Middle English. Gower was living at a pivotal time as far as the English language was concerned. When Richard II met the leaders of the Peasants' Revolt on 15 June 1386 at Smithfield, as Gower recorded in *Vox Clamantis*, the king addressed Wat Tyler in English. Following the stabbing of Tyler, Richard turned to the assembled rebels and again spoke English, making them a series of promises which were never in fact fulfilled. This is thought to be the first record of a monarch using English since the Norman Conquest. When Richard was deposed by Henry Bolingbroke in 1399, both the documents deposing him and the king's abdication speech were in English.

Four decades earlier, in 1362, the chancellor had addressed Parliament in Westminster Hall in English rather than French, introducing the idea that the vernacular should be used in official business, and contemporary records show that English was also replacing French in schoolrooms. The idea of court poets using their native tongue in their verse was also part of this important development, and the work of John Gower runs beside that of his friend, Geoffrey Chaucer. The two are linked in the tribute expressed by the poet John Lydgate around the year 1403 when he referred to 'Gower Chaucers ertheley goddes two', while the author of the 'Kingis Quair' (p. 29) dedicated their poem to the memory of 'Gowere and chaucere, that on the steppis satt of rethorike'.[5]

Although Chaucer's exact birth date is also not known, it was probably in the 1340s. He was born and bred in the City of London, the son of a vintner in Thames Street, the area near the wharves where merchants imported wine from Italy and Gascony. It is thought that he might have attended the school attached to St Paul's Cathedral, as it received in 1358 a generous benefaction of books, including works by Latin authors known to Chaucer, such as Virgil and Ovid.

For many years Chaucer worked as a servant of the Crown, beginning as a page in the household of Lionel, Duke of Clarence, the second surviving son of Edward III. In 1359, when he was in France with Edward's invading army during one of the campaigns in the Hundred Years War, Chaucer was captured and ransomed at the siege of Réthel. In 1366 he married Philippa Roet, the sister of Katherine Swynford, mistress of another of the king's sons, John of Gaunt. In time Katherine was to become Gaunt's third wife, while Chaucer enjoyed the enduring patronage of the duke.

In 1374 he was appointed comptroller in the port of London, responsible for the export tax on the lucrative trades in wool, skins and leather, working out of lodgings over the Aldgate, on the east side of the City. It would have taken no time at all for Chaucer to have crossed the river and visited Southwark and his friend John Gower. Crown patronage enabled him to travel widely in the 1370s, carrying diplomatic letters to various Western European courts. In particular, he spent time in Genoa and Florence, becoming familiar with the poetry of Petrarch, Boccacio and Dante, having accorded Gower power of attorney during his absence.

At some point Chaucer began to combine his administrative career with the writing of poetry. In the final lines of *Confessio Amantis*, Gower described how he wrote 'dites and songes glad' – courtly lyrical poetry – as a young man, but the first of his longer poems can be dated to the late 1360s when he produced *The Book of the Duchess*, his commemoration of the death of Blanche, Duchess of Lancaster, John of Gaunt's first wife. His travels abroad meant that he had an acquaintance with French and Italian poetry unmatched by any other English writer of the time, and these influences can be seen in works such as *Troilus and Criseyde*, which dates from around 1385. This was the time when he retired from his comptrollership and moved out of London to Kent, where he became a knight of the shire for Parliament.

Chaucer's place of residence in Kent is not known, but the favoured view is that it was Greenwich. Again, it was a short journey by horse for him to have travelled to Southwark to visit and dine with his friend John Gower. Here he would be able to get background material for his most famous literary work, *The Canterbury Tales*, perhaps over some of the Gascon wine donated by their mutual patron, Henry Bolingbroke.

As noted earlier, Thomas Becket was murdered in his cathedral at Canterbury on 29 December 1170 by four Norman knights, spurred into their action by the exasperated words of the king, Henry II, asking who would rid him of this troublesome priest. Condemnation of the murder ran throughout the kingdom, and through Europe, with people shocked by the violence and profanity of the crime. A cult, associated with the belief in the curative power of Becket's blood, instantly began: the first recorded miracle took place in Canterbury on 4 January 1171, with similar examples proliferating by Whitsun of that year. Two years later, Becket was canonised by the Pope, and the remorseful king encouraged pilgrimages, becoming one of the earliest to visit his tomb. By the late fourteenth century, it is estimated that around 200,000 pilgrims were making their way annually to Canterbury, and the cult had been developed into a highly organised industry.

Canterbury may have had Becket's shrine, but Londoners made him their patron saint, aware that he had grown up in the City. A memorial was created in the churchyard just north of St Paul's Cathedral, which became known as the Pardon Churchyard. Here Becket's parents, Gilbert and Matilda, were buried, and in time a chapel was founded in Thomas's memory, and this too became a pilgrimage centre.

Those who could afford the time and the expense of the pilgrimage to Canterbury officially began their journey at St Thomas's Chapel on London Bridge. Many, however, gathered in Southwark, and Chaucer chose this as the location for the starting point of his pilgrims. Borough High Street was lined with inns, which in this context were places of temporary accommodation rather than the private residences of prelates and aristocrats described earlier. Chaucer chose as his inn the Tabard, which had been adapted into a place for travellers by the Abbot of Hyde. It lay on the east side of

Borough High Street, a location now marked by Tabard House, part of Guy's Hospital.

In the Middle Ages, Southwark acted like a railway terminus, with merchants and other traders bringing their goods up from the Cinque Ports, Dover, Sandwich, Hythe, Romney and Deal, and from the hinterland of southern England. And, like a modern terminus, the inns were the equivalent of Victorian railway hotels, so that travellers could stay overnight, ready early in the morning to make their way across London Bridge when the gates were opened. In the other direction, those making their way into Kent, Surrey or Sussex could move quickly out of the metropolis.

Chaucer also names the host of the Tabard as Harry Bailly. Records dating from the 1370s show a Harry Bailly as an ostler, and possibly the same man was one of the MPs for Southwark at this time. Like many a Southwark entrepreneur, he was a man of many parts, collecting taxes, acting as a coroner and having an employee who ran a brothel. Whether Bailly actually owned the Tabard is not certain, but Chaucer as a fellow MP must have taken the name to use in this context. In the *Tales*, Bailly acts as the master of ceremonies for the journey to Canterbury, initiating a story-telling competition and offering free dinner to the winner on their return to Southwark.

Pilgrims were in a way the first tourists, undertaking their journey for pleasure, or at least for satisfaction, rather than for necessity. Chaucer sets his pilgrimage in April, when the days are lengthening and the roads more passable after the hard weather of winter. His memorable opening lines give the flavour of the excitement of the open road, with the opportunity for people to make new acquaintances and to see new places:

Whan that Aprill with his shoures soote
The droghte of March hath perced to the roote,
And bathed every veyne in swich licour
Of which vertu engendred is the flour;

3. *Chaucer's pilgrims setting off from the Tabard Inn to make their way to Canterbury.*

[When April with its sweet-smelling showers
Has pierced the drought of March to the root,
And bathed every vein (of the plants) in such liquid
By which power the flower is created;]
. . .
Thanne longen folk to goon on pilgrimages,
And palmeres for to seken straunge strondes,
To ferne halwes, kowthe in sondry londes;
And specially from every shires ende
Of Engelond to Caunterbury they wende,
The hooly blissful martir for to seke,

[Then folk long to go on pilgrimages,
And professional pilgrims to seek foreign shores,
To distant shrines, known in various lands;
And specially from every shire's end
Of England to Canterbury they travel,
To seek the holy blessed martyr,][6]

Chaucer takes twenty-nine pilgrims and, like John Gower, draws upon various levels of the society, but he has moved from the allegorical approach to individual characterisation. There are no high-born aristocrats, who would have had servants accompanying them, nor the poorest in society, who would not have been able to afford a horse to carry them. Regulations issued in 1381 set the fees for the hire of horses from Southwark: 12d to Rochester, 12d from Rochester to Canterbury, so beyond the purses of many.

Within this middle tranche of society, Chaucer presents us with a rich gallery of pen portraits, drawing upon his wide experience of people through his career serving the Crown, and, while compiling his *Tales*, observing the community of Southwark. Moreover, he gives these characterisations a wry twist. From the religious community he introduces one of his two female pilgrims, the Prioress, with her refined table manners, her knowledge of French after the manner of Stratford atte Bow in East London and her love of worldly possessions.

Two other characters from the religious community are more controversial: the Friar and the Summoner. The mendicant orders of friars were under fire at this time from those who argued that there was no theological basis for a life of poverty and that pastoral work should be exercised within the formal parochial structure. In 1356, for example, sermons were preached against friars at the open-air pulpit of the Cross in the churchyard of St Paul's Cathedral. As we have seen, John Gower was specifically critical of friars in *Speculum Meditantis*, and Chaucer tells us that his Friar is not a poor scholar, but more like a master of the Pope. The idea that pardon from sin could be purchased from men licensed by the Pope attracted the condemnation of the reformer John Wycliffe, and Chaucer would have been familiar with his views, as John of Gaunt was also his patron and protector. The prologue to 'The Pardoner's Tale' reveals the narrator's covetous nature, relating it to other sins, such as drunkenness, gluttony, gambling and swearing.

From the lay community, he introduces the Knight, privileged but also displaying integrity, modesty and courtesy, especially to women. Nevertheless, again there is a wry touch, for he presents a record of battle honours, but a recent historian has questioned the view of the Knight as a paragon of Christian chivalry, arguing that he is in fact no more than a professional mercenary, and that Chaucer based him on Sir John Hawkwood, an English freebooter whom he would have known about during his time in Italy.[7]

In strong contrast comes the Miller, bawdy where the Knight is genteel, and delivering a ribald parody of his tale of courtly love. Part of Chaucer's skill is that he chose prose and verse styles that suited every story and teller. Perhaps the most arresting is the example of the Reeve, who tells the tale of two clerks, Alan and John, 'born in the same village, name of Strother, Far in the North'. The Reeve, a carpenter by trade, clearly also comes from northern England, evident from the language that he uses, so that Alan protests, 'This lange nyght ther tydes me na reste', which has been rendered into a modern version as 'All this lang neet I shall na geet nie rest'.[8] Chaucer surely must have come across such a dialect while working as comptroller in the port of London.

The second female pilgrim is the Wife of Bath, providing Chaucer with the opportunity to look at contemporary ideas of marriage and love. Five times married, she not only demonstrates how she is able to consolidate money and power in a male-dominated society, but also challenges the claim of the superiority of celibacy, instead giving voice to female desire. Perhaps Chaucer fixed upon this wife coming from Bath because he spent some time in the early 1390s as Deputy Forester of the royal forest at North Petherton in Somerset.

The Tabard was one of the large inns located near the gates of London in the late medieval period. Ludgate Hill to the west and Bishopsgate to the north also offered such establishments, but Southwark had the greatest concentration as the one way southwards. Records show a colourful mixture of names. Perhaps the most intriguing is the Swan with Two Necks, just across Long Southwark, as the main street was often known, from the priory church. The 'necks' are 'nicks', the marks that used to be put upon the bills of swans in the Thames to show they were in the care of the Vintners' Company, as opposed to the Dyers and the Crown. Many of the inn names are heraldic – the Boar's Head that belonged at one stage to Sir John Fastolf, the Green Dragon, formerly the private London residence of the Cobham family, the White Hart, the badge of Richard II, and, most heraldic of all, the Tabard, the coat of a herald, emblazoned with the arms of the sovereign.

Chaucer says comparatively little about the accommodation and fare offered at the Tabard, apart from describing the rooms and stables as 'wide', making them 'easy, all was of the best', and the fare as 'vitaille at the beste' and 'strong wyn'. John Gower, on the other hand, is more critical in one of his descriptions of tradesmen in *Speculum Meditantis*. This has been translated as:

Concerning the Taverner I make my accusation,
That he falsely mixes the fresh wine
With the old wine of the previous year
Which lies spoiled in its cask
And is neither wholesome nor good;
This is the way with tavernkeeping[9]

Possibly his long sojourn in Southwark produced this jaundiced view.

The ancient Southwark inns were swept away in Victorian times to make way for the burgeoning railway system, but photographs survive of the Tabard shortly before its demolition. It had been rebuilt at least once because of fire but retained the galleries that looked down onto the courtyard and accommodated the bedrooms. One inn does survive, however, giving some idea of the scale of these institutions: the George, now looked after by the National Trust. This stands just south of the site of the Tabard, with the characteristically narrow street frontage forming the gateway into the front courtyard.

The courtyard runs back and back, and in its complete form would have reached stables at the very back.

An idea of what these inns must have been like can also be gleaned from two very ancient hostelries in south-west England. One is the George Inn at Norton St Philip in Somerset, approximately halfway between Bath and Frome. The second is the Old Bell at Malmesbury in Wiltshire. Both were originally linked to monasteries: the George Inn with the Carthusians at Hinton Charterhouse; the Old Bell was the abbey guest house in Malmesbury. The considerable size of these establishments may be compared with the footprint of the medieval Southwark inns. The establishments along Borough High Street were destroyed in the 'Great Fire of Southwark' in 1676 and rebuilt in the fashionable style of the late seventeenth century, but the courtyard at the back of the George Inn at Norton St Philip, dating from the fifteenth century, gives an idea of what the Tabard, for example, might have looked like in Chaucer's day, with half-timbered galleries on the first floor giving access to the bedrooms of the inn.[10]

More details can be added from other writings of the fifteenth century. One takes the form of a spurious fifteenth-century addition to *The Canterbury Tales*, with a Prologue and 'The Tale of Beryn'.[11] Chaucer's pilgrims never got to Canterbury, but in this tale they do so, and go sightseeing around the city. After the first outing, the two female pilgrims, the Prioress and the Wife of Bath, stay behind for dinner while the rest venture out again. The two women stroll along gravel alleys in the inn's gardens, savouring the railed beds of herbs, such as sage and hyssop. It is highly likely that in the fourteenth century the Southwark inns would have had such gardens, perhaps beyond the stables, for cultivating herbs, vegetables and orchard fruits for catering to the large number of guests. When the Tabard was rebuilt in 1588, records show that it had a drinking bower furnished with tables, forms and wicker lattices.

An idea of this catering is given in a French conversation manual written c.1415 by a writing master in Oxford, William Kingsmill.

He introduces six male travellers with their three servants and nine horses staying at an inn in the city. The host of the inn boasts of being able to stable and feed 100 horses altogether. The hostess, meanwhile, can offer chambers where the beds are furnished with curtains, testers, mattresses, blankets and feather pillows. She offers to provide food in-house, or to fetch from a cookshop. She has every kind of fowl, apples, pears, cheese and eggs, so that the guests choose to eat in. Breakfast consists of a robust menu of boar with mustard, beef, mutton and boiled pork.[12]

'The Tale of Beryn' is a testament to the enduring popularity of *The Canterbury Tales*. Fifty-five manuscripts survive with different versions of Chaucer's tales, in various orders, and some are beautifully illustrated. Just as William Caxton produced a printed version of John Gower's *Vox Clamantis*, so he published a version of *The Canterbury Tales* in 1478, with a second edition illustrated by woodcut images five years later. In another work by Chaucer that he printed and published, he described him as 'the worshipful fader & first founder and enbellissher of ornate eloquence in our Englissh'. Gower too was celebrated by Caxton as a father, 'full of senetence sette so frutously'.[13]

Images of Chaucer's pilgrims appear in one of the early-twentieth-century stained-glass windows in the north aisle of Southwark Cathedral. Harry Bailly leads the group out through the gateway of the Tabard Inn, watched by a chamber-maid looking down from one of the windows of the inn. Above the travellers is a tabard, bearing the lions of England and the fleurs de lys of France, the arms of the Plantagenet kings. The designer of the glass, Charles Eamer Kempe, apparently expressed reservations that a tavern should be depicted in a church but was reminded by one of the cathedral's clergymen that Christ had been born in the stable of an inn. Kempe was no doubt less concerned about the window that he designed for John Gower, which is set above the present location of his tomb. St John is shown for the poet, and St Agnes for his wife.

# 5

## The Bishop's Geese

The medieval bishops of Winchester were not only senior in the episcopal order but also, with close to sixty manors spread across the south of England, immensely wealthy. Some of this wealth was derived from an unlikely source: the licensing of brothels in Southwark, where the prostitutes came to be known as the Bishop of Winchester's geese.

Legal anomalies were a speciality of Southwark. Some parts were known as liberties, lying outside the jurisdiction of the Crown and the City. The Liberty of the Clink lay within the purlieus of Winchester House, with the bishop as owner, enabling him to allow brothels to operate on his estate. They were particularly located along the banks of the Thames, on Bankside, and were known as stews.

When exactly the bishop began to lease brothels and to gain money from so doing is not certain. This uncertainty is not helped by a retrospective claim by one of the incumbents in the fifteenth century that Henry II had in 1161 issued royal ordinances establishing Southwark as London's authorised district of prostitution. In this claim it was mentioned that Parliament supported Henry's ordinances, impossible as Parliament had not existed at this time.

Various attempts had been made to ban prostitution within the walls of the City of London. Concerns were expressed in the 1130s following a change in the constitution of the clerical establishment at St Paul's Cathedral, introducing a dean and chapter. Before this change, the canons had been able to marry, but now they were to be celibate. One effect of this change was the record growth of the number of brothels in the surrounding streets. This interesting development could not be reversed, despite proclamations of bans over the next centuries, including one in 1276–78 which seems to have been effective at the time but did not last. So, a different approach was sought, and in 1393 a proclamation officially sanctioned brothels in two parts of London only: in Cokkes Lane in Smithfield, outside the City walls but within its jurisdiction; and in the Bishop of Winchester's liberty, although it was the Borough's bailiff and his officers who were to be held responsible for the upholding of strict regulations.

This was precisely the time when John Gower and Geoffrey Chaucer were composing some of their works in English. They would no doubt have found interesting the etymology of the reference to stews. This was derived from the term for the stoves used to heat bathhouses, but the brothels were established close by the bishop's stewponds in his park at Winchester House that supplied fish such as pike and carp for his table. The earliest reference in English to a stew as a fishpond comes in 1387, about the same time that Chaucer refers to a stew or 'styve' as a brothel in 'The Friar's Tale'.

There have been various suggestions put forward as to why the prostitutes of Bankside were identified with geese. One is that they screeched like the birds, another that their arms, whitened with mercury, looked like the necks of geese. Just as Cokkes or Cock Lane in Smithfield implied sexual activity, so did some of the streets of Bankside: Maiden's Lane, Foul Lane, Codpiece Lane, along with Slut's Hole and Cuckold Court.

In issuing the ordinances of 1393, considerations of public order rather than morality were the primary concern. The Church in the

Middle Ages would appear to have viewed prostitution as a necessary evil, protecting the respectable women of the community from the lusts of men. St Augustine of Hippo, for example, had written back in the fifth century that to 'Suppress prostitution and capricious lusts will overthrow society', a view echoed later by St Thomas Aquinas when he is said to have declared: 'Towns are like the cesspool in the palace; take away the cesspool and the palace will become an unclean and evil-smelling place.'[1]

The very precise regulations contained in the ordinances reflect the concern to repress procurers who might seek to draw 'honest' women into the profession. Originally, stewholders were to be married men, whose houses were to be used only as brothels, and not to sell food, fuel or candles. They were to retain just one female servant, a laundress, and a male servant to act as an ostler. One ordinance stated that a prostitute should pay the customary rent of 14 pence per week, a high sum for the time, but the brothel keepers were subject to high rents, the lucrative income enjoyed by the Bishops of Winchester. The prostitute must be allowed to come and go at will, with the stewholder as their landlord rather than their master. There were regulations forbidding the stewholder from having within their establishment women of religion, married women, anybody suffering from sickness, or anybody who might be pregnant.

Boatmen on the Thames were forbidden to bring any man or woman to the stews between sunset and sunrise, or to tie up their boats within 20 fathoms of the shore during that time, 'lest evildoers be assisted in their coming and going'. Stewholders were forbidden to keep boats, presumably to prevent them soliciting custom.

Strict regulations also applied to the behaviour of the prostitutes. A form of sumptuary laws was published so that the women might be identified by their apparel. For example, they were forbidden to wear aprons, thought to be a garment of respectability. At one stage they were obliged to wear striped hoods but it was stipulated that these must not be coloured or trimmed with fur. It was forbidden for the women to hinder a man in the street from passing by, or to grab him by his clothing. There was to be no short-changing; they were to lie with a man until morning. Paramours were not to be kept in the brothel, and prostitutes were to absent themselves during daytime on holy days. Mirroring the regulations applied to a stewholder, if a prostitute fell pregnant, got married, joined a religious order or contracted a 'perilous infirmity', they would be evicted.

The levels of punishment were considerably greater for the prostitutes than the stewholders. They could include heavy fines, imprisonment or being ducked in a cucking stool. The last was a punishment imported from Germany, where it was used for execution, literally drowning a person in muck and excrement. In England it was used rather for humiliation. William Langland in his fourteenth-century poem *Piers Plowman* mentions just such a punishment. Prostitutes who kept a paramour, for example, were to be imprisoned for three weeks, fined 6s 8d, set on the cucking stool and expelled from the manor.

As one historian has pointed out, these regulations present a picture of model manorial governance, commercial regulation and the keeping of public order, but in practice the ordinances were often flouted. Records show that women at times were forced into prostitution. A young girl, Isabel Lane, for example, was procured in 1439 by Margaret Hathewyk 'for certain Lombards and other men unknown'. She was allegedly raped in Margaret's house and elsewhere and taken against her will to Bankside. Another case involved Thomas Bowde, who lured his servant girl across the river to Bankside.[2]

Moreover, the brothels were not confined to Bankside. Borough High Street served as the entrepot for travellers coming from all parts of southern England, providing not only victualling and accommodation with its inns, but also satisfying sexual needs. In 1433 the residents of the Borough presented a petition to Parliament complaining how former Bankside stewholders had set up similar establishments in the High Street, where thieves and other miscreants were entertained by the prostitutes.

Chaucer must have known about these, for he begins 'The Pardoner's Tale' with just such a scene, although he sets it in the Low Countries:

In Flanders once there was a company
Of youngsters haunting vice and ribaldry,
Riot and gambling, stews and public-houses
Where each with harp, guitar or lute carouses

Like Chaucer, William Shakespeare would have been familiar with the Southwark establishments, and one such makes an appearance in *Measure for Measure,* probably written in the summer of 1604. Although the play is set in Vienna it has a distinct London character, with Mistress Overdone ostensibly running a drinking-house that is, in fact, a house of ill repute, employing bawds, such as Kate Keep-Down.

It is interesting that Chaucer in his tale told by the Pardoner sets his group in Flanders, for again and again immigrants from the Low Countries are invoked in this context. During the Peasants' Revolt in 1381, followers of Wat Tyler attacked a brothel inhabited by *frows de Flaundres* near London Bridge on their rampage through Southwark. This reflects the influx of 'aliens' at this time, but it might also be interpreted as introducing an exotic element, skilled in sophisticated activities, just as French prostitutes were sometimes viewed in the nineteenth century. In the early seventeenth century John Marston wrote a play, *The Dutch Courtesan*, that was incongruously performed by the company of boy actors attached to St Paul's Cathedral.

The Tudor chronicler John Stow highlighted in his survey of London published in 1598 the peculiar medieval institution of brothels licensed by the Bishops of Winchester: 'On this [west bank of the Thames] was sometime the Bordello, or stewes, a place so called of certaine stew houses privilidged there, for the repaire of incontinent men to the like women.' By the time he was writing, attempts by the Crown had been made to tackle the increasing development of this red-light district. In 1504 Henry VII decreed the number of licences should be cut from eighteen to twelve, concerned about the spread of syphilis and other venereal diseases. Stow explained that 'These allowed stew houses had signes on their frontes, towardes the Thames, not hanged out, but painted on the walles, as a Boares head, the Crosse keys, the Gunne, the Castle, the Crane, the Cardinals hat, the Bel, the Swanne, etc.'.[3] Gillian Tindall in her book about the houses of Bankside, featuring in particular one still standing next to Cardinal's Cap Alley, noted that these black signs were painted on white-washed walls so as to be visible across the Thames. This prefigured the later practice of printing the names of wharves large and clear on the walls.[4]

Henry VIII went further than his father, suppressing the Bankside brothels altogether in 1546. The result was a dispersal of prostitutes into other parts of London. The herald Charles Wriothesley, who kept a chronicle of events running through the reigns of Henry and his successors, Edward VI, Mary and Elizabeth, made note of the effect by citing one example. He described how in July 1548 'a single woman called Founsing Besse, which was a whore of the stewes ... after the putting downe of them was taken and banished out of divers wardes of the citie. And now taken in a garden by Fynesburie Court with one of the Kinges trumpeters, which for her vicious life not yet amended was had to the counter in Bread Streete [the prison attached to the Lord Mayor's court].' From there she was taken to the pillory in Cheapside, with basins being beaten to attract public attention, and had her hair cut off at the ears, and a paper placed on her breast 'declaring her vicious living'. Bess then stood in the pillory for an hour 'which punishement hath been an old auncient lawe in this citie of longe tyme and now putt in use againe'.[5] This punishment of public humiliation reflects the medieval custom of the cucking stool.

Bess had the misfortune to be caught and punished, but many of her fellow prostitutes were able to avoid detection by turning to taverns to ply their trade. Robert Crowley, writing an epigram 'Of Bawdes', printed in 1550, warned that the suppression, just four years old, would prove ineffective:

The bawds of the stues in taverns and typling house
be turned all out; many myght be founde,
But some thing that they inhabit if officers would make search
al Englande through out. But as they are bounde[6]

The prostitutes returned in force to Bankside, and to another Southwark liberty just to the west, Paris Garden. In the twelfth century the land, under the name of Wideflete, was acquired by the military order of the Templars and after their suppression passed to the Knights Hospitallers. Wideflete, which can be translated as 'willow stream', was very marshy, lying several feet below the high-water level of the Thames, so that embanking with an earth wall was necessary. Today this topography is reflected in the names of two of the modern streets, Upper Ground and Broadwall.

The name Paris, or Parish, Garden first appears in a record in the early fifteenth century when the manor belonged for a time to Henry V's brother, John, Duke of Bedford, before reverting to the Hospitallers, and is defined as a privileged place, meaning that it was a liberty. Court rolls from the fifteenth and sixteenth centuries contain entries about women presented for misconduct, including whores and hucksters, or pedlars. During the reign of Elizabeth I it was the venue for clandestine meetings of foreign ambassadors and their agents, just across the river from the seat of government in Westminster. In 1578, for example, the Recorder for London, William Fleetwood, wrote to the Queen's Secretary of State, William Cecil, Lord Burghley, telling him how the French ambassador was holding meetings with the Bishop of Ross. The area was so densely wooded that even on a moonlit night 'one man cannot see another' amid the thickets.[7]

The Duke of Bedford built a mansion house here during his occupancy of the manor. Early in the reign of Henry VIII this was acquired by William Baseley, who set about repairing the manor from its ruinous state and draining the land around, which had flooded. Years later he made it into a public gaming place, with bowling alleys outdoors and tables for dice and cards indoors. The house and its garden were acquired by a City merchant, Francis Langley, who built the Swan Theatre on part of the site, opened in 1593 (p. 108). The area had become a centre for animal baiting, and now it would contain most of the capital's public theatres. Customers took the short boat ride across the Thames and landed at Bankside, combining on occasion a visit to all three attractions. In the words of one seventeenth-century commentator of the Puritan persuasion: 'This may better bee termed afoule dene than a faire garden . . . Here comes few that either regard their credit, or their losse of time: the swaggering Roarer, the cunning Cheater, the rotten Bawd and the bloudy Butcher have their rendezvous here.'[8]

It comes as no surprise that local prostitutes figure in plays of the period, and Ben Jonson also brought them into his verses. He wielded his satirical pen to feature one named Kate Arden. In his poem 'The Famous Voyage' he describes a wherry boat being rowed up the notoriously noxious Fleet Ditch, running north from the Thames just to the west of Ludgate Hill. He likens the stench both to that wafting from the rotting meat fed to the bears in their enclosure in Paris Garden, which he calls their college, and that experienced by being kissed by Kate:

The meate-boate of Beares colledge, Paris-garden,
Stunke not so ill, nor, when shee kist, Kate Arden[9]

Jonson had been a journeyman actor in the theatres of Paris Garden, so would have been only too aware of the strong aroma of the bears.

Another writer came to Kate's defence, albeit rather backhandedly: 'Bears are more clean than swine, and so's Kate Arden'.[10]

In 1613 the Globe Theatre on Bankside burned down after a cannon being fired during a performance of Shakespeare's *Henry VIII* set alight the thatched roof. Ben Jonson later attributed the destruction to a virulent dose of 'burning clap' from the unfortunate Kate in his poem 'An Execration Upon Vulcan'.

Another target of his accusations of transmitting venereal disease was Bess Broughton. She ran one of the most exclusive and expensive brothels in the early seventeenth century, known as the Holland Leaguer. This occupied the mansion house in Paris Garden that had in turn accommodated a royal prince, the Duke of Bedford, the gaming establishment of William Baseley, and the residence of Francis Langley, the proprietor of the Swan Theatre. Bess Broughton, sometimes known as Hollander, was said to charge £20 for dinner followed by what could be termed post-prandial amusements. This sum was considerable: a clergyman at this period might hope to earn this as his annual salary, while a schoolmaster would have to make do with around £12. It was said that leading members of the royal court were among her clients. King James would seem an unlikely contender, but his favourite, George Villiers, Duke of Buckingham, might have made the journey to Paris Garden. It was a world away from the sixpenny whoredom reputed to be earned in the taverns and alleys of Southwark.

Jonson was no respecter of a high-class courtesan. In his poem about the burning of the Globe, he linked Bess with Kate Arden:

Pox take thee, Vulcan. May Pandora's pox
And all the ills that flew out of her Box
Light on thee. And if those Plagues won't doe,
The Wive's Pox take thee, and Bess Broughton's too[11]

Bess seems to have attracted a lot of opprobrium. One well-known proverb circulating in the early seventeenth century ran, 'No Goose

4. *The brothel run by Bess Broughton in Paris Garden that was reproduced on the title page of Shakerley Marmion's play* Holland's Leaguer *in 1632.*

bit so sore as Bess Broughton', depicting her as the transmitter of venereal disease.

'Leaguer' was the name used for a military encampment, and once more a connection with the Low Countries appears; a popular rumour of the time linked the house specifically with Dutch prostitutes. Bess used the moat, portcullis and drawbridge as part of her marketing, but the defences no doubt came in useful when apprentices on the rampage attacked the Leaguer on Shrove Tuesday in 1631. This prompted a playwright, Shakerley Marmion, to write *Holland's Leaguer*, first performed in December of that year. On the title page of the printed version of the play, an image of Bess's establishment was reproduced with its defences and a small garden.

Southwark was home to a considerable population of apprentices, whose common practice it was to take advantage of their holiday on the last day before Lent to run wild and cause havoc. Marmion in his play refers directly to the 1631 incident at the Leaguer: 'Good Sir, let's think on some revenge; call up/ The gentleman's 'prentices, and make a Shrove Tuesday'.[12]

A similar incident occurred in March 1668 when apprentices attacked brothels, including that of Damaris Page, described by Samuel Pepys as 'the great bawd of the seamen'. Page was favoured by the king's brother, James, Duke of York, the Lord High Admiral. Pepys in his diary goes on to note how 'the Duke of York complained merrily that he hath lost two tenants by their houses being pulled down, who paid him for their wine licences 15 l [pounds] a year. But here it was said how these idle fellows have had the confidence to say that they did ill in contenting themselves in pulling down the little bawdy-houses and did not go and pull down the great bawdy-house at Whitehall. And some of them have the last night had a word among them, and it was "Reformation and Reducement!"'. Pepys also noted that it was said that they had 'men of understanding among them, that have been of Cromwell's army'.[13]

The Duke of York may have been merry, but the response to the apprentices' misbehaviour was savage, for it was felt that with their rallying cry they were threatening the Crown: it was only eight years after the Restoration. Four of the apprentices were hanged, drawn and quartered, and two of their severed heads were set on the southern gate of London Bridge.

It would seem unlikely that the unfortunate apprentices were preaching moral reformation, but there had been a growing chorus of disapproval from Puritans who linked prostitution with the malign influence of the theatre. As early as 1579 a writer, Stephen Gosson, produced a treatise, *The School of Abuse*, in which he described play-houses as being no more than an anteroom for a brothel: 'every wanton and his paramour, every man and his mistress, every John and Joan, every knave and his Quean, are there first acquainted and cheapen [bargain] for merchandise in this place, which they pay for elsewhere as they can agree.'[14] In the years that followed, there were many attempts to pass civil laws to condemn and punish sexual laxness. In 1650, with the Puritans wielding power in Parliament, a law was passed making adultery a felony punishable by death, and fornication punishable by three months' imprisonment. The threat was severe but, as with so many earlier attempts at control of prostitution, doomed to fail.

The bishop's geese had widely scattered, although Southwark remained one of the areas of the city most populated by prostitutes, and thus represented an attractive draw. In August 1663 Pepys wrote in his diary of a visit across the Thames to Mother Palmer's. This lady was known for a kind of ventriloquism, whereby she spoke 'in the belly', and Pepys had paid her an earlier visit and had 'good sport'. Assuming that she ran a brothel, he hoped to 'light upon some lady of pleasure (for which God forgive me)', for Pepys could never resist a sexual encounter. Instead, he spent the afternoon listening to Mrs Palmer singing, which must have been both disappointing and excruciating, for Pepys was a fine musician: 'And for her singing which she pretends to, is only some old bawdy songs, and those sung abominably; only, she pretends to be able to sing both bass and treble; which she doth, something like but not like what I thought formerly and expected now. Nor doth her speaking in her belly take me now as it did then, but it may be that is because I know it and see her mouth when she speaks, which should not be'.[15] Altogether, this visit to Bankside proved a dismal failure, with Pepys obliged to spend a shilling on wine.

Although London's West End, and in particular Soho, had become the leading red-light district, the Bankside attractions continued. One expert on London's topography suggested in the 1970s that panoramas of Southwark of the eighteenth century depicted substantial brothels moored to the south bank. There was, however, no longer a bishop of Winchester resident: the last incumbent to occupy Winchester House had been Lancelot Andrewes, who died in 1626. Moreover, the bishopric itself was for a time suppressed when Parliament considered getting rid of all cathedrals in the 1650s. On the Restoration of Charles II, the palace was returned to the bishopric, but there was also a property in Chelsea provided by Act of Parliament in 1661. With the growth of the population of Southwark and the development of industry along the river, the location probably did not appeal. Instead, the buildings were let out in multiple tenancies and grew ever more dilapidated. Some of the walls of the old palace buildings were incorporated into new structures, but a serious fire in 1814 revealed part of the bishops' great hall with its medieval rose window, as can still be seen on Clink Street. It serves as a reminder of the wealth of the see, and of the income derived from the prostitutes of Southwark.

There are just two women featured in the screen behind the high altar erected for the newly created Southwark Cathedral in 1905: St Margaret of Antioch and St Mary Magdalene. They are here because there were local parish churches dedicated to them. However, the inclusion of St Mary Magdalene is also a reminder that she was the fallen woman featured in the New Testament. And, perhaps significantly, while all the other figures on the screen look out, she alone is looking up towards the figure of Christ.

A fascinating coda to John Stow's account in 1598 of the bishop's geese in Southwark notes: 'I have heard ancient men of good credite report, that these single women were forbidden the rightes of the Church, so long as they continued that sinnefull life, and were excluded from christian buriall, if they were not reconciled before their death. And therefore was a plot of ground, called the single woman's churchyard, appoynted for them, far from the parish church [St Saviour's]'.[16]

This note has roused much interest and speculation in recent years. In the 1990s, excavations were undertaken at a site now known as Cross Bones, located on Redcross Way, by the Museum of London Archaeology Service during the construction of the Jubilee Underground Line. At the time of the Great Plague, in 1665, the land here had been acquired by St Saviour's as a plague pit, and it was subsequently consecrated as a cemetery for the poor of the parish. When it was closed in 1853, the site was described as completely overcharged with the dead, and thus burials were 'inconsistent with a due regard for the public health and public decency'. The archaeologists during their dig in the 1990s uncovered a small part of the cemetery, but even in this restricted area they found some 15,000 bodies piled one on top of another.

As early as 1795 the Redcross Way site was claimed to be the Single Women's churchyard, although Stow never specified its location beyond setting it some distance from St Saviour's. Moreover, he had been not entirely correct that the Church forbade Christian burial for unrepentant prostitutes. Ecclesiastical records identified the burial of single women, sometimes describing them as 'wenches', which might suggest they were prostitutes.[17] The question, however, remains, if this is not Stow's Single Women's churchyard, then where is it?

The site is now a lovely garden, run by the Friends of Cross Bones, full of references to the bishop's geese, such as an arcaded entry in the form of a goose wing. At the suggestion of John Constable, who was very involved with the establishment of the garden, a service is held annually by the Dean of Southwark on the nearest Sunday to the feast day of St Mary Magdalene, 22 July. The first such service, held in 2015, was described as 'An Act of Regret, Remembrance, Restoration', with the burial ground given the blessing of the Church.

Services have also been held on the eve of All Souls' Day at the end of October to honour the outcast dead. For, even if the Church did not deny Christian burial to the Winchester geese, as suggested by John Stow, these women were usually poor and led difficult lives. They risked disease and were treated with disdain and derision, often suffering heavy and humiliating punishments. In a strongly patriarchal society, their lot was a difficult one.

The cathedral, along with the Globe Theatre, has also been a venue for performance of *The Southwark Mysteries*, written by John Constable.[18] He began to publish them as a series of poems and mystery plays in 1996, casting himself in the role of John Crow, a trickster-familiar. He encounters the Goose in the Cross Bones Graveyard, where she introduces herself as 'born a Goose of Southwark by the Grace of Mary Overie, Whose Bishop gives me licence to sin within the Liberty. In Bankside stews and taverns you can hear me honk right daintily, As I unlock the hidden door, unveil the Secret History'.

# 6

## Spreading the Word

Alongside the high-ranking ecclesiastical figures and saints appearing in the screen behind the high altar of Southwark Cathedral is one man who held a more modest office, Prebendary John Rogers. Rogers, however, played a very important role in scriptural history by preserving the translations rendered into English by William Tyndale.

There had been scriptures in the vernacular in Anglo-Saxon times, but these disappeared with the Norman Conquest. At the very time that courtly poetry began to be written in English and that the vernacular was making an appearance in legal documents and in the schoolroom, in the late fourteenth century, there began a demand that the Bible should likewise be available. This demand came from the Lollards, the followers of the theologian and religious reformer John Wycliffe. There is no record of Wycliffe undertaking any actual translation; nevertheless, he was denounced for the offence of offering ordinary people the opportunity to consider the scriptures for themselves. When Wycliffe died in 1384, he was declared a heretic, and his followers, named Lollards after the Dutch for 'mutterers', faced persecution including denunciation for wanting an English Bible.

In 1411, Thomas Arundel, Archbishop of Canterbury, wrote to the Pope describing Wycliffe as 'pestilent and wretched ... of cursed memory, that son of the old serpent', and accusing him of 'devising – to fill up the measure of his malice – the expedient of a new translation of the Scriptures into the mother tongue'.[1]

Although many scriptures, along with the writings of Wycliffe, were rounded up and burnt, about 250 Bibles and New Testaments have survived. Some are large and beautifully written and decorated, while others are small and in comparatively rough hand. The centre for their covert production was among the craftsmen who lived and worked in the area just to the north of St Paul's Cathedral. These craftsmen were known as stationers because they sold books on stalls or stations within the cathedral's churchyard, and in 1403 they founded themselves into a 'Misterie', which in time became the Stationers' Company.

Despite the fact that John of Gaunt protected and supported Wycliffe, his son King Henry IV, and, even more so, his grandson Henry V, persecuted the Lollards when the movement became associated with social rebellion. Recantation and penance in St Paul's Churchyard were replaced by burning at the stake of those found guilty of heresy. One of the first to suffer this terrible fate was John Badby, at Smithfield in 1410.

The whole controversy about the Bible in English gained momentum with the invention of moveable type by Gutenberg in Mainz in 1452. It was now possible for writings to be produced not as individual manuscripts but in hundreds of copies, if not thousands. The catalyst came in 1516 with the publication of *Novum Instrumentum*, a new Latin translation by the Dutch humanist scholar, Erasmus, of the New Testament with a critical commentary and the original Greek alongside. The place of publication was the Swiss city of Basel, safe from Church authorities, but an Oxford scholar, William Tyndale, took up the Greek text and began to translate it into English.

At the time Tyndale was acting as tutor to the Walsh family in his native Gloucestershire. In the spring of 1523 he sought permission from Cuthbert Tunstall, Bishop of London, to print his translation. Tunstall's refusal spurred him to leave for mainland Europe, declaring that there was no place in England for him if he could not undertake publication. Tyndale's version of the New Testament was printed in Worms in Germany in 1525, with copies smuggled up the Rhine and into Britain. Bishop Tunstall responded to this provocation by rounding up all the copies he could find and burning them, along with the writings of the reformer Martin Luther.

By 1534 Tyndale was living in Antwerp as a guest of Thomas Poyntz, an English merchant and cousin of Lady Walsh, who had employed him in Gloucestershire as tutor to her children. Here he met John Rogers, a Cambridge graduate who was employed as chaplain to the English House in the city. Despite the sympathetic support of Henry VIII's chief minister, Thomas Cromwell, and other members of the English royal court, a combination of forces firmly opposed to religious reform succeeded in getting Tyndale arrested outside the English House in early 1536, and in the autumn he was strangled and burnt at the stake as a heretic at Vilvoorde Castle just outside Brussels. According to the martyrologist John Foxe, his final, haunting words were 'Lord, open the King of England's eyes'.[2] In a remarkably short time his wish was to be fulfilled.

In 1535 an Augustinian friar from Cambridge, Miles Coverdale, working independently from Tyndale, had translated and printed the entire Bible in English while living in Antwerp. Where exactly it was printed has been a subject of controversy, but suffice to say that the sheets were imported into England and preliminary pages were added by James Nicolson at his press in the precinct of St Thomas' Hospital, just off Borough High Street. Nicolson was a glazier by training and, despite his anglicised name, was born in the Hapsburg dominions, probably in the Netherlands. He is first recorded in England in 1518 when he was working in Cambridge, and in 1526 he was one of a group of glaziers working on the windows for King's College Chapel (p. 96). At some point he came to the attention of Thomas Cromwell, when he acted as a guarantor for the appearance in court of a man called Fyrmyne de Bos.[3]

James Nicolson is unusual in that his press was in Southwark. This location was no doubt dictated by the fact that he was part of the community of makers of stained glass, requiring him to be close to the river, as well as being beyond the City regulations.[4] He is often described as the printer of the first Bible in English. The historian Peter Blayney, however, points out that the book was printed in mainland Europe, with Nicolson adding his imprint information at the beginning, so he is better credited as the first publisher of an English Bible. Such was the demand for Coverdale's Bible that he was very soon to organise a reprint, which he made on his own press.

The connection with Cromwell is significant, for he enabled the Coverdale Bible to be imported openly, unlike Tyndale's New Testament. It is estimated that the production run for the Coverdale version was between 1,000 and 1,500 copies, each containing 284 printed sheets, so a substantial arrival. Records are mostly missing for the autumn of 1535, but on 9 September Nicolson received a single basket with unbound books valued at £4, possibly the first of a series of shipments. Cromwell would have ensured that the text was examined, for Coverdale on the title page expressed the hope that Henry VIII would accept the translation and even included a depiction of the king handing copies to his bishops. This hope became reality two years later.

Following Tyndale's death, John Rogers managed to rescue his writings and assembled a complete Bible by amalgamating the New Testament and part of the Old with a translation by Coverdale. This was first printed in Antwerp by two London merchants and issued under the name of two of Jesus's disciples, Thomas and Matthew, for Tyndale had died a heretic and thus could not be named. In time this version of the scriptures became known as Matthew's Bible and was licensed by Henry VIII.

Thomas Cromwell's ambition to place a copy of an English Bible in every parish church was gradually coming to pass, for Matthew's Bible led two years later, in 1540, to a further revision known as the Great Bible. This had as its title page a depiction of Henry VIII handing Bibles to his chief ministers, Archbishop Thomas Cranmer and Thomas Cromwell, who then passed them down to the king's grateful subjects. Ironically, at this very time the precarious balance at the Tudor court was shifting, so that Cromwell fell from power in the summer of 1540. Among the articles of accusation against him was the introduction and maintenance of Lutheran and Anabaptist doctrines: he was executed on 28 July without trial, a triumph for the religious conservatives, led by Stephen Gardiner, Bishop of Winchester.

John Rogers, the rescuer of Tyndale's texts, remained in Antwerp for several years, marrying a Flemish woman, Adriana de Weyden, before becoming pastor of Meldorf in north-west Germany. Here he met the Lutheran scholar, Philip Melanchthon, who described him in a letter: 'a learned man ... gifted with great ability, which he sets off with a noble character ... he will be careful to live in concord with his colleagues ... his integrity, trustworthiness and constancy in every duty make him worthy of the love and support of all good men'.[5]

These qualities shine through in Rogers' subsequent career, when he returned to England and became vicar of two of the leading London churches in Friday Street, where he was known for his powerful preaching. Edward VI was now on the English throne, and a Protestant reformation of the English Church was taking place. In 1551 Nicholas Ridley, Bishop of London, made Roger prebendary of St Pancras in St Paul's Cathedral. But this brief time of recognition and safety ended two years later with the death of Edward VI and the accession of Mary Tudor, who was determined to return England to the Church of Rome. Ordered to keep to his house, and accused by the Privy Council of preaching sedition, Rogers was deprived of his prebendary. After several months, he was removed by the new Bishop of London, Edmund Bonner, to Newgate Prison, where he shared a cell with the Protestant bookseller John Day. It was probably conversation with Rogers that inspired Day later to produce the great work on the persecution of Protestants, John Foxe's *Actes and Monuments*, more commonly known as *Foxe's Book of Martyrs*.

Rogers also met in Newgate other leading Protestants, including John Hooper, Lawrence Saunders and John Bradford. Their petitions to the queen for less rigorous treatment, and for the opportunity to state their case, were disregarded. Instead, in December 1554, Parliament re-enacted anti-Lollard legislation permitting the execution of heretics. Rogers, along with Bradford, Hooper, Saunders, Robert Ferrar and five others, were brought before Stephen Gardiner, the Bishop of Winchester and Lord Chancellor, in trials held in what is now the retrochoir of Southwark Cathedral.

Gardiner has gone down in history as plain-speaking and irascible, bitterly disliked by Protestants such as John Foxe, who described him as 'wily'. Although Gardiner sharply interrogated the prisoners at their trial, Rogers defended himself ably, denying that he was a heretic. It was, however, a doomed enterprise, and Gardiner and his council condemned him along with the others, delivering them to the secular power to be burnt at the stake in locations associated with their former clerical positions. Thus, Robert Ferrar, as Bishop of St David's, was executed at Carmarthen, John Hooper as Bishop of Gloucester and Worcester at Gloucester, and Lawrence Saunders, who had connections with Lichfield, at Coventry. Smithfield was chosen as the place of execution for John Rogers, and later for John Bradford.

Stained-glass windows were put into the retrochoir in the nineteenth century to commemorate the ordeal that these men went through during their heresy trials. These have not survived, but as noted earlier a statue of Prebendary John Rogers is included in the screen behind the high altar of the cathedral.

Rogers met his fate on 4 February 1555. According to John Foxe, great crowds lined the streets, rejoicing in his constancy and crying out to him to have courage. His wife Adriana chose to be at Smithfield to strengthen him against the ordeal, along with their eleven children, one born since his arrest and held at her breast. Offered a pardon on condition that he recanted, Rogers refused and exhorted the crowd to stand firm in their faith that they had been taught. When the fire took hold of his body, 'he, as one feeling no smart, washed his hands in the flame, as though it had been cold water'.[6] He was the first of almost 300 martyrs to die during the reign of Queen Mary.

Eleven months later Bishop Gardiner died at Westminster. He had survived the terrifying vicissitudes of the Tudor court and was afforded the privilege denied to so many of his contemporaries of dying in his bed. Temporarily buried in a vault in the priory church of St Mary Overie, his body then was taken from Southwark to Winchester, where he was laid to rest in a splendid chantry tomb in the cathedral.

In 1619 a very different bishop was elevated to the see of Winchester. Not only was Lancelot Andrewes different in character from Stephen Gardiner, but also the intervening seven decades had seen a complete change in the religious scene in England. Following Mary Tudor's death in 1557, her half-sister Elizabeth had returned the Church in England to the Protestant faith. Several versions of the scriptures were now available in English, including what was known as the Geneva Bible, produced with the help of Miles Coverdale, who had taken refuge in Switzerland during the reign of Mary Tudor. Geneva was the city of John Calvin, and the overtones of Calvinism evident in this version of the scriptures concerned Elizabeth's Archbishop of Canterbury, Matthew Parker. He set out to produce a text that was more comfortable with the tenor of the English Church, parcelling out parts to twelve bishops, including himself. The result was the Bishops' Bible, printed in 1568, but it was not regarded as a great achievement. The bishops involved, unlike William Tyndale, were not necessarily skilled in the translation of Hebrew and Greek. It was, moreover, a book created by a committee, often no guarantee of success.

When James I came to the throne in 1603, he found a Church divided, under increasing pressure from those of a Puritan persuasion. In an attempt to bring together the parties of the High and Low Churches and to settle some of their differences, he convened a conference at his palace of Hampton Court in 1604. The conference failed in these efforts, for his bishops proved intractable in their stance, but out of the proceedings came a commission to undertake a new translation of the Bible and, despite the lesson of the Bishops' Bible, one taken forward by the most elaborate series of committees.

Fifty-four revisers were appointed, drawn from the most distinguished scholars and divines, divided into six companies, based at Oxbridge and Westminster. Three were responsible for the Old Testament, two for the New and one for the Apochrypha. Richard Bancroft, Bishop of London, worked with the king to draw up specific rules for translators, including a system for exchanging drafts. One of these rules was of great significance: 'these translations to be used when they agree better with the Text of the Bishops. *Tindoll's, Matthews, Coverdale's, Whitchurch's* [the London merchant who printed the Great Bible of 1540], *Geneva.*'[7] Tyndale's great contribution was at last officially recognised. It has been estimated that 83 per cent of the final text of the King James Bible was from Tyndale's translations made eighty years earlier. John Rogers had been responsible for preserving many of these, from the Old Testament in particular. Without him, we would not, for example, have 'let there be light, and there was light', 'who told thee thou wast naked?' and 'my brother's keeper'.

Lancelot Andrewes was early recognised as an outstanding scholar while at Cambridge, becoming master of his college, Pembroke, which by coincidence had been the college of John Rogers. Once a year, Andrewes spent a month with his parents in London, and during this vacation he would find a master from whom he could learn a new language, so that after a few years he acquired most of the modern European languages. This combination meant that he not only was put in charge of the Old Testament as part of the

Westminster company, but also acted as a general editor for the whole project.

With the various sections of the Bible completed, a meeting was held in 1610 at the Stationers' Hall in Ave Maria Lane, just to the west of St Paul's Cathedral. Remarkably, given such a ponderous editorial structure, the resulting text was published the following year by the King's Printer, Robert Barker. It is often described as the 'Authorised Version', but there was no official pronouncement at the time, and the only truly authorised version has been the Great Bible of 1540.

Andrewes was regarded not only as a great linguist and scholar but also as a powerful preacher. James I, who considered himself a connoisseur of sermons, greatly admired his style. On 3 November 1605 Andrewes had been installed at Chichester as bishop, just two days before the uncovering of the Gunpowder Plot devised by a group of Roman Catholics to blow up Parliament during the state opening to be attended by the king. The new bishop was asked to prepare a sermon for presentation to James the following year. In this, Andrewes justified the need to commemorate the deliverance of the king and his government and defined the nature of celebrations: this was to be the foundation of the long tradition of preaching Gunpowder Plot sermons.

Although the popularity of the sermons of Andrewes dipped in the later seventeenth century when his style was regarded as outdated, it was revived 200 years later. One great admirer was T.S. Eliot, who declared himself a 'classicist in literature, royalist in politics and anglo-catholic in religion' in *For Lancelot Andrewes: Essays in Style and Order*, which he published in 1928. The previous year he had published his poem 'Journey of the Magi' that owed more than a little to Bishop Lancelot's Christmas sermon for 1622.

Andrewes' sermon ended with a consideration of the physical conditions of the arrival in Bethlehem of the Magi: 'It was no summer progress. A cold coming they had of it at this time of the year, just the worst time of the year to take a journey, and specially a long journey. The ways deep, the weather sharp, the days short, the sun farthest off, in "the very dead of winter". And these difficulties they overcame, of a wearisome, dangerous, unseasonable journey; and for all this they came.'[8]

Lancelot Andrewes died on 25 September 1626 at Winchester House. His funeral procession, arranged by the College of Heralds, was held two weeks later in St Saviour's Church, which was hung with 165 yards of black baize paid for by its parishioners. The sermon at his interment was given by John Buckeridge, then Bishop of Rochester, one of Andrewes' most intimate friends. The chapel at the easternmost end of the church's apse was chosen for his interment, in a canopied tomb in marble and alabaster, with a full-length recumbent effigy wearing the mantle of a prelate of the Order of the Garter. The memorial inscription was penned by Matthew Wren, who had studied at Pembroke College in Cambridge during Andrewes' mastership: he was the uncle of the architect Sir Christopher Wren. The monument has been moved several times and can now be seen in the south aisle of the chancel, next to the high altar (plate VII).

The death of Lancelot Andrewes was mourned right across the Church of England. The Calvinist Thomas Fuller praised his qualities as a scholar and preacher while John Milton penned a Latin elegy on his death. Particularly lavish praise was bestowed by William Laud, his successor as dean of the Chapel Royal, who wrote how the greatest light of the Christian world had been extinguished. As Andrewes' biographer points out, his 'political, theological, and liturgical influence during his lifetime had been largely a matter of quiet example imitated by sympathetic associates and admirers. Following his death, however, Laud and his circle, with the support of Charles I, pursued the systematic enforcement by episcopal and royal fiat of Andrewes' more private ideals and preferences, in the reorientation of national worship.'[9]

One way that Laud achieved this was by editing and publishing in 1629 ninety-six of his sermons, in association with Andrewes' friend,

John Buckeridge. A large number of the chosen sermons had been preached at court, giving emphasis to the authority of the Crown, while the many communion day sermons gave prominence to high eucharistic theology, as promoted by Laud first as Bishop of London, and then as Archbishop of Canterbury.

Charles I governed without Parliament from 1629 to 1640, raising money by various means that were considered by many contrary to recent constitutional developments. Financial pressure from war against the Scots forced the king to recall Parliament in the spring of 1640, but this lasted less than a month because the money was only forthcoming if grievances were settled. The result was rioting and demonstrations in London: politics combined with religion in popular revulsion against Archbishop Laud, accused of having an addiction to popery and superstition. One area of the city particularly affected was the south bank of the Thames, where apprentices marched on Laud's palace at Lambeth, and in parish churches in Southwark, where demonstrations took place against 'scandalous' members of the clergy, calling for their replacement by godly alternatives.

One of the reforms that William Laud had launched was to have rails installed to separate the congregation from the high altar. In June 1641, at St Saviour's, the church where Lancelot Andrewes had been laid to rest just twelve years earlier, what was described as the meaner sort of parishioners tore down these offending rails as a symbol of popery. At St Olave's the rails were removed on the initiative of the churchwardens, but disruption followed when zealots reviled the congregation that came up to the high altar to receive the eucharist from the curate, Oliver Whitby. From the gallery, two Thames watermen shouted 'Why do you suffer Baal's priest to give you the communion and serve you so? Kick him out of the church; kneel to a pope, hang him. Baal's priest, get ye home and crumb your porridge with your bread.'[10] Later that year a crowd of what were described as Brownists (p. 129) lay siege to a third Southwark church,

St George the Martyr, enabling a cobbler to force his way to the pulpit and to preach for an hour.

Although these demonstrations were dismissed as the work of separatist radicals, the evidence shows that protesting members of the Southwark community included the well-off as well as what were dismissed as the meaner sort. There were also many who were horrified by their actions, causing deep divisions within the parish congregations. The king had been obliged to recall Parliament at the end of November 1640, and as the political crisis deepened, he chose to sacrifice William Laud along with his chief councillor, Thomas Wentworth, Earl of Strafford. Both were impeached, with Strafford going to the block in May 1641, but Laud remained a prisoner in the Tower of London until 1644 when he, too, was beheaded. Charles had departed from London two years earlier, and the country had moved inexorably towards civil war.

The Restoration of Charles II in 1660 was achieved peacefully, with his Declaration of Breda, promising liberty of conscience in matters of religion. But serious divisions were to reappear when in the 1670s it was revealed that the king's brother and heir to the throne, James, Duke of York, had converted to Roman Catholicism. Two political factions emerged: the Tories and the Whigs. Both were terms of abuse: 'Tory' from the Irish for outlaw; 'Whig' from the Scottish Gaelic for horse thief. The Whigs claimed the power to exclude James from the throne, while the Tories supported his hereditary right, despite his choice of religious faith. James did succeed his brother in 1685, but when his Catholic queen gave birth to a son three years later, the king fled his realm after the invasion by his son-in-law, William of Orange. The debate between Whigs and Tories, however, continued, with both political and religious implications.

At the dissolution of the priory of St Mary Overie, preaching chaplains were appointed, and after the church, now known as St Saviour's, was purchased from James I by the parishioners, these clergymen were chosen by public election. This tradition lasted until

1885, when such events were deemed unseemly, attended by 'exhibitions of religious and political fanaticism'.[11] This perception was amply justified in the case of the election of Henry Sacheverell. Soon after he had been chosen by the parishioners of St Saviour's in 1709, Sacheverell was invited by the new Lord Mayor of London, Sir Samuel Garrard, to deliver the Gunpowder Plot sermon in St Paul's Cathedral. Biographers make clear that Sacheverell was a tricky individual, disliked at his Oxford College, Magdalen, for his overbearing arrogance and conceit, as well as his drunken exploits. He was also zealously High Church and Tory.

Sacheverell took as the title of his 1709 sermon 'The Perils of False Brethren both in Church and State', seizing the opportunity to accuse the Whigs of imperilling the Anglican Church by siding with nonconformists. One man attending the service in St Paul's Cathedral later recalled that Sacheverell 'came into the pulpit like a Sybil to the mouth of her cave, or a Pythoness upon the Tripod', and that his face was fiery red, with 'a goggling wildness of his eyes'.[12] As he embarked on his sermon, Sacheverell pulled no punches, declaring that he would 'open the Eyes of the Deluded People in this our Great Metropolis, being conscious of what prodigious importance it is to the welfare of the Whole Nation to have its Rich and Powerful Citizens set right their Notions of Government, both in Church and State.'

By coincidence, William of Orange had landed in England on 5 November 1688, setting in train the events of what became known as the Glorious Revolution. Thus, the tradition of the Gunpowder Plot sermon that Lancelot Andrewes had set down in 1606 now by convention made the comparison of a double deliverance from popery. But Sacheverell, intent on attacking non-conformists as well as Roman Catholics, took as his comparison the execution of Charles I on 30 January 1649: 'indelible monuments of the irreconcilable rages and bloodthirstiness of both the popish and fanatic enemies of our Church and Government . . . These TWO DAYS indeed are but one united proof and visible testimonial of the same dangerous and rebellious principles these confederates in iniquity maintain.'[13] In fact, he dismissed the threat from Catholics in the first three minutes of his sermon, and for the remainder, lasting nearly an hour and a half, he railed against what he described as sectarists and schismatics.

Against the advice of his supporters, Sacheverell took advantage of the presence of printers in the area around St Paul's Cathedral to have the text of his sermon printed. He claimed that the mayor, a staunch Tory, had authorised this, although it has never been established as the truth. Henry Clements, based at the Half Moon in St Paul's Churchyard, printed 1,000 copies in quarto to sell at 1s each, and between 35,000 and 40,000 in octavo selling at 2d per copy. A second edition followed, along with pirated editions, so that the total sale was around a prodigious 100,000, and by circulation capable of reaching the entire electorate of the time. The Whig presses now leapt into action, producing broadsheets that depicted Sacheverell flanked by the Devil and the Pope, and reminding readers that despite Queen Anne's many pregnancies, there was no direct heir to the throne, and that her half-brother, James II's son, the Pretender, in exile in France presented a constant threat.

When the Tories did well at the forthcoming general election, the response from the Whigs was to have Sacheverell impeached for preaching sedition. Despite, or perhaps because of, his provocative firebrand style of preaching, Sacheverell enjoyed huge popular acclaim. As his coach was driven each day to Westminster Hall for his trial, crowds cheered him on his way. When Queen Anne also made her way each day to Westminster, the crowds called upon her to support him. Although one of her bishops reported that the queen felt the sermon a bad one, and that Sacheverell deserved to be punished, she travelled to Southwark to hear him preach. She referred to him as 'Boanerges', the name applied by Christ to two of his disciples, James and John, because of their fiery style. The royal arms of the queen, installed in St Saviour's Church on this occasion, can still be seen in the south-west corner of the choir.

Following his trial, Sacheverell was found guilty, although his sentence, a three-year suspension from preaching and the burning by the public hangman of the text of the offending sermon, was so lenient that it was adjudged a victory for the Tories. The queen's great friend, Sarah, Duchess of Marlborough, with her firm Whig views, was furious, precipitating the break-up of their relationship. The fervid temperature of the debate is reflected by a painting to be seen over the staircase at Hanbury Hall in Worcestershire. When Sacheverell was put on trial, the trompe l'oeil painter James Thornhill was working on the theme of Olympian gods for Thomas Vernon, a barrister and a Whig in his politics. Presumably at the request of Vernon, Thornhill added to the scheme a small portrait of Henry Sacheverell held by Mercury, who leaps away from his fellow deities and is cast to the Furies to be set alight.

Sacheverell began his suspension from preaching by making a triumphal progress to Selattyn, a living in Shropshire given to him by an admirer. The journey to and from the parish took six weeks, and he managed to visit eight counties and twelve parliamentary boroughs en route. However, this marked perhaps the summit of his extraordinary career. In 1713, when he returned to Southwark and the pulpit of St Saviour's, he preached a sermon on Palm Sunday based on the text 'Father, forgive them for they know not what they do'. The choice of the words spoken by Christ on the Cross was judged by some to be blasphemous. When he went to St Paul's to speak at the invitation of the Corporation of the Sons of the Clergy in December of that year, the crowd hissed at him: a marked difference from the earlier adulation.

Although Sacheverell continued to be a chaplain at St Saviour's Church until his death in 1724, he remained a muted voice. The succession of the Hanoverian George I to the throne in 1714 resulted in the triumph of the Whig party, and the end of all hopes of preferment for High Church clergymen.

Three stained-glass windows made in the early twentieth century by Charles Eamer Kempe and his company on the theme of scriptural teachings and their dissemination are to be seen in the north aisle of Southwark Cathedral. In one, Henry Sacheverell is depicted with St Paul, holding a sword and a scroll inscribed 'in perils among false brethren', a reminder of his controversial sermon.

Alongside Sacheverell, and less controversially, are windows depicting John Bunyan and Alexander Cruden. John Bunyan would have been anathema to Sacheverell, for he was a highly influential non-conformist. Imprisoned in Bedford Gaol for his religious views, he began to write his most famous book, *The Pilgrim's Progress*, the first part of which was published in 1678, with the second following in 1684. He established a network of five dissenting congregations in Bedfordshire with satellite meetings in surrounding communities, but he preached much further afield, including in Southwark at an open-communion Baptist church established by Stephen More. In 1687 another meeting house was built in Zoar Street on land leased from the Bishop of Winchester. 'Zoar' means refuge or sanctuary, and its site is now next to Sumner Street at the west end of Bankside. It was given the name 'John Bunyan's Meeting House', but he can only have preached there on one or two occasions, for he died the year after it was set up. In the stained-glass window in Southwark Cathedral, he is depicted in a portrait medallion, below which is shown Christian from *The Pilgrim's Progress* gazing at the Cross while his burden of sins rolls away into the sepulchre behind him. Faith is shown in the lowest panel.

Alexander Cruden was an extraordinary and rather tragic figure. Born in Aberdeen in 1699, he considered entering the ministry of the Church of Scotland, but a disappointment in love, when the lady not only failed to respond to his attentions but was made pregnant by her brother, drove him into his first bout of insanity. When he recovered, he left for London, working first as a private tutor, then as a proof-corrector and as a bookseller. In 1733 he began work on his celebrated *Complete Concordance to the Holy Scriptures*, an alphabetical arrangement of the principal words contained in the Bible with citations of where they appear. This he completed four years later, presenting a copy to Caroline, George II's queen. Her death only days later, and financial problems in the production of the great work, contributed to a further mental deterioration. His life continued with a series of mishaps, and in later life he convinced himself that he had been called upon to reform the nation. When Cruden died in 1770, as a lifelong Calvinist he was buried in the dissenters' burial ground at Deadman's Place in Southwark. The stained-glass window in the cathedral has his portrait medallion along with representatives of the Old and New Testaments, including Timothy, a disciple of St Paul who, like Cruden, was renowned for his knowledge of the scriptures.

These are three very different characters, but they have been associated by their very different contributions to the evolution of scriptural study. They take their place in the tradition of this evolution that took place in Southwark over three very turbulent centuries.

# 7

# A Mixed Community

Historians looking at Southwark from the late medieval period onwards emphasise the raffish aspects of the community. One commentator begins her examination of the sixteenth and seventeenth centuries, 'it is a commonplace ... that Southwark was the most disreputable quarter of London'.[1] The area was famous for its alehouses, prostitutes, theatre players and prisons. Yet there were prosperous households in the Borough, often with important connections to the City and to the royal court, as can be seen in some of the monuments to be found in Southwark Cathedral.

One of the most impressive of these, dating from around 1616, is that of Alderman Richard Humble, a vintner. He is shown kneeling towards the high altar along with his two wives, Margaret and Isabel, while his children are depicted along the sides of the tomb (plate VI). They are all arrayed in sumptuous robes, and one of the wives sports a fashionable tall hat, possibly of beaver. When the Native American princess Pocahontas arrived in London in 1616, she was painted wearing just such a hat in her portrait, and Southwark may have been the place where she bought it, for the Borough was known for its manufacture of fine beaver headgear. Humble was not only a City merchant but also a speculative landlord, like many other men of business at this time. Pulling down old dwellings that may have been made redundant at the dissolution of the monasteries, he put up new ones of timber and lath on their foundations on the west side of Borough High Street. From the rents of these he bequeathed a goodly sum of £5 4s to the poor of St Saviour's.

In the north choir is a wall monument to John Trehearne, 'portar' to James I, with his coat of arms displaying herons as a pun on his name. 'Portar' in this context indicates that he carried keys for opening royal gates. Gentlemen Porters have been recorded for the Tower of London, but it is not known whether Trehearne was one of these. Beside him is his wife Mary, and the two figures hold a tablet with an epitaph reminding us of his royal connections:

> Had Kings a power to lend their Subject's breath,
> Trehearne thou should'st not be cast down by Death,
> Thy Royal Master still would keep thee then.
> But length of days are beyond the reach of men,
> Nor wealth, nor strength, or great men's love can ease
> The wound Death's arrows make, for thou hast these.
> In thy King's Court good place to thee is given,
> Whence thou shalt go Ye King's Court in Heaven.

Their six children are shown kneeling below. Like one of Humble's wives, the elder two girls wear tall hats. Trehearne was a freeman of the wealthy Clothworkers' Company and owned several properties in the Borough. By his will, drawn shortly before his death in 1618, he left money to the poor prisoners in the Clink and to maintain the embankment of Upper Ground.

A third memorial, in the north transept, was commissioned by William Austin for his mother, Lady Joyce Clerke, a benefactress of St Saviour's, and for his first wife. Austin was a barrister, attached to Lincoln's Inn, but he seems to have preferred the life of a writer, settling in a house in Paris Garden. He was one of the London wits who contributed prefatory verses to Thomas Coryat's *Crudities*, an account of a journey made through Europe to Venice and back, published in 1611. Austin's poetry was circulated in manuscript form among literary friends, including the poet and dramatist Ben Jonson.

Austin's memorial in the cathedral draws as its theme on the parable of the sower, with an angel of the Resurrection pointing to the sun of righteousness, and supported by the rock of Christ, from which issue a stream and a serpent. Below this are sheaves of corn and, flanking the central feature, two pastoral figures wearing sun hats, with a rake and a pitchfork, looking as if they would be more at home in a painting of rural life by George Stubbs in the late eighteenth century. The design of this unusual composition is attributed to Nicholas Stone, one of the leading sculptors of the early seventeenth century, although it has been suggested that Austin himself may have had a hand in its creation. When he died in 1634, he was buried below the memorial, with an epitaph that can be translated from the Latin as 'an Angel in his thoughts, a Daedalus in his actions … a miracle of patience in illness, an example of faithfulness in death'.

One of the most prosperous, and generous, members of the community has a much more discreet memorial, just a tablet on the wall in the north choir, hidden behind a startling figure of a decomposing cadaver in stone, thought to be the *memento mori* of one of the medieval priors. The tablet records Thomas Cure, master of the Saddlers' Company and saddler to three monarchs, Edward VI, Mary Tudor and Elizabeth I, who died in 1588. A man of considerable means, he represented Southwark in Parliament, owned a ship and acquired a variety of properties. These included the former monastic property, Waverley Place, bought from Viscount Montague, which lay adjacent to the new churchyard of St Saviour's. In addition, he purchased several inns: the Red Lion, the Cross Keys, the Estridge (Ostrich) Feather and the King's Head, among others. In 1580 he bought for his son the manor and liberty of Paris Garden. Rather than requesting a grand monument, he used his wealth to become one of the major benefactors of the parish church of St Saviour's created at the dissolution of the monasteries.

The Augustinian priory of St Mary Overie had surrendered to Henry VIII in the autumn of 1539 and was dissolved the following year. Unlike some of the other religious houses, notably the Carthusian monastery in Clerkenwell, where the prior and his monks putting up resistance were treated with savage brutality by the king, the passing of Southwark priory had been a peaceful one. It had never been a large house, and the number of canons had dwindled to twelve. These along with the prior, Bartholomew Linstead, received pensions at the dissolution.

In 1540 Stephen Gardiner, as Bishop of Winchester, arranged for the building to begin its new existence as the parish church of St Saviour, leased by the Crown to the former parishioners of St Mary Magdalene, the little church nestling in its shadow, and of St Margaret in the High Street. An Act of Parliament passed the following year formed the parishioners into a Corporation, consisting of thirty vestrymen, of whom six were churchwardens, given the authority to appoint two members of the clergy. They were charged with the protection of the church building and its furniture, and one of their first acts was to create a doorway between St Saviour's and St Mary Magdalene, which thus became a side chapel. St Margaret's was thereafter used as a Sessions Court, a Court of Admiralty and a prison. The churchwardens were also given the responsibility of managing the parish estates and looking after the poor.

Thomas Cure was responsible, along with other members of the Corporation of St Saviour's, for the foundation of a grammar school for the instruction of thirty boys of the parish. In 1559 the parishioners sold some of their silver plate to fund a lease on the church. One of the conditions of this lease was that within two years they should establish a building for the school and employ a schoolmaster. A temporary place for the school was organised in the church house

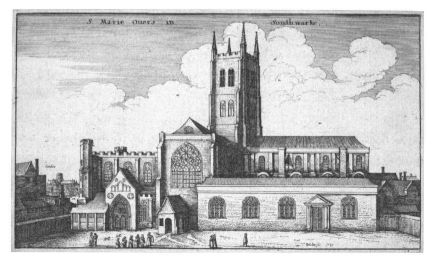

5. *An engraving dated 1647 showing the Church of St Saviour and Mary Overie, with the former parish church of St Mary Magdalene incorporated into the south aisle.*

of the former parish of St Margaret, funded by renting out the Lady Chapel of the former priory to a baker.

Letters patent were obtained from Elizabeth I in 1562. The original document is in Latin, but a nineteenth-century translation into English runs:

> Whereas our well-beloved subjects, William Emmerson, John Sayer, Richard Ryall, Thomas Cure, John Oliff, Thomas Pulter, Thomas Bill, Thomas Osborne, Richard Baptist, William Browker, Christopher Cambell, and William Gefferson and other discreet and very honest inhabitants of the parish of St Saviour within Our borough of Southwark, in our county of Surrey, of their godly affection and good disposition for the bringing up, institution, and instruction of children and younglings of the said parish, at their no little cost, labour and charges, in laudable form and order, have of late ordained and erected in the aforesaid borough and parish a Grammar School in the which the children

and younglings, as well of rich as of the poor, being inhabitants within the aforesaid parish, are instructed and brought up liberally and prosperously in grammar, to the common utility of all the inhabitants of the parish aforesaid, as we are credibly informed.[2]

The high master, Christopher Ockland, along with the 'younglings', boys only, of course, then moved into part of the former lodgings of Lady Cobham, which was now the Green Dragon Inn, just south of St Saviour's Church, land today occupied by Borough Market. Thomas Cure became the chief figure on the board of governors of the school. Ockland was paid £20 per annum, and boys from St Saviour's parish were admitted for a fee of half a crown, 2s 6d. Those from the neighbouring parishes of St Olave's and St George's could pay a fee to the high master to arrange a schoolmaster for their instruction. St Olave's got its own grammar school in 1571.

A later governor of St Saviour's Grammar School was John Bingham, who died in 1625. Like Cure, he was a saddler, for there was a considerable demand for saddles and other riding accoutrements for the many inns and their extensive stables in Southwark. The counter for the sale of leather lay in Paris Garden. Sometimes knows as the Skin Market, it was located next to the modern Globe Theatre, close to the river. Bingham's monument on the south wall of the transept of the cathedral proudly describes him as 'a good benefactor to this Parrish and Free Schole'. He was also a member of a group of merchant vestrymen known as the Bargainers. They organised in 1611 to purchase the church and rectory from the Crown for £800. James I was most impressed that they were able to do so, which suggests that he had imbibed the raffish school of thought as far as Southwark was concerned.

In 1584 Thomas Cure had also been responsible for drawing up the ordinances and statutes for a range of almshouses, a 'College or Hospital for the Poor'. Sixteen poor people were nominated from the Boroughside part of the parish by the churchwardens, the vestry, the overseers of the poor and the minister of St Saviour's. Each pensioner received the weekly sum of 20 pence, a generous amount, along with free fuel, bread and accommodation. Extra payments were added 'at sundry times as Easter, Christmas, in cold weather and when some of them were sick and paid to keepers to attend and look after those that were sick'. The residents of the college were expected to 'labour daily on the working days according to their ability of body and former manner of honest life' on pain of fines and expulsion. Their tenure was for life unless a pauper married or was expelled for bad behaviour.[3]

When Cure died in 1588, in his will he left money and land in Park Street for the almshouses, which survived until 1868 when they were demolished to make way for a new railway line. Relocated first to West Norwood and in 2005 to Purley, they are still in operation, run by the United St Saviour's Charity. Cure's generosity is recalled annually in a service organised by the charity, held in June in Southwark Cathedral.

Where Cure led, others followed, and more parishioners left money for further houses to be built in Park Street. The Elizabethan actor and theatrical entrepreneur Edward Alleyn at his death in 1616 left money for ten houses to be built in Soap Yard, next to Park Street. Alleyn today is best known for his foundation of Dulwich College, but earlier in his life he lived in Southwark, worshipping at St Saviour's and serving as a vestryman and keeper of the church's token books. These were the written records of the attempt by officers of the parish in the final weeks of Lent to require the heads of households to purchase tokens for Easter communion. One token was issued for every person over the age of sixteen within a household, and these were to be turned in at the church by communicants. Altogether, 144 token books for St Saviour's survive from c.1571 to 1643, providing a unique record of an English parish of the period.[4]

In 1605 Edward Alleyn purchased the manor of Dulwich and moved there. Mindful of Cure's foundation at Southwark, he endowed a 'hospital' for twelve poor scholars and twelve poor persons, known as the College of God's Gift. The association of Alleyn with both Southwark and Dulwich was to prove invaluable when, in the 1880s, St Saviour's Grammar School had fallen upon hard times. The Charity Commission who were reorganising the endowment of Dulwich College identified the intention of Alleyn towards other institutions he had supported during his lifetime and by his will, so that the grammar school's survival was ensured and it was amalgamated with that of St Olave.

There were many poor people in the Borough, but like many a community, there were also prosperous men who felt it was part of their Christian duty to help those less fortunate and to provide them with opportunities. Of course, it was the 'deserving poor' to whom they were offering their charitable support.

One of the striking elements of the Southwark community was the large number of 'strangers' and 'aliens'. 'Strangers' was the term usually applied to men and women from different parts of the kingdom, while 'aliens' were those from mainland Europe. They were drawn to Southwark through geographical convenience, but also because it was outside the City and thus beyond its regulations, enabling them to work there without being members of the City guilds. These men and women created wealth by their endeavours, as a Venetian commentator noted at the beginning of the sixteenth century: 'These great riches of London are not occasioned by [Southwark's] inhabitants being noblemen or gentlemen; being all on the contrary persons of low degree and artificers who have congregated there from all parts of the island, and from Flanders, and from every place'.[5]

Aliens had been present in Southwark for centuries, including two Jews until Edward I expelled them from England in 1290. From the fourteenth century the dominant group was the 'Doche', German speakers (Deutsch), particularly from Flanders. Recognising the skill of Flemish weavers, Edward III encouraged them to settle, and even granted them the right to have their own guild, despite protests from the City. Chaucer would have heard their accents, for in the prologue to 'The Cook's Tale' he quotes 'sooth pley, quad play [true jest, bad jest] as the Flemyng seith'. At one stage, part of the parish of St Olave's was known as 'Burgoyne' because so many weavers from the dominions of the Duke of Burgundy had settled there.

Contemporaries all too easily characterised Flemish immigrants as brewers and prostitutes, but these men and women brought with them a wide range of occupations, including goldsmiths and jewellers, and workers in leather. They were mostly tolerated by the local community, and xenophobia, when it arose, came rather from the City and elsewhere. Thus, in 1381, as the men of the Peasants' Revolt passed through Southwark, they attacked a brothel of Flemish women before crossing over London Bridge and targeting any Flemings they could find in the City. Breweries presented a natural target, as they were easy to identify and provided the beer to quench thirsty rebels and City apprentices on the rampage.

As ever, it is a court case that provides us with a portrait of an alien in Southwark: Henry Leeke, who was also variously known as Bleke, Hoke, Deryk Leke and Dyeke van Leeke. Like so many Southwark businessmen, he was not only involved in the brewing industry but also raised livestock and traded overseas. In 1531, complaints against him included that he had thrown filth and dung from his cattle into the Thames. Other accusations included that he sold diseased meat to poorer neighbours and to Southwark butchers and imported his hops through devious means. But if true, this bad behaviour clearly paid, for he bought property along the riverside for wharves, and when he died in 1560, he left in his will £8 per annum for the free grammar school to be founded in the parish of St Olave's.[6]

Skilled craftsmen continued to be welcomed by the Crown, and by the merchants of London, despite their concerns about City regulations, for their provision of luxury products. This movement gained momentum when Henry Tudor secured the throne, having defeated and killed Richard III at the Battle of Bosworth Field in 1485. Henry had spent years in exile in Europe, including Burgundy, and, realising that it was often easier to import craftsmen rather than their products, brought in from the Low Countries portrait-painters, scholars for his library, and tapestry-weavers and makers of stained glass for his palaces. A temporary economic downturn in Flanders combined with Henry VII's encouragement brought the glazier Barnard Flower to London, and by September 1496 he was working for the king at Woodstock Palace in Oxfordshire.

There had been strong opposition to alien craftsmen from the City guilds, including the small Company of Glaziers. They had persuaded Richard III during his brief reign to pass 'An Act against Strangers Artificers' and to issue an annual 'Return of Aliens' to be completed by any foreigners who were working in England. Henry Tudor, however, was not likely to prove sympathetic. Although Flower was obliged to live in Southwark, Henry allowed him to employ four assistants rather than the two usually stipulated for aliens. The glazier took up residence in the precinct of St Thomas' Hospital, worshipping in the chapel, which had become a parish church by 1496.

In 1505, with the death of the king's Royal Glazier, an Englishman, Flower was given the position with an annual retainer of £24. In the same year Henry Tudor was persuaded by his mother, Lady Margaret Beaufort, to take up the project of the completion of the chapel of King's College, Cambridge, founded some sixty years earlier by his 'beloved uncle', Henry VI. When Henry Tudor died in 1508 the task was inherited by Bishop Richard Foxe of Winchester. Flower had provided stained-glass windows for Winchester Cathedral, so they already had a working partnership.

For King's Chapel they had to fill twenty-six soaring Perpendicular windows with a programme of biblical scenes. Richard Foxe was in some ways like one of his predecessors at Winchester, William of Wykeham, a great builder, with attention to detail and a determination to carry through a project to a successful conclusion. Just as William of Wykeham had founded New College at Oxford, so in 1517 Foxe established Corpus Christi College at the university. Known as 'Foxe's beehive', it was established along humanist lines, with the introduction of the teaching of Greek, and possibly of Hebrew.

Flower must have made the short journey from St Thomas' Hospital to Winchester House on many occasions to confer with Bishop Foxe on the iconography for the King's Chapel windows. They chose that each window should show associated Old and New Testament scenes, so that for example the Temptation of Eve in the Garden of Eden was set above the Annunciation of the Virgin Mary, the Ascent of Elijah above Christ's Ascension, and so on. In the centre of each window, flanked by the biblical scenes, space was left for messengers carrying captions, which Foxe may have obtained from his friend, Erasmus. The bishop had a particularly fine private library, and the sources for the images came from woodcuts in two of his books, *Biblia Pauperum* (Books of the Poor) and *Speculum Humanae Salvationis* (The Mirror of Man's Salvation) along with engravings from his collection. A sketch known as a vidimus ('we have seen') was then made by the glazier or by a designer. Remarkably, two of these have survived, rediscovered in 1964, of Peter and John healing the lame man, and of the death of Ananias.[7]

Once the subjects were agreed, and vidimuses made, cartoons were commissioned from leading Flemish artists, such as Bernard van Orley, or, most famous of all, Dierick Vellert. Coloured glass was imported from Germany, and in the workshops in Southwark these were transformed by the most mysterious of crafts into the wonderful images that we still marvel at. There were two ways by which the finished windows, crated up and protected by straw, might be transported to King's College. The journey could have been made by horse-drawn wagons on the road, but this was fraught with the possibility of breakages. More likely is that they were taken to the Thames-side wharves just downstream to avoid the rapids of London

Bridge, and transported by ship to King's Lynn, and then down-river by barge to Cambridge.

At some time before 1510, Flower was joined in the precinct of St Thomas' Hospital by Galyon Hone from Antwerp, and later by two other Flemish stained-glass craftsmen who had anglicised their names, James Nicolson and Francis Williamson. Nicolson was to combine his skills with printing, publishing works that included in 1535 Coverdale's version of the English Bible (p. 73). Williamson is recorded as importing 'painted papers' and barrels of ink, so would appear to have helped Nicolson in his printshop.[8] This may seem an unusual combination of trades, but the process whereby Flower and Bishop Foxe organised the King's Chapel windows demonstrates links between the two.

At Flower's death in 1517, Hone duly succeeded him as the King's Glazier and continued the mammoth task of producing the windows for Cambridge. However, by the 1530s the religious climate was changing, with the growth of demand for reform of the English Church. Maybe anticipating trouble ahead, Hone acquired naturalisation and permanent residence in England in 1535. Even so, the London Company of Glaziers was determined to have him arrested, which they did on at least two occasions. The religious reformers, moreover, condemned richly coloured stained-glass windows along with elaborate vestments and plate as smacking of idolatry. During the reign of Edward VI, wall paintings were to be whitewashed and windows smashed.

This change is reflected by Hone's subsequent fortune. While in 1541 he had a grand house next to St Thomas' Hospital, with an extensive garden, five servants and an estate valued at £40, ten years later, shortly before his death, the estate had dwindled to 40 shillings. The glorious episode when Southwark produced some of the world's finest stained-glass was at an end.

Other creative artists were alive and well in Southwark, however, and arriving in greater numbers to escape the increasing religious persecution from the Hapsburgs in their Netherland dominions. One example is the painter, jeweller and goldsmith Hans Eworth, who arrived in Southwark from Antwerp in the mid-1540s. His first studio, where he employed another immigrant as an apprentice, was in the parish of St Thomas, before moving to the liberty of Montague Place. This was the site of the refectory and cloisters of the former priory church, acquired at the dissolution by Sir Anthony Browne, whose son became Lord Montague. The prior's house was probably turned into the family residence, while other buildings became the workshops of various artisans. During his time in England, Hans Eworth painted some of the finest portraits of the royal family and of their leading courtiers, far superior to any produced by native artists.

The memorials for Richard Humble and John Trehearne mentioned earlier were made by Flemish masons from what became known as the Southwark School of Monuments. The best-documented work-shop was founded by Garrett Janson or Johnson, who first arrived in London in 1571 in Fishmonger Alley on the north bank of the Thames before moving his premises several times and settling, like Eworth, in Montague Place. The distinguishing features of the work of Janson and his fellow Flemish sculptural masons was to work in alabaster and to use marbling for colour and richness of effect. While the English monument sculptors had produced altar tombs with recumbent effigies, with or without a canopy, and free-standing or against a wall, the Flemish craftsmen introduced kneeling figures. The monument of Richard Humble and his family is typical of this style, and has been attributed to another major Flemish workshop, that of the Cure family.

The founder of the Cure workshop was William. He was probably Dutch but not a religious refugee. A Return of Aliens made in 1571 recorded him as living in Southwark, having been in England for thirty years, since coming over during the reign of Henry VIII to work on the extraordinary palace of Nonsuch in Surrey. Marriage to an

Englishwoman meant that his sons were eligible for admission to one of the City Companies, and they duly joined the Marblers', who were absorbed into the Masons' in 1584. The Humble monument is said to be the work of William Cure of the third generation of the family.

Another group of alien craftsmen specialised in the manufacture of tin-glazed earthenware known as Delftware. The first such premises in London were located in Duke's Place in Aldgate, just east of the City, established in 1571 by Jacob Jansen. However, one of the important factors in making the pottery was access to a good source of water for washing and processing the clay, which was imported in barrels from East Anglia. Glazes were brought from mills at Ravensbourne and Wandsworth. By around 1615, therefore, Jacob Prynne, who had been working at Duke's Place, was established in Montague Place, with the Thames conveniently nearby. Other manufactories or pothouses of Delftware were soon established at Pickleherring, close to where Tower Bridge now crosses the river, and further to the east, at Rotherhithe, with more springing up along the southern bank of the Thames. London became the centre for pottery until the eighteenth century, when larger-scale manufactories were established in Staffordshire.

The Southwark pothouses supplied a wide range of products, such as floor tiles, drug jars for apothecaries and physicians, and tableware for domestic use. Because the ware was able to withstand moderate heat, cups were made for caudles and possets, warmed and spiced drinks, and the exotic beverages that became highly fashionable in the seventeenth century, coffee, tea and chocolate. Archaeological excavations at the three sites have unearthed fragments of wares that show that, while Pickleherring and Rotherhithe copied Dutch designs, vessels from Montague Place reproduced the Chinese style, either copied directly from Chinese porcelain, or from tin-glazed copies from the Low Countries.[9]

Southwark Delftware manufacturers found an enthusiastic market from aristocratic and prosperous middle-class households. So too did another product displaying conspicuous consumption: woven silk. A remarkable example of an alien skilled craftsman was Reasonable Blackman, who set up as a weaver in Southwark some time around 1579. West African in origin, he was probably enslaved by the Spanish and taken to Antwerp, one of Europe's great silk-weaving centres, with the second-largest black population after Lisbon. While under Spanish rule, the status of Africans was mostly that of enslavement, but some men and women were able to gain their freedom through manumission.

The weaver's unusual name is a mystery. He could have invented it to advertise the reasonable prices of the silks that he produced, or it could have been a Christian name received at baptism. Among Protestants, women often had names such as Prudence or Charity, while one seventeenth-century preacher was memorably christened Praise-God Barebone. Even Reasonable's surname may not have been adopted because of his colour. He was certainly a Protestant, for he bought two sacramental tokens for St Saviour's Easter communion in 1579 and later bought more for St Olave's Church. This suggests that Reasonable was a religious refugee. The modus vivendi that had existed in the southern part of the Netherlands under the rule of Emperor Charles V had evaporated with the intolerance of his son, Philip II of Spain, leading to a series of uprisings against his Catholic clamp-down. It is estimated that around 50,000 Protestant refugees arrived in England during the latter part of the sixteenth century, some of them bringing the art of weaving in silk.

This arrival was a timely one, for the demand for silk clothing and accessories was high, with Queen Elizabeth I in the vanguard. In 1561 she received her first pair of stockings from a 'silk woman', Alice Montague. Silk women were gentlewomen who made accessories known as narrow wares, rather than manufacturing on a large scale. The queen declared she would no longer wear cloth stockings, but only silk, and her courtiers and wealthy merchants' wives followed suit. There were sumptuary laws that dictated that apparel should befit certain status, but these were flouted.

The Puritan Philip Stubbes, ever ready to condemn luxury, wrote in 1583: 'you shall have those which are neither of the nobility, gentility, nor yeomanry, go daily in silks, velvets, satins, damasks, taffettas and such like, notwithstanding that they be both base by birth, mean by estate and servile by calling'.[10] Stubbes would not have been mollified in his outrage to find that silk was extensively worn by actors. Philip Henslowe, owner of the Rose Theatre, made lists in his diary of the costumes kept between 1591 and 1609: 274 items in silk or lace. Perhaps Reasonable Blackman was one of his suppliers.

Blackman was married by 1587, a sign that he was prospering. According to the token books, he lived in the West Side of the parish of St Saviour's in 1579, but his eldest child, Edward, was baptised in February 1587 at St Olave's, so he had moved, possibly on marriage. Four children followed, with the last, John, baptised at St Saviour's. Parish registers sometimes recorded the name of the mother, but Blackman's wife does not appear. It is thought that she was a white Englishwoman, for there were so few people of African descent in London at this time. In her study of 'black Tudors', Miranda Kaufmann doubts that they suffered discrimination: Londoners were xenophobic rather than racially intolerant. This was to be a later phenomenon.[11]

However, life in London was hard on the Blackman family, with two of their children, Jane and Edmund, dying of the plague in 1592. Recurrent outbreaks of the bubonic plague had hit the city during the sixteenth century, but this one was particularly severe, probably arriving via the West Country from Portugal. The theatres were shut, and there was a general lock down, but Southwark was especially affected, built on marshy ground with houses crammed together. Thomas Dekker described with ghastly exuberance how Death had pitched his tent in the 'sinfully polluted suburbs', deploying his army leaders of 'Burning Fevers, Boils, Blaines, and Carbuncles', who in turn led a rank and file of 'dumpish Mourners, merry Sextons, hungry Coffin-sellers, scrubbing Bearers, and nastie Grave-makers'.[12]

James Balmford was the curate of St Olave's, where young Jane and Edmund Blackman were buried. In *A Short Dialogue Concerning the Plagues Infection* published in 1603, he described how some victims lost their minds, leaping out of windows or running into the River Thames. He attributed the spread of the disease to the 'bloudy errour, which denieth the Pestilence to be contagious', warning people not to 'go commonly abroad and thrust themselves into company'.[13] The chronicler John Stow claimed that in the two years between December 1592 and 1594, 10,675 Londoners succumbed to the plague, around 8.5 per cent of the population.

Plague was no respecter of persons. The Coleman family, who lived on the east side of Borough High Street, was a relatively prosperous household of tallow chandlers and salters, but Giles Coleman died in the plague epidemic of 1625.[14] That outbreak also claimed the dramatist John Fletcher, who was buried in St Saviour's. A touching memorial in the cathedral dating from 1652 records a young girl, Susanna Barford. It begins: 'The No-such of the world for Piety and Vertue in soe tender years'. It is thought that her parents were from the theatre community and that she too was a plague victim. The verse continues, 'This world to her was by the traged play. She came and saw't, dislik't and pass'd away.'

So great were the number of deaths from the plague in the sixteenth and seventeenth centuries that special pits had to be dug. During the reign of Elizabeth I, one was located in Deadman's Place, in part of what is now Park Street, and in 1665, during the Great Plague, what is now known as the Cross Bones Graveyard was commandeered by St Saviour's for the excessive number of parishioners' bodies. Into such mass graves were interred the prosperous craftsmen and artisans, alien and native, and of course the poor of the Borough, in this truly mixed community.

# 8

# Entertaining London

When William Baseley, Henry VIII's bailiff for Southwark, acquired the lease of the mansion house in Paris Garden in the early sixteenth century, he used it as a dwelling, as noted earlier. As he worked on its repair, he realised that it stood in very marshy ground, so it was not suitable for residential development. However, he spotted the potential of the location for public gaming. In 1547 he obtained a licence to install 'the games of boulles or bowlinge, cardes, dyze and tables', despite the fact that these recreations had recently been forbidden by Act of Parliament, and that Baseley would appear to have been a member of that Parliament.[1] This marked the beginning of Paris Garden and Bankside as a centre for entertainment.

Just before Baseley's introduction of skittle and bowling alleys and gaming tables, a small bullring was built at St Margaret's Hill, which was soon superseded by a larger one on Bankside, along with one for baiting bears. Henry VIII came here to watch the baiting of these animals by dogs, a sport apparently introduced to England by Italians as far back as the reign of King John at the beginning of the thirteenth century. A topographical panorama drawn in 1588 shows rings for the unfortunate bulls and bears. They were also baited in pits in an open arena at the centre of buildings, with galleries around for the spectators. These proved the ideal form of building for another kind of entertainment – public theatres.

The first dramatic performances in London were held in churches. When Mary Tudor returned her realm to the Church of Rome, religious plays were performed in the parish church of St Olave, for example, with children recorded as taking part. Courtyards of inns were also the location for plays, first of a religious nature but then taking on secular themes. In the 1570s, however, purpose-built theatres began to appear in London. Taking advantage of the fact that he was beyond the reach of City censorship and taxation, James Burbage in 1576 erected a playhouse simply called 'The Theatre' in Shoreditch, with The Curtain in Finsbury Fields following two years later.

Theatres also began to appear in Southwark, again safely beyond the jurisdiction of London's civic authorities. The first of these was at Newington Butts, in the southern part of the Borough, which took its name from the practice of archery there. This playhouse may have opened as early as 1576, organised by Jerome Savage, a leading member of a company of players that had Ambrose Dudley, Earl of Warwick, as their patron.

During the 1560s, theatre companies under the patronage of members of Elizabeth I's court had begun touring around the country, just as the queen herself took part in magnificent progresses, visiting favoured courtiers. Stratford-upon-Avon in Warwickshire was visited by two theatre companies, the Queen's Players and Worcester's Men, in 1564, the very year of the birth of William Shakespeare. In the years that followed, the town received at least thirteen visits from such companies, so that Shakespeare grew up in an environment offering a repertory of drama.

In 1575 the queen was entertained at Kenilworth Castle by her great favourite, Robert Dudley, Earl of Leicester, with nineteen days of spectacular events. These were open to all, so Shakespeare may well have made the short journey to Kenilworth to watch a water pageant held on the castle's lake. When he came to write *A Midsummer*

*Night's Dream* some twenty years later, Shakespeare perhaps recalled details of the pageant along with a rather less refined performance by the Coventry townsmen of their traditional Hocktide play, which was also presented at Kenilworth that summer.

Robert Dudley, like his brother Ambrose, gave his name to a company of players, as did so many other courtiers, providing a dazzling array: Leicester's Men, Warwick's Men, Worcester's Men, Lord Strange's Men, Essex's Men, Derby's Men, Lord Berkeley's Men. All of these, along with more official companies such as the Queen's Players, the Lord Admiral's Men and the Lord Chamberlain's Men, were to perform plays at the Southwark playhouses from the 1570s onwards.

In 1585 Philip Henslowe leased from St Saviour's parish a garden known as 'the Little Rose' on Bankside and built a theatre that was opened two years later. Businessmen in Southwark diversified into many projects, but Henslowe takes the laurel for his range of activities. Although he was a freeman of the Dyers' Company, this would seem to be the one trade that he did not practise: his investments included starch-making, property speculation and pawnbroking, as well as being a theatre financier. Brought up in the Ashdown Forest in Sussex, where his father was master of the game, he retained interests in the sale of its wood. He was also a member of the court circle, which was to prove useful when dealing with difficulties over his playhouses. Henslowe lived all his adult life in the Clink Liberty, in a house located somewhere near the prison, and took an active interest in the running of St Saviour's parish, serving as a vestryman, churchwarden and overseer of the poor. He was also a governor of the grammar school.

Henslowe's various interests are shown in his diary, which is really a book of accounts. Kept between 1591 and 1609, it provides a vivid picture of theatrical life, showing the loan of money for playbooks and costumes, for licences for performances, and for keeping the Rose Theatre in good repair. It also gives us a picture of some of the Southwark community. His pawnbroker customers were from all levels of society, from 'My Lord Burte', who is thought to be either Baron Willoughby, whose family name was Bertie, or William Herbert, later Earl of Pembroke, through to a woman selling herbs in the market. He dealt mostly through agents, notably Goody Watson, but the entries of the transactions are in Philip Henslowe's own hand.

One of the most intriguing of the entries is the loan of 11 shillings made in January 1593 to the daughter of a midwife. The complexity of the Elizabethan wardrobe is shown by a doublewrought 'rebato', a stiff collar to support a ruff, a cap of wool and a cross cloth, a linen cloth worn across the forehead. In addition, she pawned a gilt box containing a looking glass, a new comb, a pair of scissors, three ear picks and a pair of small compasses. Poignant are the references to the pawning of rings. One, a little hoop of gold with the poesy 'hope helpeth heaviness', was given in April 1594 against the sum of 5 shillings.[2]

The Rose Theatre was smaller than the other London venues but, with easy access from the City across the Thames, it proved so successful that in 1592 Henslowe set about enlarging it to make room for around 500 further spectators. The original shape, a regular polygon of fourteen sides, now took on a distorted egg shape. An archaeological investigation of the site in the late twentieth century revealed that portions of the foundations were littered with fruit seeds and hazel nuts. These were not the detritus from playgoers' snacks but deliberately laid with cinder and earth to provide a tough floor surface. During the building works, the hazels were brought from the nearby soap house, one of the biggest of its kind in London, where they were crushed for their oil.

In the same year, Henslowe's stepdaughter married the actor Edward Alleyn, and the two men formed a highly successful partnership at the Rose. Various troupes had performed at the theatre, but by 1592 Alleyn was the leader of the Admiral's Men, so that they became the resident company, performing many of the plays of Christopher Marlowe. With his physical stature – Alleyn was well over 6 feet tall – and strong voice, his particular talent lay in powerful characters such as Tamburlaine, Doctor Faustus, and possibly Barabas in Marlowe's *Jew of Malta*. One contemporary noted, 'his eyes are lightning, and his words are thunder'.[3] In the late 1590s the Rose was showing signs of age, so Henslowe and Alleyn decided that the show must go on while repairs were made, but in a different part of London. The Fortune Theatre was built on the north bank of the Thames, just beyond London Wall in the parish of St Giles, Cripplegate, an area well known to Alleyn during his youth. The theatre was opened in 1600.

Alleyn and Henslowe shared an interest not only in the theatre but also in baiting of animals. Dramatic performances at the Rose alternated with spectacles of bears being pitted against mastiff dogs. In 1598 the two men made plans to acquire the mastership of the bears – a court appointment and a lucrative one, given the popularity of the sport. Initially they were thwarted in their aim, but from 1604 they held a joint patent of the office. Alleyn even baited lions before King James at the Tower of London.

Meanwhile, a second playhouse had been built close to the Rose on Bankside in 1594–95. Francis Langley had acquired the manor of Paris Garden, and he erected the Swan Theatre on its eastern edge, accessible from the river via the Falcon landing stairs. Proximity to the Thames was now clearly key – the playhouse at Newington Butts was being demolished at the very time the Swan was going up. The Dutch traveller Johannes de Witt celebrated it as the largest and most magnificent of all London's playhouses, with a capacity for an audience of 3,000. Constructed in flint concrete, it had wooden supporting columns that de Witt described as so cleverly painted that they would deceive the most acute observer into thinking they were of marble. De Witt also drew a sketch of the interior, which survives in a copy, the only visual image known to exist. The dating suggests that it may depict members of the Lord Chamberlain's Men, who are thought to have played there in 1596.

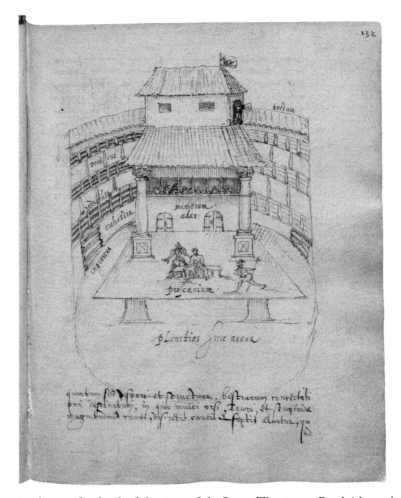

6. *A copy of a sketch of the stage of the Swan Theatre on Bankside made by the Dutch traveller, Johannes de Witt, c.1596.*

Langley does not come down as a pleasant character, and this seems to have affected the success of his playhouse. Originally apprenticed as a draper, he was turned out by his master for taking inappropriate liberties, but he managed somehow to secure his freedom of the Company and became the alnager or searcher of woollen cloths for the City. No sooner had he taken up this lucrative office than he became embroiled in lawsuits, accused of extortion and fraud. He also pursued a career as a money-lender, and it was through the default of a loan that he acquired Paris Garden from the Cure family (p. 89).

Langley's desire to maximise his profits brought him serious trouble when a play, *The Isle of Dogs*, was performed at the Swan by Lord Pembroke's Men in 1597. One of the authors, Ben Jonson, was imprisoned for producing a satire 'containing very seditious and slanderous matter', according to the court record, while the second, Thomas Nashe, beat a hasty retreat from London. Jonson was soon released, but Langley had incurred the wrath of the powerful Secretary of State, Robert Cecil. In fact, Langley was already in trouble with Cecil, implicated in the theft of an enormous diamond from a Spanish ship captured by English seamen in 1592, a scenario worthy of an Elizabethan drama in itself. Langley managed for a time to evade Cecil's grasp, but a series of failed ventures drove him into bankruptcy. He was forced to sell the manor of Paris Garden, along with its playhouse. He died penniless in 1602, leaving his widow with six children and a batch of lawsuits, and was buried in St Saviour's churchyard.

In the same year, the Swan was embroiled in another scandal, concerning a play advertised by an author in financial difficulties, Richard Vennar, entitled *Plot of the Play Called England's Joy*, in honour of Queen Elizabeth. According to Vennar, it was to consist of nine scenes to be performed by men of good birth, scholars by profession, and the spectators paid in advance a substantial 2s 8d for a seat. Vennar appeared on stage, delivered six lines of prologue, but was then arrested for debt by bailiffs. A rather different story was given by John Chamberlain in a letter sent to his friend Dudley Carleton, in which he suggested that Vennar, having got the seat money, set off across the Thames but was apprehended. 'In the meane time the common people . . . revenged themselves upon the hangings curtaines chaires stooles walles and whatsoever came in theyre way very outrageously and made a great spoyle'.[4]

A calmer and happier course was steered by the third theatre to be opened on Bankside. When James Burbage died in 1597, Giles Allen, the owner of the land in Shoreditch on which The Theatre had been built, refused to renew the lease. Theatres were increasingly becoming the target of attacks from Puritans. One in particular, John Stockwood, proved a fierce critic, giving two fiery sermons at St Paul's Cross in 1578 and 1579 condemning the acting profession. Burbage's playhouse he described as 'the gorgeous Playing-place *erected in the fields*' before comparing it to 'the old heathenish *Theatre* in Rome, the showpiece of all beastly and filthy matters'.[5] He went on to speak out against other pastimes and entertainments that he felt diverted people from studying the scriptures.

Condemnation continued to be exercised both in sermons and in publications, so that Allen, a Puritan, was adamant in his refusal to renew. On 28 December 1598, while Allen was enjoying Christmas at his country house, Burbage's two sons, Richard and Cuthbert, along with their players and friends, dismantled the theatre and took the material to a warehouse on the waterfront near Bridewell. Once the weather turned warmer, the woodwork was ferried across the Thames to some marshy ground to the south of Maiden Lane in Southwark, and a new playhouse was erected: the Globe.

The Burbage brothers were already financially stretched, as their father had in 1596 bought premises at Blackfriars to create an indoor playhouse, but residents in the former monastic complex had protested, making it impossible to proceed. Therefore, Richard and Cuthbert invited some members of the Lord Admiral's Men, including William Shakespeare, to become stakeholders in the new Bankside theatre. As the company had been together for five years, they were more stable than other troupes, and they had Shakespeare as their playwright. In the spring of 1599 he worked on a new drama, *Julius Caesar*, and this would seem to be the first play to have been performed at the Globe.

The Swiss traveller Thomas Platter saw a performance that September, noting that it was 'very pleasingly performed'. More forthcoming and enthusiastic was the poet John Weever, who took to verse:

So have I seen, when Caesar would appear,
And on the stage at half-sword parley were
Brutus and Cassius. Oh, how the audience
Were ravished with what wonder they went hence[6]

Southwark is full of associations with the Bankside theatres. There is some debate as to when William Shakespeare moved here, with some experts suggesting that he was residing somewhere in Paris Garden from 1596. Once the Globe was being erected, he took up lodgings in the Clink Liberty, so that he was close at hand to participate in the decisions to make the most of the building's dramatic potential. Little wonder, therefore, that his plays are redolent with characters that he encountered on the streets of Southwark. In the mid-twentieth century a stained-glass window was created by Christopher Webb for the nave of the cathedral. It takes as its concept the biblical Tree of Jesse, with Shakespeare as the root, in a Bankside meadow, with Prospero, Ariel and Caliban from *The Tempest* as the central light. The left lancet depicts characters from Shakespeare's comedies, including Falstaff from *The Merry Wives of Windsor*, while the right lancet has figures from his tragedies, including *Othello* and *Richard II*.

Shakespeare often carried his audiences out of London into all manner of locations, including a forest glade outside Athens for *A Midsummer Night's Dream* and, most incongruously, Bohemia for *The Winter's Tale*, but the characters which he placed in these exotic places would nevertheless have been familiar. It would be highly unlikely to come across Caliban in Borough High Street but perfectly possible to meet merchants' wives like Mistress Ford and Mistress Page from *The Merry Wives of Windsor* at Southwark market or negotiating with the laundresses who worked along the bank of the

Thames. Some of the merchants of Southwark could have been fretting about the fate of their ships and cargoes as they gathered on the quays by London Bridge, just as Antonio listened for news on the Rialto in *The Merchant of Venice*. A clear reference to the prostitutes of Southwark is made in *Troilus and Cressida* when Shakespeare talks of 'some galled goose of Winchester', galling indicating syphilis.

Perhaps the most typical of all Southwark characters is introduced in *The Winter's Tale*, written in 1610 or 1611. Shakespeare presents us with Autolycus, the roguish pedlar who was wont to steal laundry drying on bushes and hedges, snapping up 'unconsidered trifles'. This is not to suggest that Southwark produced such sneak thieves, but the pedlar or chapman was a common sight in the Borough.

The servants in Leontes' household describe how Autolycus brought love ballads to country girls, and he might have also carried almanacs and chapbooks, small cheap publications. Autolycus himself adds more details of the contents of his pack:

Lawn as white as driven snow,
Cyprus black as e'er was crow,
Gloves as sweet as damask roses,
Masks for faces, and for noses,
Bugle-bracelet, necklace amber,
Perfume for a lady's chamber;
Golden coifs and stomachers
For my lads to give their dears;
Pins and poking-sticks of steel,
What maids lack from head to heel ...[7]

All these goods would have been obtainable from the shops that lined London Bridge. Along with Cheapside, this was one of the city's high-class shopping areas. In 1578 a French visitor wrote of 'a great and powerful bridge, the most magnificent that exists in the whole of Europe. It is built entirely of ashlar and completely covered with houses which are all like big castles. And the shops are great storehouses full of all sorts of very opulent merchandise. And there is nowhere in London which is more commercial ... And there is no bridge in the whole of Europe which is on a great river like the Thames and as formidable, as spectacular and as bustling with trade as this bridge in London.'[8]

The first houses and shops installed on the bridge in the thirteenth century (p. 31) were two storeys in height, but over the years they were rebuilt higher and higher, usually of timber to minimise weight, and cantilevered out over the Thames. In the fourteenth and fifteenth centuries the dominant trades were haberdashers, glovers, cutlers, bowyers and fletchers. The haberdashers offered a wide variety of goods, such as combs, purses, spectacles, bracelets, looking glasses, headgear, writing materials, laces and pins, just as Autolycus mentioned in his list. In the seventeenth century all these trades except haberdashery declined, but the bridge shopkeepers were joined by hosiers and silkmen, and grocers offering dyes, spices and apothecary goods.

The first record of a bookseller on the bridge comes in 1595 with Thomas Gosson. He and his successors sold cheap popular writings such as ballads, broadsides, newsbooks, histories and romances, jest books and pious works. Samuel Pepys built up a collection of just such publications in the late seventeenth century, cataloguing them in his library as Vulgaria, Penny Merriments and Penny Godlinesses. He visited balladmongers on the Bridge, such as Josiah Blare at the Looking Glass, John Back at the Black Boy, and Charles Tias at the Three Bibles. Their wares may have been cheap, but there was considerable demand among an increasingly literate market. The inventory of Charles Tias, taken in 1664, shows that he had books and ballads stored in the shop, with more in a lower chamber on the street, the hall, the garret and even on the stairs. Altogether there were just under 10,000 books ready to go out, most priced at under 6d, but with Bibles at 10s and 4s, and the equivalent of 37,500 ballad sheets.

In 1686 John Back announced in the back of one of his books that he 'Furnisheth any Countrey Chapman with all sorts of Books, Ballads, and all other Stationary-Wares at reasonable Rates'. The 'country chapmen' congregated in Southwark, collecting the various goods that they wished to sell in preparation for setting out across southern England. Margaret Spufford in her study of chapmen compiled a survey of their locations in various parts of London. She found that the largest group were in Southwark and Newington in the 1680s, with a second concentration in West Smithfield, on the north-west side of the City.[9]

Southwark establishments were customers of the London Bridge shops; for example, cloth finishers buying dyes, and the physicians at St Thomas' Hospital acquiring the spices for their medicines. But it was the chapmen who represented a significant proportion of the trade. The late seventeenth-century trade card of the grocer John Shakemaple at the Anchor shows that he supplied chapmen who had horses with ropes and cords, cart saddle trees, whips, rugs and packthread. Ralph Bodman, trunkmaker, had a shop in 1675 appro- priately called the Pedlar and Pack. Records of some of the chapmen show the catchment area for Southwark. William Oliver, for example, was a chapman selling in the Salisbury area. He bought from grocers and girdlers, who would have supplied him with belts, in the 1610s. Robert Streete 'hath sought to get his liveing by buying and selling in Darking', Dorking in Surrey. He purchased from a grocer and a mercer on the bridge. Debts owed to Thomas Ruck, a haberdasher on the bridge, include people from Kent, Sussex, and Croydon and Wandsworth, both then in Surrey.[10]

Shakespeare does not specify whether Autolycus had a horse or travelled on foot. Chapmen with horses were in the minority, and this was very much a young man's trade, for their packs would have been weighty and they had to travel considerable distances.

While Autolycus is perhaps the character of Shakespeare's most specifically associated with Southwark, the figure that appears in three of his plays and is eulogised in a fourth is Sir John Falstaff. Originally, Shakespeare had called Prince Hal's drinking companion Sir John Oldcastle, a real-life character who became Lord Cobham, a Lollard gentleman revered as a martyr of the Protestant faith. Under pressure from Oldcastle's Elizabethan namesake, William Brooke, Lord Cobham, pertinently the Lord Chamberlain, Shakespeare was persuaded to change the name to Falstaff. Just to make matters even more complex, Shakespeare had some years earlier, in the first part of *Henry VI*, included in the cast of characters Sir John Fastolf, 'a cowardly soldier' in the French Wars in the 1430s. The real Sir John Fastolf, who had a residence in Southwark, had in fact fought with distinction in those same wars (p. 34).

These complexities were no doubt lost on the audiences who took Shakespeare's Falstaff to their hearts. One of the playwright's contemporaries, Leonard Digges, wrote of *Henry IV Part One*, 'let but Falstaff . . . and you scarce shall have a room, All is so pestered'.[11] These playgoers probably had met just such a character, with his companions Bardolph and Pistol, in one of the Southwark inns, along with Mistress Quickly, the hostess of the Blue Boar, which the playwright set on the other side of the river, in Eastcheap. According to Nicholas Rowe, the seventeenth-century editor of Shakespeare's works, Queen Elizabeth was so pleased with the character of Falstaff that she 'commanded him to continue it for one Play more, and to shew him in Love'. The result was *The Merry Wives of Windsor*.[12]

By the beginning of the seventeenth century, Shakespeare was prospering as a stakeholder in the Globe Theatre, and in 1604 he moved northwards to lodgings in Silver Street, near to the Barbican and the church of St Giles at Cripplegate. This location would have made it easy for him to set off on the road to Stratford-upon-Avon, but there was also a theatrical community here. Henslowe and Alleyn had their Fortune Theatre, and parishioners of St Giles included the playwrights Ben Jonson, Thomas Dekker and George Wilkins, who was to become Shakespeare's last collaborator. In the nearby parish of

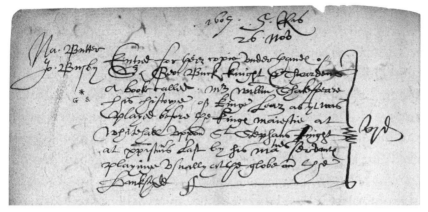

7. *An entry in the register at Stationers' Hall in 1607 of a 'booke called Master William Shakespeare his "historye of Kinge Lear" as yt was played before the kinges maiestie at Whitehall uppon St Stephen's night at Christmas Last by his maiesties servantes playing usually at the "Globe" on the Bankyside'.*

St Mary Aldermanbury lived his actor friends John Hemminges and Henry Condell, who produced the First Folio of his plays in 1623.

Still to be seen in the graveyard of St Giles is the tomb of William's nephew, Edward, who died in 1607. He was the son of the playwright's youngest brother, Edmund, sixteen years William's junior, who had come from Warwickshire to London in the 1590s to take up acting. Little is known about Edmund Shakespeare, but he had an affair with an unknown woman, hence the child. Edmund himself died just four months after his son and is buried in what is now Southwark Cathedral. According to the churchwardens' accounts, he was buried 'with a forenoon toll of the Great Bell', costing the sum of 20 shillings, and it is thought that William paid for this.

Close by the ledger stone commemorating Edmund are those of two dramatists, John Fletcher, who died in 1625, and Philip Massinger, who died in 1640. Fletcher is known as one half of a famous duo of collaborating playwrights, with Francis Beaumont, but he worked with several others, and wrote no fewer than sixteen of his own. With Shakespeare, for example, he wrote *The Two Noble Kinsmen* and *Henry VIII*. The first reference to Philip Massinger in theatrical terms comes in 1613, when he wrote from Clink Prison to Philip Henslowe, asking him for £5 owed to himself and two fellow prisoners for an unidentified play. In the early 1620s he worked closely with Fletcher, a partnership that ended with the latter's death from the plague (p. 103). Massinger went on to write two plays that poked fun at the affectations of the rising City merchant class, *A New Way to Pay Old Debts* and *The City Madam*, so it is ironic that his last resting place is close by some of the targets of his satire. Massinger and Fletcher are described by a contemporary as great friends, which may explain why they share a grave.

In the summer of 1613, the Globe Theatre had been destroyed when a cannon set off during a performance of Shakespeare and Fletcher's *Henry VIII* misfired. A contemporary recounted how 'some of the paper or other stuff, wherewith one of [the cannon] was stopped, did light on the thatch, where being thought at first but idle smoke, and their eyes more attentive to the show, it kindled inwardly, and ran like a train, consuming within less than an hour the whole house to the very ground.'[13] Luckily, nobody was killed, though 'one man had his breeches set on fire, that would perhaps have broyled him, if he had not by the benefit of a provident wit, put it out with a bottle of ale': an appropriate remedy for Southwark.

The Globe had a thatched roof because, when the Burbages and their players dismantled The Theatre back in 1599, they did not take the roof tiles, which were too heavy to be easily transported. The Globe was rebuilt, and at the same time Henslowe decided to open yet another theatre on Bankside, on the site of his bear garden. It was optimistically named Hope, but this could apply neither to its future for drama nor for the unfortunate animals that were baited here with increasing frequency in place of the plays. Both the Globe and the Hope were closed down by the Puritans in 1642. The theatre at Newington Butts, too far to the south, had disappeared by 1594, and the Rose was torn down in 1606. Like the Hope, the Swan was given over to displays of bear-baiting and sword-fighting, and by 1632 it was described as having fallen into decay, compared by the playwright Shakerley Marmion to 'a dying swan, [that] hangs her head and sings her own dirge' in his play, *Holland's Leaguer* (p. 64).

One Southwark resident watched the decline of the Bankside theatres with dismay: John Taylor, known as the Water Poet. He came to London sometime in the 1590s, having abandoned his grammar school education in Gloucester because he found Latin impenetrable, and was apprenticed to a Thames waterman. This was probably in Southwark, where a quarter of St Saviour's parish – around 40,000 men, according to the chronicler John Stow – were employed in the trade. Their boats could be used as communal taxis, with prospective passengers gathering at the Thames-side stairs. They would respond when the waterman shouted 'Eastward Ho' to go downriver, or 'Westward Ho' to go to Westminster or further upstream, and these cries were to become the title of two Jacobean plays. London Bridge was narrow, the roadway only 15 feet in width, choked with traffic, so that many people preferred to use the services of the watermen to make even the brief journey across the Thames. On Bankside, within less than a mile stretch, there were fifteen stairs and other docking places. What purports to be one of the original ferryman's seats is still to be found by what was Bear Garden Stairs.

Taylor led an exciting life. Shortly after completing his apprenticeship, he was pressed for the navy and was present at the siege of Cadiz conducted by the Earl of Essex in 1596. Other adventures included walking to Braemar in Scotland, making various expeditions to mainland Europe and attempting to sail in a boat made of paper to Queenborough on the Isle of Sheppey in Kent, with two dried stockfish tied to the canes for oars. This last venture, which nearly proved fatal, was to promote the virtues of hempseed.

When not undertaking these adventures, John Taylor settled in Southwark, worshipping at St Saviour's Church, and he is said to have chosen as his regular boat route Bankside, Whitehall and the Old Swan stairs. He became the overseer for the Waterman's Company, whose hall still stands on Upper Thames Street, and acted as spokesman when it was decided to present a suit to James I against the new theatres that were being erected north of the river, such as Henslowe's Fortune at Cripplegate and, after residents' protests were overruled, the indoor theatre at Blackfriars. The lucrative trade to Southwark was being seriously threatened. Despite sympathetic words from the king's ministers, nothing was achieved.

However, Taylor had become acquainted with the actors, writers and playgoers as he ferried them across to Bankside, and he began to write, starting with verses published as *The Sculler, Rowing from Tiber to Thames* in 1612. He recognised the publicity value of a waterman of lowly rank aspiring to poetry, and he played on it to secure complimentary verses from poets, though Ben Jonson, whom he claimed as a friend, did not comply. One of Taylor's verses derided the traveller Thomas Coryat, setting off a heated pamphlet war and probably not endearing him to fellow parishioner William Austin, who had contributed prefatory verses to *Crudities* (see p. 89).

Taylor also opposed any idea of building more bridges across the Thames, writing:

Carroaches, coaches, jades, and Flanders mares,
Doe rob us of our shares, our wares, our fares:
Against the ground we stand and knock our heeles,
Whilest all our profit runs away on wheels

He ended his days on the north bank of the Thames. An unswerving supporter of the king, he ran an alehouse, the Crown, in Covent Garden, changing its name to the Mourning Crown after Parliament executed Charles I in 1649.

But the watermen were still able to take their customers across the river to Southwark to attend baiting of animals. Pepys noted in his diary on 14 August 1666, just a fortnight before the Great Fire of London: 'After dinner I went with my wife and Mercer to the Bear-Garden, where I have not been, I think of many years, and saw some good sport of the bull's tossing of the dogs – one into the very boxes. But it was a very rude and nasty pleasure.' Unlike many Londoners, Pepys found such displays not to his liking. He was joined in this by his fellow diarist John Evelyn, who attended a bull-baiting entertainment in 1670 and found it 'rude and dirty'.[14]

Pepys was more approving of the prize fighting that had become such a feature of Bankside. In May 1667 he recorded:

> stopped at the Bear-garden Stairs, there to see a Prize fought. But the house so full, there was no getting in there; so forced to [go] through an alehouse into the pit where the bears are baited, and upon a stool did see them fight, which they did very furiously, a butcher and a waterman. The former had the better all along, till by and by the latter dropped his sword out of his hand, and the butcher, whether or not seeing his sword dropped or I know not, but did give him a cut above the wrist, so as he was disabled to fight any longer. But Lord, to see how in a minute the whole stage was full of watermen to revenge the foul play, and the butchers to defend their fellow, though most blamed him: and there they all fell to it, to knocking and cutting down many on each side. It was pleasant to see, but that I stood in the pit and feared that in the tumult I might get some hurt. At last the rabble broke up, and so I away.[15]

The baiting of animals, fighting of men and the services of the brothels continued on Bankside, but the brief, glorious time of the theatres was gone. The cavalcade had moved on. The best epitaph to this period comes, unsurprisingly, from the pen of William Shakespeare. In 1611 he wrote his final play, *The Tempest*, performed at the Blackfriars Theatre. Prospero's speech towards the end of the play is often described as Shakespeare's farewell to London and its theatres, but it can particularly be applied to the actors' departure from Southwark:

> Our revels now are ended. These our actors,
> As I foretold you, were all spirits, and
> Are melted into air, into thin air:
> And like the baseless fabric of this vision,
> The cloud-capp'd tow'rs, the gorgeous palaces,
> The solemn temples, the great globe itself,
> Yea, all which it inherits, shall dissolve,
> And, like this insubstantial pageant faded,
> Leave not a rack behind. We are such stuff
> As dreams are made on . . .[16]

# 9

# Brave New World

O brave new world,
That has such people in it!¹

Shakespeare's famous lines in *The Tempest*, where Miranda thrills at
the discovery of a whole world beyond the island on which she has
grown up, were written at the very time that the English were beginning to found colonies across the Atlantic in North America. An
intriguing range of people from Southwark played their part in these
early communities.

In 1585 Sir Walter Raleigh organised an expedition to establish
the first permanent settlement on Roanoke Island, in what was
named Virginia after the queen. Unable to lead the expedition
himself because Elizabeth would not release him from the royal
court, he sent in his stead the mathematician and expert on naviga-
tion Thomas Harriot to accompany Ralph Lane, who was to become
governor of the colony. Both men returned to London the following
year, but their intention of sending supplies to Roanoke was
confounded when England became embroiled in war with the
Spanish, with Philip II launching his armada of invasion. So it was
not until 1590 that a relief party arrived back at Roanoke, only to

find the settlement abandoned: the fate of these first colonists remains unknown.

An attempt to re-establish foothold in Virginia proved more successful and abiding when a settlement was created in 1607 on the Jamestown River, named in honour of the new king, James I. A charter drawn up two years later described the investors in the Virginia Company as 'divers Knights, gentlemen, merchaunts and others of our cittie of London', and their hope was to discover precious metals.[2] This proved a failure, but trade of various types was begun. Recognising the burgeoning demand for tobacco in England, plantations were established, using the native type of tobacco which proved poor and bitter in taste.

In the summer of 1609 one of the ships making for Virginia, the *Sea Venture*, was driven aground by what was described as a 'dreadful tempest' onto the uninhabited island of Bermuda, or 'of the Devils', as it was sometimes known. Aboard this ship was the poet and shareholder in the Blackfriars Theatre, William Strachey. He later recorded the adventure in a letter back to London, which was undoubtedly known to William Shakespeare when he wrote *The Tempest* in 1611. Another passenger aboard the stricken ship was George Yeardley from Southwark. The son of a merchant tailor, he had been baptised in St Saviour's Church in 1588. Choosing not to follow his father into the mercantile community, he had served as a soldier in the Netherlands, and he was accompanying his commanding officer, Captain Thomas Gates, newly designated governor of the colony of Virginia.

A third passenger was John Rolfe, an energetic entrepreneur who spent the enforced period stranded on Bermuda acquainting himself with the kind of tobacco grown in the Caribbean, *Nicotina tabacum*. Discovering that this was sweeter than the Virginian type, he arranged for plants to be brought from Trinidad and began to cultivate them. When two smaller boats were built, enabling the settlers finally to leave the island and to make their way to Jamestown, he took the tobacco plants with him. After Rolfe sent a small amount of his yield to London in 1612, the trade in tobacco took off rapidly. King James had published in 1604 an attack on the smoking of the noxious weed, *The Counterblaste to Tobacco*, condemning the 'manifold abuses of this vile custom'. The royal commercial instincts, however, prevailed, overcoming his prejudices: the Virginian tobacco trade was to become hugely important for England. John Rolfe married as his second wife the Powhatan princess Pocahontas and brought her to London, where she caused a sensation at the royal court.

To keep the fortunes of the Virginia Company commercially afloat, lotteries were held. This practice dated back to Elizabeth's reign, when her chief minister, William Cecil, needed to find money for the repair of England's harbours. He got the idea from the Low Countries, where the mercantile cities raised funds for military and municipal projects. The lottery office was located in St Paul's Churchyard, with the prizes announced on walls and doors of the City. The investors in the Virginia Company decided to overcome their financial difficulties by holding a lottery in 1612, and although the idea took time to take off, and ticket sales were initially low, gradually it took root, and lotteries were held annually thereafter, supported by their royal charter. A ballad composed when the first Virginia lottery was held encouraged different groups to take part, such as farmers, City merchant venturers, the royal family and women seeking a husband:

You Maydes that have but portions small
to gaine your Mariage friend,
Cast in your Lottes with willing hand,
God may good fortune send.
You Widowes, and you wedded Wives,
one litle substaunce try:
You may advance both you and yours,
with wealth that comes thereby.[3]

One copy of the company's broadside for the lottery of 1616 survives, showing two Native Americans with tortoises at their feet, and silver cups and sacks of coins promised to the winning ticket holders.

When the King James decided to cancel this vital source of revenue, bankruptcy threatened, drawing George Yeardley back to London to confer with officers of the company. He also wanted to encourage more rapid settlement of the colony by replacing military rule with civil government. The following year Yeardley was appointed governor, implementing various reforms instilled in a document known as the 'Great Charter' that provided for representatives to be elected to any assembly for the enactment of laws: the first such legislative body in an English colony. Among the money-making schemes that were developed with Yeardley's encouragement was one to send potential brides to the new colony, thus ensuring its long-term viability by providing the settlers in Virginia with ties of family and children. Was he inspired to adopt this scheme by the ballad quoted above?

In 1621, fifty-six women, 'young and uncorrupt', were sent over to Jamestown. One of these came from Southwark. Margaret Dauson, Suffolk born, was a servant to Elizabeth Stevenson, the wife of a Southwark leather-seller. The sacramental token books for St Saviour record an Edward Stevenson from Boroughside purchasing tokens for himself and his wife in 1620 and 1621. Elizabeth vouched that Margaret Dauson, then aged twenty-five, had long lived as 'a good and faithfull servant' with the household.[4]

The first contingent of women sailed on the *Marmaduke* in May 1621. Margaret was part of a second, larger group that boarded the *Warwick* in September, en route to a new life in America, with a bridal price of 150 lbs of tobacco. The women embarked from Billingsgate quay and were rowed downstream to Gravesend. From here they began the long voyage, arriving at Chesapeake Bay and making their way to the mouth of the James River in midwinter. It had taken between three and four months to make this crossing.

Thereafter, we do not know what happened to Margaret Dauson, though it is possible that she was the woman with the same Christian name from the *Warwick* who married a smith from Lincolnshire, Ezekiah Raughton. Also possible was that she perished in the 'Great Attack' launched on Good Friday 1622, when the Powhatan Confederacy led by Opechancanough killed a substantial proportion of the Jamestown community. This was to avenge atrocities that had been meted out by the settlers on the native population, and to try to drive the settlers from their lands forever. Shakespeare's Miranda, having been brought up isolated from society, took an innocent view of humanity which was all too removed from a reality such as this violent clash of cultures. Whatever her fate, Margaret Dauson must have found unimaginably startling the contrast between the tiny infant colony in the midst of exotic wilderness, and the teeming, raucous streets of Southwark.

More women were to follow in the years to come. Contemporary ballads suggest what might have motivated them to make the perilous journey. One was the prospect of a marriage and financial security, as in these lines:

The Maidens of London are now in despaire,
How they shall get husbands, it is all their care,
Though maidens be never so vertuous and faire,
Yet old wealthy widowes, are yong mens chiefe ware.
Oh this is a wiving age
Oh this is a wiving age[5]

Another motive might be, like that of Chaucer's Canterbury pilgrims, a desire to travel and to expand what were inevitably narrow horizons, especially for women living in a patriarchal society. A mid-seventeenth century ballad reflects this with an alluring invitation:

Come all you very merry London Girls,
that are disposed to Travel,

Here is a Voyage now at hand,
will save your feet from gravel,
If you have shooes you need not fear
for wearing out the Leather
For why you shall on shipboard go,
like Loving Rogues together,
Some are already gone before
the rest must after follow
Then come away and do not stay
your guide shal be Apollo.

The 'merry London Girls' were promised that on board ship they would be plentifully supplied with 'bisket salt-Beef and English Beer, and Pork well boyld with Peason', and once arrived, there would be gold and silver mines to make their fortune.[6]

A very different motivation lay behind the transatlantic voyages that began the year before the first Jamestown brides set sail. In the summer of 1620 the *Mayflower* set off from London to make landfall at Cape Cod in Massachusetts. Many of the men and women aboard this ship and those that followed were making the perilous journey for religious reasons. They were part of a wider Puritan movement, which had existed in the Church of England since Tudor times. Some within this movement, rather than remaining in the Church of England and hoping thereby to undertake reform from within, chose to form separate ecclesiastical communities, and thus came to be referred to as separatists.

Separatists adopted a very different structure from that of the Church of England. In 1550, when the Dutch Church received the recognition of the firmly Protestant Edward VI and took over the former priory of Austin Friars in Old Broad Street in the City of London, it established the right of the congregation to elect their own pastors, elders and deacons. Inevitably, this church fell foul of Mary Tudor and her determination to return England to the Church of Rome: its Pastor, John Rough, was burnt at the stake. However, the principle had been established, and clandestine meetings of separatists were held, despite attempts to suppress them by Elizabeth I as Supreme Governor of the Church of England.

One leading separatist, Robert Browne, was fortunate to enjoy the friendship and protection of the queen's chief minister, William Cecil, Lord Burghley. Browne was an advocate of the fundamental principle that church members should be believers, entering a covenant of membership with their 'gathered' church as opposed to their parish. Browne lost credibility when he chose to recant his ideas and became headmaster of St Olave's grammar school in Southwark. His former followers, however, continued to embrace the principles that he had introduced and were described as Brownists.

In 1587 a group of Brownists attending a meeting in the City of London were arrested as recusants or dissenters and committed to the Bishop of Winchester's prison in the Clink. When a leading separatist, Henry Barrow, visited one of the group, John Greenwood, he was promptly detained on the orders of the Archbishop of Canterbury, Richard Whitgift, who was virulently opposed to the separatists' egalitarian views on religious matters. Greenwood spent his incarceration writing pamphlets, smuggled out of the Clink hidden in the clothing of Cicely, his wife's servant. His tone was uncompromising, likening the Church of England to a harlot sitting upon the waters and murdering saints. It can thus be said that the first separatist English Church began in the Clink, and when Greenwood and Barrow were granted a temporary reprieve, they held meetings at a house in Deadman's Place, founding the Southwark Independent Church.

In December 1592 Greenwood was arrested with another leading separatist, Francis Johnson, at a meeting in a house on Ludgate Hill. Three months later another raid was made on premises in the village of Islington, to the north of the City. From the records of interrogation we get a picture of some of the men and women who had taken up these religious views. Several of them were from Southwark:

Robert Abraham, leather dresser, and Christopher Diggins, weaver, from St Olave's parish; Daniel Buck, scrivener, Thomas Micklefeld, joiner, Robert Rippon and Robert Stokes from St Saviour's parish; and Quinton Smyth, a Southwark feltmaker who was arrested for distributing pamphlets. The women on the list yield little information beyond their names, though it is sadly noticeable how many of them died in Newgate as a result of the bad conditions prevailing there. The interrogators found that almost all the people arrested were literate, for it was very important to these Protestants that they be able to read the scriptures for themselves.[7]

The following year, London was in turmoil, with the plague raging and hostility mounting against Archbishop Whitgift, characterised by separatists as the great enemy of God. When a second wave of arrests of Brownists took place, Barrow and Greenwood were taken to Tyburn for execution, but so many supporters thronged the streets that a postponement was decided upon. Nevertheless, a matter of weeks later the two men were hanged together on the Tyburn Tree, while another leading separatist, John Penry, suffered the same fate on a gibbet at Thomas-a-Watering by the Old Kent Road. It was so called because this was where some of Chaucer's pilgrims were thought to have met up en route to Thomas Becket's shrine in Canterbury.

Although some Brownists decided to emigrate to Holland, the numbers continued to increase in London. While the Bishop of London declared there were 200 Brownists in the capital in 1601, the Spanish ambassador reckoned the figure to be over 5,000. The estimation of the much larger number, and the popularity of the movement, is backed up by a reference made by Shakespeare in *Twelfth Night*. Sir Andrew Aguecheek, asked to decide whether to act with courage or calculation, responded 'It must be with valour; for policy I hate. I had lief be a Brownist as a politician'.[8] Shakespeare could rely on his audience to understand his drift.

Not all the episcopacy was so hostile to the ideas of the dissenters. Bishop Thomas Bilson of Winchester, along with the vicar of

St Saviour's, Edward Phillips, had some sympathy with their views about purifying the Church. One of the congregation of St Saviour's, Henry Jacob, corresponded with both the bishop and the Brownist leaders. He was part of the group of Puritans looking at how the Anglican Church could be more accountable, although wanting to stay within it. However, when James I called his conference at Hampton Court Palace in 1604 to try to find a way of resolving disputes, Jacob found the bishops refused to compromise. Not to be defeated, Jacob in 1609 wrote *An Humble Supplication for Toleration and Liberty* addressed to the king, who noted its contents, as did the London merchants who were looking for settlers for further colonies to be established in North America. Jacob himself became a Brownist in 1610, and six years later he established his own church in Bankside, using the Brownist method of asking each potential member for a statement of personal faith, followed by agreement to the church covenant.

The community in Southwark was strong, for it included some of the religious refugees that had fled in the past from the parts of the Netherlands controlled by the Spanish. A particular interchange took place between the community in London and that in Leiden, where the authorities were tolerant. This was to change when in 1612 King James joined what was known as an Evangelical Union with the Dutch and Germans as a counterbalance to a Catholic alliance between France and Spain. One condition of the union was that the independent English Church congregations in Holland should be outlawed. This provided the impetus for the separatists to become pilgrims, and to set off for liberty to the New World, beyond the reach of the king and his bishops.

Apart from the physical perils involved in such a journey, there were many organisational difficulties to overcome. Very substantial investment was required, as was the permission of the king. After the Virginia Company failed to put together a scheme and the king agreed to 'connive', investors from London's mercantile community opened negotiations with Thomas Weston, a shipowner in Rotherhithe, to hire a ship. The separatists represented an attractive proposition to these investors, for they were hardworking and, as many of them were craftsmen, practical. The ship that Weston offered for the voyage was the *Mayflower*, capable of carrying around a hundred passengers with a crew of twenty or thirty. She embarked from either Blackwall or Wapping on the Thames in July 1620, meeting up in Southampton with a smaller ship, the *Speedwell*, which was carrying around fifty pilgrims from Leiden. The *Speedwell* proved to be unseaworthy, so that in Dartmouth some of the passengers were transferred to the *Mayflower*, which sailed on alone to Massachusetts.

The passenger list for the *Mayflower* has been carefully examined and research undertaken into the people named. Southwark is represented only by John Billington and his family, and Edward Doty, a servant of a City merchant. Given the strength of religious separatism in the Borough, this tiny number strikes a curious note. The explanation of this inconsistency lies in an incident that had occurred in 1618 when the Jacob Church in Southwark was raided by the authorities, and Francis Blackwell, who had taken over as leader following Henry Jacob's immigration to Virginia, was arrested. Blackwell then struck a deal, giving the names of all the separatists. The Archbishop of Canterbury, George Abbott, was delighted at this betrayal, for it enabled him to block these potential pilgrims from joining the voyage aboard the *Mayflower*. Billington and Doty were described as 'profane' passengers, as their departure for America was not on religious grounds.

In 1621 the *Fortune* made the same voyage to Massachusetts. She was much smaller than the *Mayflower*, with thirty-five passengers in all, of whom we know the names of twenty-eight. Several of them were from Southwark. Two, Clement Briggs and Robert Hicks, were fellmongers, removing the skin from sheep before tanning, yet another reminder of the importance of the local leather industry. Hicks was aged about forty when he sailed, and his wife and family followed on the *Anne*, which, with the *Little James*, made the crossing in 1623. Among the passenger list of these two ships are several more pilgrims from Southwark, including Timothy Hatherley, one of the venture investors of the *Mayflower*, and the memorably named Kempton Menassah, originally from Northumberland but now a member of the Jacob Church.[9]

In the years that followed, more pilgrims from Southwark made their way across the Atlantic, alienated by the developments in the Church of England under Charles I and his Archbishop of Canterbury, William Laud, which they regarded as Romanising (p. 80). One such was John Lothropp, originally from Yorkshire, who became a curate in Kent during the first years of the seventeenth century. In 1623, however, Lothropp renounced his orders, and the following year he became the pastor of the Jacob Church in Southwark. Within a few years he had landed in trouble with William Laud, at the time Bishop of London. He was arrested by the bishop's pursuivant in April 1632 and jailed in the Clink with some of his adherents when they were found at worship in a private house in Blackfriars. While he was in prison Lothropp's wife died, leaving his six children in dire poverty. Eventually, he was released on bail with the warning that he should not frequent conventicles. Within six months, in September 1634, he was in Boston with some of his followers.

As so often happened in those times of intense religious feeling, the community was fractured by disagreements. Records, however, described John Lothropp as a man 'studious of peace', eventually settling with his second wife Anna in Barnstaple, Massachusetts, where he died in 1653. His great legacy was a personal one: he had many descendants, estimated at more than 80,000. These include six US presidents – Millard Fillmore, James A. Garfield, Ulysees S. Grant, Franklin D. Roosevelt and the two George Bushes. Other descendants include the poet Henry Wadsworth Longfellow, artists Louis Comfort Tiffany and Georgia O'Keefe, actors Clint Eastwood and Shirley Temple, financier John Pierpont Morgan and the lawman 'Wild Bill Hickok'.

An American legacy of a rather different kind was provided by John Harvard. The son of a Southwark butcher, he was born in 1607 and baptised in St Saviour's Church. His father, Robert, was a vestryman and churchwarden of St Saviour's, as well as serving as an overseer of the poor and a governor of the parish grammar school, which John almost certainly attended. The Harvard family was large: John was the fourth of nine children, but diseases, including the plague, carried off his father and several siblings. John's mother, Katherine, married twice following Robert's death in 1625. Her third husband was Richard Yearwood, a wealthy Borough grocer and a relative of Sir George Yeardley, the governor of Virginia (p. 124). With her remarriages, Katherine significantly increased the family's resources, and this enabled John to study at Emmanuel College in Cambridge.

Emmanuel was the first wholly new college to be founded in Cambridge since the Reformation, in 1584, and was strongly Calvinist in intention. Sir Walter Mildmay, Elizabeth I's Chancellor of the Exchequer, stipulated that it should be designed solely for ordination candidates. A famous story tells that when questioned by the queen about creating a Puritan foundation, Sir Walter replied 'No, madam; far be it from me to countenance anything contrary to your established laws; but I have set an acorn which when it becomes an oak, God alone knows what will be the fruit thereof'.[10]

Whether this story is true or not, one of the fruits of Emmanuel was John Harvard. Mildmay had disapproved of perpetual fellowships and warned against regarding the college as a permanent abode, instead encouraging the graduates to look forward to spreading the knowledge acquired beyond its walls. Following the death of his mother in 1635 and that of his last remaining sibling in 1637, John Harvard became the primary heir to the family's considerable assets, which included rental properties and an inn, the Queen's Head in Borough High Street. He was thus in the position to be able to liquidise these assets and to join the group of emigrants from Emmanuel – thirty-five in all during the 1630s and early 1640s –

who made their way to New England. He must have already taken holy orders, although there is no record of his ordination. By August of 1637 he had arrived with his wife in Charlestown in Massachusetts, and duly became teacher at the church there, working with the pastor, Zechariah Symmes, also an Emmanuel man.

While Harvard settled into his new home, a college was being set up a few miles away in Newtown, which was renamed Cambridge in 1638. The first Master was yet another Emmanuel graduate, Nathaniel Easton. The foundation of a college for the transfer of learned culture was considered vital for new colonists, and James I had ordered his English bishops to raise funds so that the Virginia Company might build one at Henrico, named in honour of his son, Henry, Prince of Wales, on the James River just below Richmond. That project was brought to an abrupt end by the 'Great Attack' in 1622 that had left many colonists dead, including the man in charge of the development, and the site was annihilated. When John Harvard died in 1638 he left half his estate and his large personal library of about 400 books to the infant Massachusetts college. He thus contributed to one of its central requirements, the mastery of Latin, Greek and Hebrew and a detailed knowledge of the scriptures. In recognition of these gifts of money and books, the general court voted that the college should be named Harvard in his honour.

The money from Harvard's estate was indeed generous, but perhaps above price was his bequest of books to what was the only college in North America. The college tried to acquire other collections, sending out requests to both sides of the Atlantic. England, however, was plunged into civil war, and so these pleas went unheeded. Students had to rely on handwritten texts copied from the college's collection and borrowing books from local patrons. The first class graduated in 1642, an event celebrated in a book published in London the following year, *New England's First Fruits*. This described evangelisation results, including the conversion of Wequash Cooke, allegedly the first Native American adoption of Protestant Christianity in

New England. Unfortunately, all but one of John Harvard's books were consumed by fire in 1764, but by then the university had built up collections from elsewhere.

Connections between Southwark and North America continued to proliferate. While George Yeardley was buried in Jamestown, Virginia, John Lothropp in Barnstaple and John Harvard in Charlestown in New England, the burial site of a Native American is in the churchyard of Southwark Cathedral. Mahomet Weyonomen, from the Mohegan tribe of Connecticut, came to London in 1735 to petition George II for restoration of their tribal lands. When settlers had first taken the land at the beginning of the eighteenth century, Mahomet's uncle, Owenoco, made the voyage to England, and Queen Anne's commission had found in his favour. However, this was ignored by the governor of the Connecticut colony. Moreover, further encroachments had taken place, leaving the Mohegans unable to subsist. Taking lodgings in the City of London, Mahomet's entire party succumbed to smallpox before the petition could be presented to the king. While the City authorities were happy to bury Mahomet's European companions, room had to be found for his body in St Saviour's churchyard, on the other side of the river. In November 2006, Her Majesty Queen Elizabeth unveiled a carved granite boulder from Connecticut in the churchyard as a reminder of this shameful chapter in the history of Britain's colonial history.

The Separatist Church in Southwark, established at the end of the sixteenth century by Henry Barrow and John Greenwood in Deadman's Place, moved to a building in Union Street in 1788. Here it served a poor community, developing a significant following, but was threatened with the loss of its lease. Fundraising was led by the pastor, John Waddington, who proposed that the new church building be named in honour of the Pilgrim Fathers. Building began in 1850 and was completed fourteen years later, but it was destroyed in aerial bombardment in 1941. Although it enjoyed a short post-war existence in a new home on the corner of Great Dover Street and Spurgeon

Street, this too came to an end. The building can still be seen, but is no longer used as a church.

However, one connection between Southwark and the early history of North America has been cherished. The chapel in the north choir of the cathedral is dedicated to the memory of John Harvard as a tribute to his contribution to the cultural beginnings in New England. This project was the inspiration of Joseph Choate, the US Ambassador to St James from 1899 to 1905. A Harvard alumnus, he encouraged the university to commemorate Harvard's link and to refurbish the chapel. Choate commissioned John La Farge, the distinguished American artist, to design the stained-glass window in the chapel. It takes as its main theme the baptism of Christ, alluding to John Harvard's baptism in St Saviour's Church in 1607, accompanied by the arms of Harvard University and those of Emmanuel College, Cambridge.

The theme of pilgrimage has been adopted for the north entrance to Southwark Cathedral, looking towards the Thames, the beginning of so many voyages into the great unknown.

# 10

# Medical Matters

Buildings of gleaming glass and steel dominate the area just south of London Bridge. These include not just the soaring Shard, which has been described as the cathedral's other spire, but also Guy's Hospital. Peel back at least ten centuries and there was a very different landscape, but one that included a hospital within the priory church of St Mary Overie.

According to Peter des Roches, the Bishop of Winchester, writing in 1212, an 'ancient spital, built of old to entertain the poor, has been entirely reduced to cinders and ashes'.[1] If the legend of an Anglo-Saxon nunnery recorded by the Tudor chronicler John Stow is based on fact, the hospital could indeed have been ancient (p. 10). Certainly, the Augustinian priory founded at the beginning of the twelfth century by Bishop Giffard of Winchester included a hospital to the south of the church. The Augustinian order was outward looking, anxious to serve God in His Church but to serve too the needs of those among whom its monks lived. When Thomas Becket was canonised following his murder in Canterbury in 1170, the hospital was named in his honour. The two ancient London hospitals still going strong today are St Thomas', now in Lambeth, and St Bartholomew's, north of the City, also founded by the Augustinians.

A plan of Christ Church in Canterbury dating from around 1165 shows the area around the church and priory, with orchards, flower gardens and a herbarium, or herb garden. This last would have been organised by the infirmarer, with lay brothers and gardeners to maintain long, narrow beds of herbs. At St Mary Overie, which was not a large house, the infirmarer could even have been assisted by some of the canons. Some idea of the types of herbs that were grown here to be made up into medicines, simples or compounds, and ointments and plasters can be deduced from a list of plants in the physic garden at St Gall Monastery in Switzerland, drawn up three centuries earlier. These record traditional medicinal herbs such as lovage, sage, rue, pennyroyal, mint and rosemary. Also included in the list are roses, grown on trellises, which might be distilled to make sweet waters, and flag irises, whose roots could be ground up to produce sweet powders. Mallows could provide poultices to be applied after bloodletting. Poisonous plants that were used for narcotics were usually kept in a separate area that would be kept locked by the infirmarer. A herb garden has recently been planted to the south of Southwark Cathedral, containing some of these medicinal plants.

The fire described by Peter des Roches began on London Bridge and spread down to Southwark, killing many: the figure of 3,000 has been suggested. When Bishop Peter organised the rebuilding of St Thomas' Hospital, he moved it from south of the priory church to a site on the east side of the High Street, where the air was said to be sweeter. The hospital occupied a site of about 9 acres, with its own chapel, which in time became St Thomas's parish church, the tower of which is still to be seen in St Thomas Street.

The medieval hospital, staffed by a mixed order of Augustinian monks and nuns, was funded by charitable donations. Following the devastation of the Black Death in the fourteenth century, the concept of purgatory grew ever more potent in the minds of men and women, and generous contributions to the hospital were thought to speed the supplicant's journey through to heaven. One such donation came from Alice de Bregerake: 'Know all men, present and future, that I, Alice de Bregerake, moved by divine piety and for the welfare of my soul, as well as those of my ancestors, have given ... to St Thomas the Martyr ... property ... for free and perpetual charitable uses; rendering therefore to me and to my heirs yearly, one rose on the feast of St John [the Baptist, 24 June].'[2]

The make-up of the staff of the hospital is provided in a tax survey taken in 1295, naming six brothers who were priests, five lay brothers and five sisters, looking after forty sick inmates. While the brothers played a religious role, the sisters did the nursing. Each new patient was washed and had lice removed before being given clean sheets, although patients were expected to share beds. When the Bishop of Winchester, William of Wykeham, made a visitation in 1387, he found that the food and drink were both insipid and inadequate, that the number of staff had been allowed to decline, and that valuables had been pawned.

The poet John Gower, who spent the last years of his life residing in the priory of St Mary Overie (p. 44), in his will in 1408 left money to the hospital: to the master, 40 shillings; 6s 8d to each of three brethren; 3s 4d to the professed sister; 1s 8d to each nurse; and 1 shilling to each patient. At almost the same time, Richard Whittington, the very rich City mercer and famous Mayor of London, was providing funds for all manner of charitable causes. To the hospital of St Thomas he gave money for a ward of eight beds for 'young women that had done amiss, in trust of good amendment', adding that this should be kept secret so that it in no way affected their marriage prospects.[3] A century later, in 1507, the hospital's master, Richard Richardson, bought extra land and added a new ward or almshouse for poor men. These were usually local residents who could not support themselves through age or infirmity.

The presence of St Thomas' Hospital may have influenced the printer Peter Treveris to set up his press in Southwark in 1525 and to print as his initial publications two books in folio on medical matters.

*8. The title page of Peter Treveris's* Grete Herball, *published in 1526: the first herbal in the English language. Men are gathering herbs and grapes, accompanied by Adam and Eve.*

His name, Treveris, suggests that he came from Trier, now in Germany but then part of the Hapsburg Empire, and he could have been a political refugee. His first book was *Handywerk of Surgery*, written by Hieronymus of Braunschweig, published in the year that Treveris set up the press, and in 1526 he produced *The Grete Herball*, translated from the French.

Infirmarers in medieval monasteries might have manuscripts with notes about medicinal herbs and remedies, and if they were exceptionally lucky, these might contain identifying images, but now Treveris was providing the first printed herbal in England with woodcut illustrations. It has an elaborate title page, showing a man picking grapes and another filling a basket with herbs, while Adam and Eve appear at the bottom of the image, wearing fantastical plant

9. The imprint page from Treveris's herbal, indicating that his printshop was
'in Southwarke . . . [at] the sygne of the Wodows'.

headgear. The final leaf of the book carries an equally elaborate device announcing the address of Peter Treveris at 'the sygne of the Wodows' over the bridge in Southwark. 'Wodows' or 'Woodwoses' were wild men and women of the woods, here shown in all their hairy glory.

The book contains nearly 500 small woodcuts, mostly of plants, although there are also figures of animals and minerals. These to modern eyes are rather primitive, but they must have been valuable aids to identification. A few years earlier, in 1518, Henry VIII had granted a charter for the foundation of the Royal College of Physicians at the instigation of his physician, Thomas Linacre. This, along with the medical staff of St Thomas' Hospital and St Bartholomew's Hospital, provided a market for the books of Peter Treveris.

Richard Richardson, the master of St Thomas', was succeeded by a very different character, Richard Mabott. We have not only a list of his misdemeanours, but also a vivid picture of what life could be like in Tudor Southwark. In 1536 Thomas Cromwell, Henry VIII's chief minister, described St Thomas' as a bawdy house. This was the time when he was presiding over the dissolution of the monasteries, so a damning view might be expected, but evidence bears him out. Parishioners laid a whole raft of complaints against Mabott. One assertion was that he and the brothers were maintaining improper persons within the precinct of the hospital, at the same time refusing relief to poor persons in sickness, even those prepared to pay. A pregnant woman, denied lodging, died at the church door. Often Mabott quarrelled with his staff, stabbing one in the hand so that the constables and bailiffs were obliged to intervene. He even turned communal lavatories, known as laystalls, into gardens, which he then leased out. Perhaps to add allure to these gardens, Mabott broke into the substantial garden of the glazier Galyon Hone (p. 98) and stole sixty young bay trees.

Mabott's mistress, Julian Foster, was put in charge of the sisters, and when the father of one of the brothers called her a harlot on

London Bridge, he got him consigned to the King's Bench Prison. Even Edith Percke, who kept a brothel in Lambeth where he had set up Julian, had reproached him for his behaviour. In all, he was described as acting like a lord, king and bishop. Despite this, he died in office in 1539, and it was his successor who surrendered the hospital as part of the dissolution of religious institutions the following year. Richard Gresham, the father of the famous Sir Thomas, tried to persuade Henry VIII to allow the City governance of St Thomas', along with three other hospitals.

This proposal failed, but in 1552, during the reign of Edward VI, with 'the miserable state of the sick and infirm poor men lying begging in public streets', a new hospital combined with a poor house was opened under royal charter.[4] At the time of the dissolution of the monasteries, Henry VIII had demanded that the shrine in Canterbury Cathedral of Becket, the man who had dared to defy his monarch, Henry II, should be destroyed. Now, the dedication of the Southwark hospital was changed to that of St Thomas the Apostle.

Nicholas Ridley, Bishop of London, gave a sermon on the subject of charity in the presence of Edward, as a result of which the young king founded Christ's Hospital in the dissolved Greyfriars monastery in Newgate Street, just to the north of St Paul's Cathedral. The aim was to get waifs and children of all ages off the streets of London and to equip them with an education and skills. At the same time, Bridewell Royal Hospital was founded in the former palace on the north bank of the Thames to cater for vagabonds and petty criminals of all ages. Bridewell was often referred to as the 'bawdy court', while the illnesses all too often treated at St Thomas' were venereal, so that it was known as the 'bawdy hospital'.

Although the three institutions, St Thomas', Christ's Hospital and Bridewell, were to go their separate ways, they are thus linked by this founding history, and by a certain element of bawdiness. City merchants took up the governorships of the three foundations. One example is the very wealthy Francis Barnham, a leading member of the Drapers' Company. Between 1559 and 1576 he served alternately as governor of the Bridewell and of St Thomas'. Having acquired some of the lands of the dissolved priory of St Mary Overie, he endowed the property to the infant Christ's Hospital: Barnham Street, which leads south from Tooley Street, is a reminder of this gift.[5]

The records of St Thomas' Hospital are rich in social detail. We learn that in the early seventeenth century the physicians employed a herbwoman to provide the raw materials for the remedies that the apothecary prescribed to the patients. The difference in status between the medical men and the 'workers' is clearly demonstrated by their salaries. In 1629 it was noted that the apothecary was paid £60 per annum, the surgeon £35 and the doctors £30, while a man employed to cut bladder stones – a common problem thought to be exacerbated by the adulteration of bread by mixing chalk into the flour – received £15 and the herbwoman a mere £4. The apothecary was expected to pay for the ingredients of his drugs out of his salary, so the herbwoman may have received additional money on top of her modest wages. The herbs were acquired in bulk, with wormwood coming by the horseload, others by the lapful, bundle, bag or flasket, so the woman clearly cultivated her herbs in the style of market gardening.

The herb garret of the old St Thomas' Hospital, overlooking the former operating theatre, can still be visited, entered just by the church tower in St Thomas Street. Many of the recipes are to be found there, such as one for 'snail water' to cure venereal disease, dating from the early eighteenth century and evidence that venereal disease continued to pose a serious problem for St Thomas'. The recipe shows how the large quantities of herbs were used: a pound and a half each of wormwood, ground ivy and cardus thistle, and half a pound each of pennyroyal, juniper berries, fennel and aniseed. The herbs were mixed with three ounces of cloves and cubebs, eight gallons of spring water and spirit of wine, six gallons of snails and three gallons of earthworms. They were then distilled in an alembic to make what today sounds a truly appalling concoction.

In the early eighteenth century a second hospital was established next door. The funding was given by Thomas Guy, who had become a governor of St Thomas' in 1704. Guy was probably born in 1644, the son of a lighterman and coalmonger working on the Thames. The Guy family were members of the Anabaptist community in Horsleydown, on the eastern side of Southwark. Anabaptists were considered the most extreme of the separatist groups, believing that their members should be baptised only as adults and incurring intense hostility from the religious establishment. The uncertainty of his date of birth is due to the fact that it was not entered into the records. After apprenticeship to a bookseller, Thomas Guy became a member of the Stationers', although he came into conflict with the company over the monopoly of printing the scriptures. He had been contracted by Oxford University to become their printer, meeting the demand for cheap, mass-produced Bibles, but when he began to bind up psalms with them, he was ousted from the Stationers' Company in 1691. By that time, however, he had established himself in the trade, amassing a fortune of £15,000 and provocatively naming his shop in the Stocks Market in the City the Oxford Arms.

Guy comes down as a complex and controversial character. Although he did not follow his father's dissenting stance, instead becoming a member of the Church of England, he clearly was a non-conformer in many ways. A contemporary bookseller, John Dunton, in his biographical accounts of his fellow publishers, characterised him as a miser, although this may have reflected jealousy of his business acumen. From the 1670s, Guy had dealt in seamen's pay-tickets, a high-risk commodity which formed the beginning of the national debt. In 1710 these tickets were put into the South Sea Company, which three years later was granted a monopoly to supply African slaves to islands in the 'South Seas' and to South America.

At this time the British were embroiled in war with Spain and Portugal, the countries that controlled most of South America, so there was little prospect that such a trade could take place. The stock of the company, however, rose greatly, and by 1720 Thomas Guy is said to have possessed £45,000 of the original expanded stock when the South Sea Company took on 60 per cent of the national debt. He began to sell his shares when their value trebled, getting rid of the last when that value reached sixfold, just before the bubble burst. Thus, while the nation, great and small, members of the royal family and modest wage earners, reeled as a result of the financial crash, he had acquired a vast fortune. The connection with the South Sea Company has recently brought Guy into considerable disrepute, and at the time of writing, the hospital is preparing a statement of the historical context to be put with his statue in the front courtyard. It cannot be disputed, however, that the money gained was to be used for the incalculable benefit of many generations to come.

Greatly influenced by his doctor friend Richard Mead, in 1721 Guy bought land from the governors of St Thomas', intending his new hospital to be part of the same foundation. When the building reached its second storey, however, he decided it should be separately administered. The roof had just been completed when he died in December 1724. Having never married, he left the bulk of his fortune to the hospital, with the intention that it should accommodate four hundred sick persons deemed to be incurable and ineligible for treatment elsewhere, with a ward for twenty incurable lunatics also established. So, while St Thomas' dealt with acute cases, Guy's would care for long-term conditions. An Act of Parliament was to be secured by his executors and trustees to incorporate them with the governors of St Thomas' and to purchase lands, ground rents and estates to maintain the hospital for the sick poor. Guy was originally buried in the parish church of St Thomas, but his remains were moved to the chapel of Guy's, with a monument designed by John Bacon.

Richard Mead was one of the most influential doctors of his day, becoming the royal physician. Like Guy, he was born into a dissenting family, and he also became a member of the Church of England. His range of interests was wide, including mathematics and archaeology.

In 1703 he was elected physician to St Thomas', an unpaid position that nonetheless enabled the incumbent to develop clinical experience with a variety of patients and to gain personal access to the wealthy and influential individuals who formed the governing board of the hospital. By becoming a reader in anatomy for the Company of Barber Surgeons, which was well paid, he was able to continue his work at St Thomas' until in 1715 he resigned and was named a governor. Thomas Guy had originally been one of his patients, and now he persuaded him to use his wealth for the foundation of the new hospital.

Samuel Johnson wrote of Richard Mead that he 'lived more in the broad sunshine of life than almost any man', with many friends and a good bedside manner.[6] He took the opportunity of the new and enlarged premises in Southwark to improve conditions for the patients. Good records have survived of the staff employed in the hospitals, including a man to kill the bed bugs. We also have the regulations imposed on patients, such as only one patient in a bed at one time, and strict demarcation of the wards for men and women. Guy's new hospital flourished. When Mead died in 1754, he was laid to rest in the Temple Church, while a monument to him was erected by his son in Westminster Abbey.

There was, however, long-standing scepticism about physicians in general. A trenchant judgement had been delivered by one seventeenth-century lady: 'Kitchen physic I believe is more proper than the Doctor's filthy physic'.[7] Treatments could be very expensive and often drastic, with theories based on purgative drugs and blood-letting. Apothecaries were often at odds with physicians, and Richard Mead, despite his popularity, was criticised for taking himself to a coffee house where he would receive reports from apothecaries about patients and write up prescriptions which the apothecaries then fulfilled. He was by no means the only physician to do so.

Some people therefore turned to unconventional medicines offered to them by unqualified practitioners or quacks. One such was

I. Oil painting by Claude de Jonghe of Old London Bridge in 1650. On the left, on the north bank of the Thames can be seen the Tower of London and the church of St Magnus the Martyr. On the south bank the churches of St Olave and of St Saviour, now Southwark Cathedral, are depicted.

II. A painting by an unknown artist, probably Dutch, showing London c.1630 viewed from Southwark. Between the churches of St Saviour and St Olave is the northern end of Borough High Street and the gateway onto London Bridge, adorned with the decapitated heads of traitors.

iii. The great screen in the cathedral, erected in 1520 by Bishop Foxe of Winchester and restored in the early twentieth century, when the niches were filled with statues of people with historic connections to Southwark. The top row includes Bishop Anthony Thorold, St Olaf, Bishop William of Wykeham, Cardinal Henry Beaufort, Prior Aldgood of St Mary Overie and Bishop Edward Talbot. The lower row includes Prebendary John Rogers, St Thomas Becket, John Gower and Bishop Peter des Roches.

iv. Stained-glass window in the retrochoir of Southwark Cathedral recalling the tradition that a convent originally stood on the site, founded by Mary, the daughter of the ferryman.

V. *(above)* The monument to the poet John Gower in the north aisle of the cathedral.
VI. *(right)* The early seventeenth-century monument of the Humble family in the cathedral's north choir aisle.

VII. The effigy of Bishop Lancelot Andrewes of Winchester on his tomb now in the south choir aisle of Southwark Cathedral.

VIII. A street performance of scenes from *Oliver Twist* that took place in May 1928 in Mint Street.

IX. William Hogarth's painting of 1733 of Southwark Fair, filled with the various performing acts that congregated in the Borough every year in September. He brilliantly brings together the rural and the urban, with glimpses of the Kent and Surrey countryside beyond the church of St George the Martyr.

x. The Lions part leading the parade through Borough Market to celebrate Apple Day in October. Behind Sonia Ritter is the Berry Man, the autumnal incarnation of Green Man, with the Mayor of Southwark.

XI. The great hall of Winchester House, the medieval episcopal palace in Clink Street. The great rose window may have been the work of the master mason, Henry Yevele.

XII. Southwark Market from Hugh Alley's *Caveat* of 1598, showing a section of Borough High Street, viewed from the east. Market holders are seated under columns indicating the sources of their produce. On the left is the market hall, which in fact stood in the middle of the High Street, and a remarkable multi-pillory for offenders.

XIII. The ornate interior of the Hop Exchange on Southwark Street, from an early twentieth-century illustration in *The Chronicle*.

XIV. Detail from the monumental panoramic view of London drawn by J.H. Banks in 1843. London Bridge Station is shown by the south end of John Rennie's new bridge, set up high, with tracks built on arches. On the other side of Borough High Street is St Saviour's Church with Thomas Cure's almshouses in front.

xv. A view of twenty-first-century Southwark, with the Shard dominating the skyline. It has been described as the cathedral's other spire.

xvi. The Globe Theatre, brainchild of Sam Wanamaker and Theo Crosby.

Lionel Lockyer, whose monument in the north transept of Southwark Cathedral celebrates both his virtues and the pills that he offered for sale. A broadsheet published after his death in 1672 described him as 'an authoriz'd physician and chymist' with 'at least Forty Years Experience and Practice, both in England and most Foreign Parts'.[8] He apparently lived the last years of his life in St Thomas', but it is doubtful that he ever practised in the hospital itself.

His most notable product was Lockyer's pills, for which he claimed miraculous qualities, including sunbeams as an ingredient. In an anonymous letter of endorsement, it was also claimed that he had demonstrated his pills before King Charles II in 1664. His successful marketing stung a rival, George Starkey, into publishing a tract entitled *A smart scourge for a Silly Sawcy Fool*, in which he questioned the authenticity of the endorsement and mocked Lockyer's poor Latin. Despite this, Lockyer's nephew took over the sale of his pills after his death in partnership with an apothecary and successfully sold them wholesale in bulk batches at a price of 4 shillings for a hundred.

The monument in the cathedral is a grand one, although it has been pointed out that the anatomical details of his semi-recumbent form are incorrect. The epitaph reads:

Here Lockyer: lies interr'd enough: his name
Speakes one hath few competitors in fame:
A name soe Great, soe Generall't may scorne
Inscriptions which doe vulgar tombs adorne.
A dimunition which most mens mouths rehearse.
His virtues & his PILLS are soe well known ...
That envy can't confine them under stone.
But they'll survive his dust and not expire
Till all things else at th'universall fire.
This verse is lost, his PILL Embalmes him safe
To future times without an Epitaph

10. *A seventeenth-century broadsheet advertising Lionel Lockyer's pills,*
*which he claimed had sunbeams among their miraculous qualities.*

Also in the cathedral, one of the stained-glass windows of literary figures connected with Southwark, installed in the north aisle, is a depiction of the Irish writer, Oliver Goldsmith. In fact, his connection with the Borough was a medical one. After travelling around Europe, he began to work in an apothecary's shop in Southwark and in 1756 tried to set up a practice on Bankside, although there is no record of him having a professional degree. It is said that he had patients aplenty but earned no fees. Goldsmith's life was plagued by lack of money, not helped by his enjoyment of gambling. The journal publisher Ralph Griffiths took him on as a reviewer and hackwriter, so he joined the Grub Street community, and Dr Johnson acted as his friend and champion, selling the manuscript of his novel *The Vicar of Wakefield* to the bookseller, John Newbery, and thus saving Goldsmith from being arrested for debt.

Newbery, who revolutionised the publishing of books for children, is thought to have employed Goldsmith to write anonymously *The History of Little Goody Two Shoes*, in which the heroine's father died because he could not obtain Dr James's Fever Powder. Booksellers often sold patent medicines alongside their publications, and Newbery was particularly keen on Dr James and his powder, prominently displaying them in advertisements. It is deeply ironic, therefore, that Goldsmith himself probably died in his mid-forties in 1774 having consumed huge doses of Dr James's Fever Powder, which contained mercury, lime and other noxious substances.

Given the rather brief medical connection between the Borough and Goldsmith, it is odd that another literary figure with medical connections does not feature in the Southwark Cathedral windows. John Keats, having been apprenticed at the age of fourteen to an apothecary, arrived at Guy's Hospital in 1814 and was registered as a student the following year. The distinguished physician Astley Cooper placed him under his own dresser of wounds in lodgings at 28 St Thomas Street, just across from the church. Keats was clearly an able pupil, for he was appointed a dresser in his own right just before his twentieth birthday. This was a responsible position, for a dresser was expected to cope with overnight emergencies and take charge of surgical cases that arrived in the morning before the surgeon himself arrived. He would have dealt with victims of accidents, drawn teeth, applied lotions, plasters and leeches where required, and performed minor operations.

During this period, Keats kept medical notebooks, which are packed with ideas, illustrations and phrases that were to reappear in his poetry. Keats' sonnet 'O Solitude' was composed at this time and was to be the first of his poems to be published, in May 1816. The noisy, dirty environment in which he spent his day is reflected in the lines:

> If I must with thee dwell,
> Let it not be among the jumbled heap
> Of murky buildings ...

This sentiment reflects a note that he sent to his schoolfriend Charles Cowden Clarke, who was coming to visit him at lodgings into which he moved the following autumn: 'Although the Borough is a beastly place in dirt, turnings and windings, yet No. 8 Dean Street is not difficult to find; and if you would run the gauntlet over London Bridge, take the first turning to the right'.[9]

Keats also attended lectures at St Thomas'. These, too, would appear to have been conducted in a jumbled heap. A surgeon, John Flint Smith, has left us an account of one such lecture: 'the first two rows ... were occupied by ... dressers, and behind a second partition stood the pupils, packed like herrings but not so quiet, as those behind were continually pressing on those before, and were continually struggling to relieve themselves of it, and not infrequently to be got out, exhausted. There was a continual calling out of "Heads, Heads" to those about the table whose heads interfered with the sightseers. The theatre, which dealt mainly with amputation, was closed down before antiseptic surgery was invented.'[10]

The surgeon Flint Smith does not make clear whether the lecture described above featured medical attention on a living body or a corpse that was being dissected. Physicians were obliged to resort to criminal sources for their corpses, because it was thought that the dissection of the body and the dispersal of parts inhibited true resurrection on Judgment Day. The presence of the two hospitals in Southwark posed longstanding problems for the local churches and the security of their churchyards. In 1788, for example, the vestry of St Saviour's was concerned about the security of the Cross Bones, where the parish poor were given burial. A reward of five guineas was offered for information leading to conviction of what were known as Resurrection Men. When this reward did not bring results, it was deemed necessary to build stronger walls round the graveyard and to fortify them with broken glass. Nevertheless, reports of grave-robbing continued into the following century.

We even know the identity of some of the corpses that Keats dissected. One was Ben Crouch, a former prize-fighter, another Bill Butler, ironically a dealer in bones and teeth. The room in which the dissections were performed was large, but crowded with up to 200 students. The stench of the rotting flesh was intense, and the work hazardous: Astley Cooper warned against getting an infection from a cut. By 1817 Keats had had enough of experiencing this rough-and-tumble way of life, and he declared that he would forsake the medical profession and retire to Hampstead, where a group of poets had established themselves around James Leigh Hunt.

The amity between the medics of St Thomas' and those of Guy's broke down in 1825 when the latter were denied entry to the operating theatre. A janitor was knocked down in the affray that opened up war between the two communities, and although this was eventually calmed down, they never met again in the same theatre. The combination of the two hospitals finally came to an end in 1862, when St Thomas' left its ancient site on Borough High Street following its purchase to make way for the railway viaduct from London Bridge Station to Charing Cross. The hospital took up its present site by the river at Lambeth nine years later. Before its departure from Southwark, in 1860, the Florence Nightingale School of Nursing was established, with students living in-house and attending classes at St Thomas'. The school became the model for many training establishments throughout the United Kingdom and the Commonwealth during the latter half of the nineteenth century.

Now an academic faculty within King's College, it is based in Waterloo Road.

Another nursing connection with Southwark comes with Isabella Gilmore, the sister of the artist and designer William Morris. Widowed at the age of forty in 1882, and having no children, Isabella decided to train as a nurse at Guy's Hospital. Her mother, supported by her many siblings, was fiercely opposed to this. Isabella, however, was made of stern resolution and, with encouragement from William, undertook the training, becoming a ward sister. The matron of Guy's, Victoria Jones, not only considered her a first-rate sister but also recommended her in 1886 to Bishop Thorold of Rochester, then responsible for Southwark, as suitable to found an order of deaconesses in his diocese. After initial reluctance, Isabella 'received the call', working with Thorold to revive the ancient order of deaconesses that existed in the Early Church alongside the male order of deacons. Once more, Isabella had to overcome opposition, again from her mother, but now also from some clergy.

She stipulated that her deaconesses should be 'well-educated gentlewomen', unmarried or widowed. A special blue dress was organised for the women to make them instantly recognisable, and as a sign of dedication, trainees were expected to live in an institution for three months, followed by a year as probationers. She laid emphasis on the importance of visiting the poor in a spirit of friendship, and offering practical help. Probationers therefore had to become proficient in housework, cooking and sewing and attend a course of nursing. Some of them chose to do this at Guy's.

William once said to his sister, 'I preach socialism – you practise it'. She was, moreover, echoing the role of the Augustinian canons, and perhaps the shadowy nuns who had undertaken such work centuries earlier at Southwark. At first, it was difficult to find suitable women, but five were ordained at St Saviour's in 1892, and by 1906, the year after it became a cathedral, the number had risen to forty-five. Isabella Gilmore died in 1923, and the following year a bas-relief in her honour was placed in the south transept of Southwark Cathedral.

Morris could have made his remark about another Southwark medical figure, Dr Alfred Salter. While completing his medical training at Guy's Hospital in 1896, Salter observed in his daily journey from his home in Blackheath the dire poverty of the docklands of Bermondsey. As a junior doctor at Guy's he became known as 'Citizen Salter' for his militant socialist views, deciding to become a general practitioner and devote himself to the medical and social needs of Bermondsey, which was particularly afflicted with illnesses such as tuberculosis that resulted from poor diet, and infectious diseases such as typhoid and cholera caused by poor sanitation. The surgery that he set up on Jamaica Road grew into one of the largest medical practices in the country, while Salter became Labour MP for Battersea from 1924 to his death in 1945. He made a formidable team with his wife Ada, Southwark's mayor in 1920. During their lifetime, slums were demolished and replaced by housing estates alongside open spaces. Medical matters were the byword for this eastern part of the borough of Southwark.

# 11

## Yards of Ale

The playwright Thomas Dekker, writing in 1608, claimed that there were suburbs of London where 'a whole street is in some places but a continued ale-house, not a shop to be seen between a red lattice [the indication of an alehouse]'.[1] This was no exaggeration as far as Long Southwark was concerned. A survey taken two and a half centuries earlier had noted twenty-seven purveyors of drink, some of them brewers, some tapsters, and a vintner.

As noted earlier, the inns that lined Borough High Street were large-scale establishments, offering accommodation, and were therefore the equivalent of today's hotels. Alongside them were alehouses and taverns, some of which also operated as brothels. Some offered wine: for example, the Bear-at-the-Bridge-Foot, just at the south end of London Bridge, is mentioned as a wine tavern as early as 1359.

Ale, however, was the ubiquitous drink in Southwark, and much safer than water because the fermentation undertaken in brewing made it resistant to infection. Even children were given a weak form of ale, 'small beer'. The physician Andrew Boorde wrote in his *Dyetary of Helth* in 1542, 'Water is not holsome sole by it selfe, for an Englysshman'.[2] A brewhouse is recorded in the medieval inn of the Abbot of Hyde which in due time developed from ecclesiastical lodgings into a different kind of inn, Chaucer's Tabard. Brewhouses would have been part of other monastic establishments, including the priory of St Mary Overie. Often a bakery was situated adjacent to the brewery, for both processes required the use of malt or other grains and of yeast. This may explain why the bakery for the household of Henry VI was located next to the priory.

In a domestic context, brewing was undertaken by women, known as 'ale wives', and ale was the general term given to the fermented drink that resulted from the malted grain and water. As this could deteriorate fairly rapidly and develop a sour taste, aromatic herbs, known as gruiting, were added. Examples of gruiting herbs include alehoof, or ground ivy, and alecost, or costmary – their names indicating one of their uses.[3]

The addition of hops to the fermentation may well have been introduced by immigrants from the Low Countries, who arrived in Southwark in the fourteenth century. Their hopped beers did not find favour with all. Boorde, for example, wrote that beer, being the natural drink of the Dutch, made them fat and inflated their bellies. A century later, the Water Poet, John Taylor, expressed characteristically strong views on the subject, describing beer as 'a Dutch Boorish Liquor, a thing not knowne in England, till of late days an Alien to our Nation, till such times as Hops and Heresies came amongst us, it is a saucy intruder in this land ... And now in late days it is much used in England to the detriment of many Englishmen'.[4]

Despite this opposition, hopped beers became the norm, enjoying an important advantage over ale because of the preservative quality of the hops. Small beer may have been given to children, but Southwark beer was known for its strength. In *The Canterbury Tales*, Chaucer has the Miller setting off on the pilgrimage in an inebriated state:

'Now, hear me' said the miller, 'all and some!
But first I make a protestation round
That I'm quite drunk, I know it by my sound:

And therefore, if I slander or mis-say,
Blame it on ale of Southwark, so I pray . . .'[5]

One Southwark brewer of Dutch descent was Nicholas Weblying, a tenant of a property adjacent to St Thomas' Hospital. In 1578 he was contracted by the hospital to supply beer to the inmates, who were entitled to a daily ration of three pints for two months, a quart at dinner and a pint at supper. But Weblying's beer was so strong that the poor, who were in the hospital as a refuge rather than for medical care, would become inebriated and go 'abroad, especially on Sabothe day, and abuse themselves in the taverns and alehouses, to the great displeasure of Almighty God, and the misliking of the Governors'.[6]

Concern about divine displeasure resulting from the proliferation of drinking establishments appears in the records of St Saviour's in the late sixteenth and early seventeenth centuries. Keepers of the sacramental token books would visit households within the parish to sell tokens for attendance at Sunday church. When these were not redeemed, the churchwardens might visit the premises of the absentees. Anyone found in the inns during the actual hours of the services and those who were serving them the drink were presented at the visitations of the Bishop of Winchester, convicted and fined. At least 88 victuallers, vintners and innkeepers between the years 1632 and 1640 were presented for 209 offences connected with receiving guests during these hours. In one swoop in the summer of 1634, the innkeepers of the George, White Hart, King's Head and the Queen's Head were among thirty suppliers of drink presented at the visitation of Bishop Walter Curle.

It is the inns that are here being scrutinised and implicitly criticised for distracting good Christians on the Sabbath. Alehouses came under even heavier criticism, especially from Puritan preachers. Christopher Hudson, for example, declared in 1631: 'Alehouses are nests of Satan, where the owls of impiety lurk and where all evil is hatched, and the bellows of intemperance and incontinence blow up'.[7] The alehouse and tavern were often considered a threat to public order, as well as corrupting conventional family life. Ben Jonson in his play *Every Man in his Humour* has Kiteley, a City merchant, protesting that his brother-in-law, Wellbred, and his riotous friends are turning his home upside down:

> He makes my house here common, as a mart.
> A theatre, a public receptacle.
> For giddy humour, and diseased riot:
> And here, as in a tavern, or a stews.
> He, and his wild associates, spend their hours,
> In repetition of lascivious jests,
> Swear, leap, drink and dance,
> and revel night by night[8]

Such measures do not appear to have damaged the enthusiasm for drinking within Southwark, and many customers came from outside the Borough. Pete Brown in his history of beer, focusing on the George, *Shakespeare's Local*, suggests that one feature that attracted visitors was the decapitated heads of traitors. These were displayed on spikes on the South Gate of London Bridge from 1577 until the gruesome attraction was moved to Temple Bar in Fleet Street at the Restoration.

A visit to an alehouse on the comparatively rural Bankside would have been a treat for Londoners, able there to enjoy the view of the north bank, with the medieval cathedral of St Paul's dominating the skyline, albeit shorn of its soaring spire after lightning destroyed it in 1561. But when Samuel Pepys made his way to one on 2 September 1666, it was to take in a very different view, of the City engulfed in flames. He recorded in his diary:

> we to a little alehouse on the Bankside over against the Three
> Cranes, and there stayed till it was dark almost and saw the fire

grow, and as it grew darker, appeared more and more, and in Corners and upon steeples and between churches and houses, as far as we could see up the hill of the City, in a most horrid malicious bloody flame, not like the fine flame of an ordinary fire.... We stayed till, it being darkish, we saw the fire as only one entire arch of fire from this to the other side of the bridge, and in a bow up the hill, for an arch above a mile long. It made me weep to see it.[9]

Southwark was spared on this occasion because, although the fire began in Pudding Lane, right next to London Bridge, there was a fire break on the bridge itself as a result of an earlier conflagration. However, Southwark was to experience its own 'great fire'. This started in an oil shop on Borough High Street between the George and the Talbot (the new name for the Tabard) and raged for a day in May 1676. Despite the intervention of Charles II, who repeated his role of supervising measures to fight the blaze that he had first brought into action in 1666, much of the High Street, with its medieval inns, was razed to the ground.

When the inns were rebuilt, most of them became even more extensive. While the Tabard/Talbot and its neighbours were providing accommodation for travellers on horseback and wagoners and pack-horses bringing supplies to London, the inns being constructed after 1676 also had the new stagecoach traffic in mind. The first stage-coach is thought to have travelled from Chester in 1657, and the Royal Mail also carried passengers as well as the post in their coaches.

Twenty years earlier, the ever-fertile mind of John Taylor, the Water Poet, had produced a *Carrier's Cosmographie*. This is a highly abbreviated form of its title, which takes up the whole of the page. In essence, it provided a list of the London inns and hostelries that catered for the coaches. Not surprisingly, a section is devoted to Southwark, and the routes from Kent, Sussex and Surrey. Ten inns are listed: the Falcon, the Catherine Wheel, the Greyhound, the Spur, the Queen's Head, the White Hart, the King's Head, the Green

Dragon, the Tabard or Talbot, and the George. For the last, he noted: 'comes every Thursday the carriers from Guildford, Wonnerch, Godhurst, and Chiddington in Surrey, also thither out of Sussex on the same days the carriers of Battle, Sandwich and Hastings'.[10] We are left in no doubt of the importance of the trade for Southwark.

Take a walk down the east side of Borough High Street today, and the size of the inns is clear, for although all but the George have gone, the lanes that originally led into their yards survive, in names such as the Queen's Head and the White Hart. The entrances off the main street are wide and would have had a high arch to allow the coaches and wagons, loaded high, into the courtyards. Today these lanes end in the buildings of Guy's Hospital, but originally they would have extended back even further, around 300 feet away from the high street, ending with a drainage ditch. Stabling for over 100 horses and for the parking of wagons would have been located at the back, with galleried courtyards in front.

Traffic such as wagons and stagecoaches were not allowed across London Bridge. Even without these large vehicles, progress along the narrow road was incredibly slow, and it sometimes took up to an hour to get from the south to the north bank. In 1722, tolls were introduced, and thirty years later, directions for traffic to keep to the left, the beginning of Britain's curious distinction from most of the rest of the world. Moreover, the gates were closed at night until the mid-eighteenth century, when the houses on the bridge were pulled down, along with the gateways. The royal coat of arms that used to adorn the South Gateway can now be seen over the door of the King's Arms in Newcomen Street.

The inns along Borough High Street not only provided an impor-tant terminus for traffic but also offered all kinds of businesses and services. The George, for example, provided the venue in the late eighteenth century for auctions of different kinds of property, such as horses, fleets of river barges, carriages and even freehold country estates. It was the place where committees met to organise elections.

Inquests were held here. The landlord advertised in 1789 that he was taking orders for Mr Ryman's cardiac tincture to cure disorders of the head and the stomach, including faintness, hiccups and wind. The medicine would be dispatched by the Reigate coach. As Pete Brown points out, the Southwark inns doubled up as town halls, community centres and eBays.[11]

But, of course, the inns were above all termini for travellers and their goods. One of the supplies that was brought in great quantities was hops for brewing. Kent, 'the Garden of England', had the soil and climate particularly favoured for their cultivation, and they were transported first by packhorse, then by river, and eventually, in the nineteenth century, by rail. A large-scale consumer of hops was a brewery established in 1616 in Deadman's Place, hard by the Globe Theatre, by James Monger under licence from the Bishop of Winchester. This was taken over by Josiah Child, who greatly expanded its business when he secured a contract to supply beer and other services to the navy. By 1659 he was provisioning East India Company ships and had become a controlling shareholder in the company.

The brewery, named the Anchor because of Child's nautical connections, passed in a zigzag route through the family and was acquired in the eighteenth century by Ralph Thrale, MP for Southwark and Master of the Brewers' Company. When he died in 1758, one obituary described him as the greatest brewer in England. His son, Henry, enjoyed a more mixed reputation. In the early 1770s he invested heavily in plant, the latest steam machinery for raising water, and architecture, including individual stabling for his seventy dray and mill horses. It was not only Thrale's horses that benefited but also the cows of Southwark. The grain from the Anchor and other breweries and distilleries in the area was acquired by cowkeepers, and by the early nineteenth century fourteen cowsheds were identified by the vestry of St Saviour's parish.[12]

However, one of Henry Thrale's innovations proved a disaster. In 1772, in an attempt to best rival London brewers such as Whitbread, he became involved in a scheme suggested to him by an incompetent chemist that beer might be brewed without malt or hops. Luckily, the Anchor Brewery was also producing a brew called Intire Porter, manufactured on such a scale that it made sense for the local drinking establishments to buy it in, rather than brew themselves. Porter was a dark, rich drink, much appreciated by the residents of Southwark.

Henry Thrale had married Hester Salusbury in 1763: it was not a union made in heaven, for she was an intelligent, lively woman, while all contemporary reports describe him as dull, vain – 'the Southwark Macaroni' – and a womaniser. Hester's father had warned that she should not be exchanged for a barrel of porter, but his death had left her mother and uncle determined to proceed with the marriage. Soon after their wedding, Dr Johnson was introduced to them, and he became very much a feature of their social life both at the house next to the brewery in Deadman's Place and at their country retreat in Streatham. Hester Thrale worked with Johnson on several of the subjects of his *Lives of the Poets*, and when Henry stood for Parliament to represent Southwark in 1765, the two collaborated on the writing of his election addresses. Thrale gained the seat, but Hester lost the child that was born shortly after the election, one of many such losses that she was to endure. In the following year, Johnson had an emotional breakdown and moved into rooms offered by the Thrales in their homes in Southwark and Streatham, referring to them as his 'Master' and 'Mistress'.

When Henry Thrale got into financial trouble with the scheme for producing beer without the vital ingredients, Samuel Johnson took up a role in the counting house and helped Hester to rescue the situation. Together they raised money from friends and her family and regained the confidence of the demoralised workforce at the brewery: she later wrote that the men would not live with Mr Thrale but would do anything for her.

Brewing establishments had long been the target of rioters: during the Peasants' Revolt in 1381 and Jack Cade's march upon London in

1450, pillaging of alehouses took place to quench thirsts and inspire further acts of recklessness, and apprentices would often go for the same targets during celebrations such as May Day. On Friday 2 June 1780 a crowd of 50,000 assembled in St George's Fields, planning to march on Parliament with a petition against the repeal two years earlier of anti-Roman Catholic legislation, organised by Lord George Gordon, an MP and leader of the Protestant Association. Groups of demonstrators, however, broke away and launched themselves on a programme of destruction. In Southwark they attacked prisons, the Marshalsea, King's Bench and the Clink, freeing the inmates before setting fire to the buildings. They also threatened the Anchor Brewery, because Henry Thrale was known to be sympathetic to the Catholic cause.

The hero of the hour, according to Dr Johnson's biographer, James Boswell, was John Perkins, the brewery's chief clerk. Seeing the freed prisoners, still wearing their chains, he declared it a shame that men should be degraded by such a heavy load and said that he would furnish them with a horse for that purpose. Such an unexpected line halted the rioters in their tracks, and Perkins then distributed 50 pounds' worth of meat and porter. By the time troops arrived, the rioters were giving toasts to John Perkins and the Anchor Brewery, and they departed leaving the buildings intact. Hester Thrale wrote of 'the astonishing Presence of Mind shewed by Perkins in amusing the Mob with Meat & Drink & Huzzaes, till Sir Phillip Jennings Clerke could get the Troops'.[13] When some hopeful rioters returned in case there was any food and drink left, the troops were in firm occupation.

Henry Thrale died of apoplexy the following year, so Hester decided to sell the brewery to a Scottish-American financier, David Barclay. Recognising the value of John Perkins, Barclay gave him a share in the equity if he agreed to remain and to run what was now known as the Barclay Perkins Brewery. Dr Johnson, named an executor by Henry Thrale, is depicted in an unexpected scenario by James Boswell in the midst of the brewery 'hustling about with an ink-horn and pen in his buttonhole, like an exciseman, and on being asked what he really considered to be the value of the property, answered, "We are not here to sell a parcel of boilers and vats, but the potentiality of growing rich beyond the dreams of avarice".'[14]

As a resident of Deadman's Place, combining his writing and his business skills in the Anchor Brewery, Dr Johnson is duly commemorated in the stained-glass windows in the north aisle of the cathedral. Below his medallion portrait is Christ before Pilate and, aptly for a lexicographer, an anagram, *Quid est Veritas? Vir est qui adest* ('What is the truth? It is the man who is before you'). And further below, King Solomon, father of wisdom and knowledge, is shown reading a book.

While the Gordon Rioters spared the Anchor Brewery in 1780, a disastrous fire destroyed the buildings in 1832. Barclay, Perkins & Co. duly rebuilt on a huge scale over many acres. It became one of the sights of London, but one sightseer did not find it a pleasant experience. Marshal Julius von Haynau was regarded as the most hated man in Europe as a result of his brutal treatment of those who rebelled against Austrian rule in Hungary and Italy. He was particularly cruel towards women, ordering those suspected of sympathising with rebels to be whipped. He was even disliked by his own men, who referred to him as the Hapsburg Tiger, so that his career in the army came to an abrupt halt. Deciding to go on a tour of Europe, he made the mistake of putting his name in the visitors' book of Barclay Perkins in September 1850. He was unaware of how avidly British working-class men read their newspapers, and he had already narrowly escaped mob violence in Brussels. When clerks spotted his name, they sent word round the brewery.

As the general and his companions crossed the yard, a large force of labourers and draymen ran out with brooms, throwing mud and dung, and shouting 'Down with the Austrian butcher'. Haynau was cornered in the street, and when he tried to hide in a dustbin, he was dragged out by the beard and pelted. Eventually, he made his escape to the sanctuary of the George Inn on Bankside.

The misadventure created an international incident, with Queen Victoria obliged to apologise to the Austrian emperor, but the British press were proud of the action of the draymen. A verse in *Punch* ran:

Our Baron bold, who wopp'd the fair
Of hanging who had the knack, man.
Came over here to England, where
He could have no ladies to whack, man,
For gibbet and halter in vain he sigh'd
At hanging unable to play, man,
So in quest of amusement, a visit he tried
To BARCLAY AND PERKINS' draymen

When the Italian revolutionary hero, Giuseppe Garibaldi, visited England in 1864, he ensured that he, too, visited Barclay Perkins Brewery, to thank the men for their action. A decorative plaque showing the general and two draymen wielding horse whips is to be seen today in Park Street.

The year 1828 is regarded as marking the peak of the stagecoach era, when the larger, horse-drawn omnibus began to replace the short-stage carriage. But all too soon a new mode of transport was to change radically the character of Southwark and the role of the inns: the train. The London & Greenwich was the first railway in the capital, with a part opening from Deptford to Bermondsey in February 1836 and reaching London Bridge that December. The impact of the railway on the topography and community of Southwark will be considered in Chapter 13, but here we must look at its particular effect on the inns of Borough High Street.

A vivid picture of the inns at this pivotal moment is provided by the pen of Charles Dickens, who knew Southwark only too well. In *The Pickwick Papers*, published in 1837, he wrote:

There are in London several old inns, once the headquarters of celebrated coaches in the days when coaches performed their duties in graver and more solemn manner than they do in these times; but which have now degenerated into little more than the abiding and booking-places of country waggons.... In the Borough especially, there still remain some half-dozen old inns, which have preserved their external features unchanged, and which have escaped alike the rage for public improvement, and the encroachments of private speculation. Great, rambling, queer, old places they are, with galleries, and passages, and staircases, wide enough and antiquated enough, to furnish materials for a hundred ghost stories, supposing we should ever be reduced to the lamentable necessity for inventing any, and that the world should exist long enough to exhaust the innumerable veracious legends connected with old London Bridge, and its adjacent neighbourhood on the Surrey side.[15]

Yet Southwark remained the centre of the hop industry. There had been a hop market in the City at Little East Cheap by Tower Hill, but practical access to it was rendered impossible by the bottleneck of London Bridge. The houses that made the traffic so slow were finally removed between 1758 and 1762, and the two central arches were replaced by a single span. However, it became clear that a completely new structure was required, and a design competition was held. Thomas Telford submitted a scheme for a single-span cast iron bridge that would indeed have been spectacular to behold. It was shelved because not enough was known about the technical factors involved. Instead, a new bridge of just five stone arches, designed by Sir John Rennie, was built by his son slightly upstream, and in 1831 the ancient medieval structure was demolished. Access on the south side was still from Borough High Street. Nevertheless, the bridge continued to be a crowded thoroughfare: a census held in 1859

11. 'Old Inns of Southwark': four of the famous inns on Borough High Street depicted in the final years of their existence; the lone survivor, the George, is shown on the lower right.

estimated that in 24 hours the bridge was crossed by 20,498 wheeled vehicles and 107,074 pedestrians.

The hops were now arriving either by river or by rail to London Bridge Station, and factors were based nearby, some in the high street inns. Visual reminders of them can still be seen, such as the elaborate frontage on 63 Borough High Street announcing the presence here in the nineteenth century of William Henry and Herbert Le May, hop factors.

In 1866 the Hop Exchange was built at the top of Southwark Street. Although not functioning as a trading floor today, its magnificent structure is quite breathtaking to behold. Forty Corinthian iron columns form an arc curving along the street. Entry to the Exchange is through wrought-iron gates decorated with scenes of hop-picking, while a stone eagle stands atop, looking south towards the fields of Kent. Inside is the original dealing floor, with a glass roof allowing natural light that would have shone on the factors and merchants dealing below. Tiers of balconies still give access to offices on four levels (plate XIII).

The creation of the Hop Exchange dealt yet another blow to the ancient high street inns, for the hop factors who had previously had their offices in them now lost out to the establishment in Southwark Street. Evans & Co., for example, were based in the George. In 1869 they filed for bankruptcy, while a second hop merchant, J. Preston and J. Morton, was dissolved the following year. Inevitably, demolition began of the inns along the high street. The coming of the railway had severely damaged their raison d'être and now the land at the back of the inns was wanted for expansion of the lines into London. Guy's Hospital was also expanding and buying up land.

There was a recognition that Southwark, and indeed London as a whole, was losing a significant part of its history with the demolition of its ancient inns. In 1875 the Society for the Photographing Relics of Old London was formed, taking the Oxford Arms in Warwick Lane, just to the north of St Paul's Churchyard, as its first project.

This inn, which had been the location for theatrical performances from Elizabethan times, had survived the Great Fire of 1666. The fine photographs taken in 1875 show the dilapidated ancient galleries from which audiences watched plays, with the dome of Wren's cathedral shimmering in the background. Demolition followed soon after the images were captured. The Society then turned their attention to the Southwark inns, and the photographs of the White Hart and the Queen's Head show that their galleries, too, were in a state of near collapse, 'like punchdrunk fighters, or ancient knights with withered skin and sunken eyes beneath their rusty armour'.[16]

The famous Tabard/Talbot, for example, was put up for sale but, when there were no takers, it was demolished in 1878, to be replaced by warehouses and a gin palace which featured 'vertical drinking'. Six years later an article was published in the *Magazine of Art*, lamenting the situation: 'Nothing shows the changes that are almost weekly taking place in London, and transforming the city so much, as the rapid disappearance of its ancient inns. Only eight or ten years ago these were nearly all in existence, unaltered and undisturbed . . . Four only of the old pattern remain and their days, or hours in one case, are certainly numbered.'

In fact, there is one survivor from this period of destruction: the George Inn. Originally built in the late fifteenth century, and sometimes known as the Syrcote or Surcoat, it burnt down along with the other inns on Borough High Street in the Great Fire of Southwark in 1676, and it was then was rebuilt. In 1849 it was sold to Guy's Hospital, who demolished the back section of the inn as part of their expansion scheme, but retained the front giving onto the high street and allowed the George to continue as a public house. Twenty-five years later, the Great Northern Railway Company (later to become LNER) bought the inn to use for railway warehousing. Like a cat with nine lives, however, it continued to be a drinking establishment, operating under a series of licencees. In 1935 Leslie and Harold

Staples took over the lease. They were known as the 'Cheeryble Brothers' because of their enthusiasm for the works of Charles Dickens and were inspired by the George's connections with the novelist, including a description in *Little Dorrit*. The brothers began making many improvements, so that LNER decided to offer the property to the National Trust in 1937.

Visitors to the George today can enjoy not only a glass of ale but also performances of Shakespeare's plays 'at barrel top', as Ben Jonson put it, viewed from the galleries. There is also a coffee room, installed in the eighteenth century when that drink became highly fashionable, lined with private drinking apartments. Today it provides some idea of the 'yards of ale' that dominated the high street over the centuries.

While the physical buildings were such a feature of Southwark, so too was the pungent smell of fermenting hops, latterly emanating from two extensive breweries. The Barclay & Perkins Anchor, lying behind Bankside, was joined downriver by another brewery in Horsleydown, rather confusingly also called the Anchor, established in 1787 by John Courage. The artist and writer Grace Golden visited the sprawling Bankside Anchor Brewery in the early 1930s and described how the various buildings were connected by suspension bridges:

> On the west side of Park Street is the mash tun house. Out of the lower part of the tall windows a man shovels the 'brewers' grains' into a waiting cart. They are a valuable ground fertilizer. . . . This brown residuum is from the mash tuns, the great cylindrical iron vessels where the malt extract, the basis of the beer, is prepared. The dome-like lids of these cylinders, divided into sections which can be raised separately, give to the whole a fantastic petal formation uncannily resembling some giant flora.

Although the technology had advanced, the scene that Grace Golden is describing resembles the fantastical images that the French artist

*12 & 13. Gustav Doré's engravings of the Anchor Brewery in 1872. The gigantic tuns he compares to elephants, against which the workers look like flies. A nightmarish scene is evoked by the image of the men working in the mash tun.*

Gustave Doré made sixty years earlier for *London: A Pilgrimage* that he produced with Blanchard Jerrold. Golden continued:

> Men, barefooted and stripped to the waist, stand among the grains, shovelling them towards tubes through which they are sucked to the outer wall. The malt and hops from the Company's maltings in Norfolk and hop-fields in Kent are unloaded at the wharf at Bank End, and conveyed to the brewery through pipes ... On the other side of the road is the yeast house where the liquor is fermented in great tanks – yeast, yeast, everywhere; the cold store for the hops, and the cellars where the barrels are filled and stored – a very sea of casks. The production of the three kinds of liquor, ales, porter and stouts, and lager (introduced in 1922) is carried on in different sections of the brewery.[17]

In 1955 the two companies merged to become Courage, Barclay & Co., but seven years later Barclay's closed and the sprawling works were demolished, leaving only the Anchor Inn as a reminder. This demolition brought large-scale brewing in Southwark to a close, and it is now craft beers that are made in the Borough.

# 12

# A Centre of Commerce

W e talk of 'the Borough' without perhaps thinking why it is so called. As noted earlier, in the ninth century a *burh,* a separate township, was established by Alfred the Great in Southwark, and this was to send two members to Parliament from 1295. One historian has characterised Southwark through the centuries as a headache to Londoners: a haven for criminals, an asylum of undesirable industries and residences, an administrative anachronism, but also, significantly, a commercial rival to the City with a considerable population to support that commerce.[1]

In the 1520s Southwark was one of the wealthiest towns in England, ranked twelfth in taxable wealth, higher than important market towns like Colchester, York, Lincoln and Winchester. By the beginning of the eighteenth century, its population was greater than that of Norwich or Bristol. A century later, it had an estimated population of 95,000, more than the rapidly growing industrial towns such as Manchester, Birmingham or Liverpool.

As a centre of commerce from the late Middle Ages, the Borough could boast an annual fair. Southwark has many things in common with Smithfield, diametrically opposed in location across the City: a medieval religious house, an ancient hospital and, in time, the attractions and hazards of a fair. St Bartholomew Fair in Smithfield, given its royal charter in the twelfth century, was originally a cloth fair, held at the end of August, following the Feast of St Bartholomew. Southwark Fair may have grown out of this, with a royal charter granted by Henry VI in 1444.

This was ratified eighteen years later by Edward IV. The charter specified that the people of Southwark could have an annual fair for three days, 'that is to say, the seventh, eighth, and ninth dayes of September, to be held together with a court of pie powder, and with all liberties and free customs to such fair appertaining'.[2] A court of pie powder was a special tribunal organised by a borough on the occasion of a fair or market, dealing with disputes between merchants, theft and acts of violence. It could provide swift justice for attendants at the fair who might not be permanent residents. Its curious name comes from the dusty feet, or *pieds poudrés*, of travellers. The court of pie powder for Smithfield was held in a tavern, the Hand and Shears, so the one for Southwark may well have taken place in one of the several inns on Borough High Street. The three days specified coincided with the Feast of the Nativity of the Virgin Mary, so it was sometimes referred to as Our Lady Fair. Its first location was by the priory church, which was dedicated to St Mary.

The original fair was intended to be an open-air market with a variety of functions, including the hiring of labourers for the beginning of the agricultural year. Southwark attracted not only people coming in from the rural communities of Kent, Surrey and Sussex, but also residents of the City, out to enjoy themselves. By the seventeenth century, Southwark Fair had become a big occasion. A proclamation from Charles I linked it with the fairs of St Bartholomew and of Stourbridge, outside Cambridge, as 'one of the three great fairs of importance unto which there is extraordinary resort out of all parts of England'. Its duration had increased to fourteen days, and the fair moved south for more space, first to St Margaret's Hill, and then to the edge of St George's Fields.

Although concerns about the spread of plague suspended the fair three times in the 1630s, the Puritans did not secure long-term closure, rather surprisingly, given the mayhem that often took hold. The two great seventeenth-century English diarists, John Evelyn and Samuel Pepys, have given us pen portraits of their visits.

Evelyn went to the fair on 13 September 1660, travelling westwards from his estate at Sayes Court in Deptford:

> I saw in Southwark at St. Margarite's [sic] faire ... Monkyes & Apes daunce, & do other feates of activity on the high-rope to admiration. They were galantly clad alamode, went upright, saluted the Company, bowing & pulling-off their hatts. They saluted one another with as good grace as if instructed by a Daucing Master. They turned heales over head, with a bucket of Eggs in it, without breaking any; Also with candles (lighted) in their hands, & on their head, without extinguishing them, & with vessells of water without spilling a drop.

Evelyn was visiting just three months after the Restoration of Charles II, so may have made the journey to Southwark in celebration, for he goes on, 'I also saw an Italian Wench daunce to admiration, & performe all the Tricks of agility on the high rope, all the Court went to see her. Likewise, here was (her) Father, who took up a piece of yron canon of above 400 pounds weight with the haires of his head only.'

Just as cabinets of curiosity were a source of fascination in the seventeenth century, so too were freak shows. Evelyn tells of 'a monstrous birth of Twinns, both femals & most perfectly shaped, save that they were joyn'd breast to breast, & incorporated in the navil, having their armes throwne about each other ... We also saw a poore Woman that had a living Child of one yeare old who had its head, neck, with part of a Thigh, growing out about *Spina dorsi*.'[3]

Samuel Pepys had made his first recorded visit to the fair two days earlier, crossing by boat from the City and landing at the tavern the

Bear-at-the-Bridge-Foot. He was to return eight years later and, like Evelyn, was fascinated by the different entertainments on offer. One was a puppet show telling the story of Richard Whittington, the young man who came to London in the late fourteenth century and not only made his fortune as a mercer but also became three times Mayor. Whittington had given some of his wealth to St Thomas' Hospital among many other charitable acts (p. 140), and thus his story was popular in London folk memory. Pepys remarked of the puppet show how pretty it was to see, and 'how that idle thing doth work upon people that see it, and even myself too'.

He moved on to a booth to view 'Jacob Hall's dancing on the ropes, where I saw such action as I never saw before, and mightily worth seeing'. A bystander took Pepys to a nearby inn where the music for the act was based. They were joined there by the tightrope walker 'with whom I had a mind to speak, whether he ever had any mischief by fall in his time. He told me, "Yes, many, but never to the breaking of a limb". He seems a mighty strong man.'

Leaving him with a couple of bottles of wine, Pepys departed with a waterman, Payne, who guided him back to the Bear on the Thames, where his own waterman, Bland, was awaiting him. The diarist had taken the precaution of leaving with Bland his gold and other valuables to the value of above £40 'which I had about me for feare of my pockets being cut'.[4] This was a wise move, for the fair was a notorious place for cutpurses, and for thieves in general. In 1683 legal records show that Mary Dorril was arrested at the fair and whipped for stealing a gown. Later, Thomas Bostock was transported for the theft of a handkerchief: his defence was inebriation, which he attributed to being at the fair.

The interconnection between the fair and Southwark's drinking establishments was naturally close, and the courtyards of the inns became part of the entertainments. In 1715, for example, a tragic opera, *The Siege of Troy* by Elkanah Settle, was performed at the booth of Mrs Mynn in the yard of the Queen's Arms. Cassandra, the daughter of Priam and Hecuba cursed by Apollo with the gift of doom-laden prophecy, was the central character, reflected by the alternative title of the play, *The Virgin Prophetess*. Dramatic effects were achieved of the city of Troy in flames. Settle was well known for his 'drolls', or comic shows. That year he was employed by Mrs Mynn to dress up as a dragon in green leather in *St George for England*.

In 1728 John Gay's wildly popular *Beggar's Opera* was brought to Fielding's booth at the Blue Maid Alley in the Talbot Inn. Much of the action of the opera takes place in Newgate Prison, and now it was being performed in an area which housed several prisons. Moreover, in an intriguing combination of reality and imagination, the actor John Spiller was performing in a neighbouring booth. Spiller's extravagant way of life had brought him into debt, and in 1722 he had taken shelter in the debtors' liberty of the Mint. Gay made him a character in *The Beggar's Opera* as Matt of the Mint, with his song, 'Fill every glass, for wine inspires us'.

Before the fair held in 1732, the entrepreneurs Lee and Harper advertised their forthcoming production of *Jeptha's Vow and the Fall of Phaeton* to be performed at their booth on the bowling green behind the Marshalsea Prison. They promised that this combination of Old Testament Jeptha, who sacrificed his daughter, and the Greek classical myth of the fall of Phaeton, killed while trying to drive his father's chariot across the sky, would be augmented with comic scenes featuring the Commedia del'Arte characters Punch, Harlequin, Scaramouche, Pierrot and Columbine. John Harper was a comic actor who specialised in performing at summer fairs a fat man dancing, so may well have taken the part of Punch or Scaramouche.

These characters, along with many other figures and acts, are depicted in William Hogarth's great painting *Southwark Fair*, of 1733. Hogarth had been brought up in Smithfield so was familiar with the acts put on at St Bartholomew's Fair, many of which transferred to Southwark. His painting *Southwark Fair*, now in the Cincinnati Gallery of Art in the United States, is huge, measuring

3 feet by 5 feet, and packed with detail (plate IX). The painting was acquired from Hogarth by his friend Mary Edwards, a lady of determined independence who managed to achieve liberty by wiping out an unfortunate marriage, thus retaining her estate at a time when property was in the hands of a husband.

Hogarth subsequently produced an engraving of the scene, which he put up for sale with his series *A Rake's Progress*. There are satirical messages contained within the work, concerning contemporary disputes between theatrical companies and possibly an attack on the Prime Minister, Robert Walpole, but it also provides a fascinating insight into the cultural and physical character of Southwark in the early eighteenth century.

The distant landscape is rural, the Kent and Surrey countryside, while the foreground is uncompromisingly urban. This mixture also applies to the visitors to the fair, with rustic figures fascinated by the pretty drummer girl announcing an imminent event, and drawn to the gaming table, no doubt with unhappy results. Some of the acts described by Pepys and Evelyn are here, although we are spared the images of the conjoined twins and the deformed child. An acrobat is suspended on a rope, for example. A mountebank eats fire to attract attention to his assistant, dressed as a clown, hawking patent medicines. There are fashionable theatrical performances on offer, such as Settle's *Siege of Troy*, advertised by a painted cloth of a white horse, hanging in front of the church tower of St George the Martyr. Underneath is a stand on a scaffold with actors and actresses, some dressed as Commedia del'Arte figures. On the left is another painted cloth, this time showing Shakespearean characters, including Sir John Falstaff and Pistol. Underneath, another stand crowded with more actors and actresses has collapsed, a typically Hogarthian detail, ignored by the figures below. In peril is a table displaying pottery, possibly the Delftware that was a particular feature of Southwark.

On the right, Hogarth has included the conjurer and juggler Isaac Fawkes. Although Fawkes died in 1731, he had created for the

London fairs a fantastical entertainment, 'The Temple of the Muses', in association with Christopher Pinchbeck, a maker of clocks and automata as well as the inventor of a kind of alloy that simulated gold. For the 1733 fair in Southwark, this was advertised as diverting 'The Publick with the following surprising Entertainments at their great Theatrical Room at the Queens Arms joining to the Marshalsea Gate ... The diverting and incomparable Dexterity of Hand, perform'd by Mr Pinchbeck who causes a Tree to grow out of a Flower-Pot on the Table, which blossoms and bears ripe Fruit in a Minute'.[5]

In this same year of 1733, trouble broke out, and a woman was trampled to death in the crowd. Ten years later, the wealthier residents of the area went to court 'to preserve the Morals of their Children and Servants from being Corrupted', according to the *Daily Post*. The popular response was a riot, which so alarmed the authorities that the site of the fair was moved northwards, to close by the Mint, and it was stipulated that the duration should be strictly limited to three days. Flouting the rules continued, however, so eventually it was decided that the fair should be closed down. On 19 September 1763, when several stallholders tried to set up their booths, they were expelled. Three hundred years of commercial trading, entertaining and generally enjoying life was at an end.

The Southwark Lady Fair, however, was only one part of the commercial activity of Southwark, albeit with a high profile. Throughout the year a street market flourished, established even earlier than the fair, in the thirteenth century, just outside the hospital of St Thomas. In fact, in time there were two markets in the Borough as a result of the complex manorial system. The one associated with St Thomas's lay on the east side of the high street within the Great Liberty, under the jurisdiction of the Archbishop of Canterbury. This specialised in the selling of corn and traded three days a week, on Wednesday, Friday and Saturday. The second market fell within the Guildable Manor and was thus administered by the Crown. This offered a wider range of produce, trading on Wednesdays and Fridays.

The presence of two markets so close to the City and offering strong competition disturbed the authorities there. Citizens were forbidden to cross London Bridge to buy merchandise, and there were prosecutions for the offences of forestalling, regrating and ingrossing. Forestalling was the prevention of goods coming onto the open market, thus driving up their price. Regrating was the buying and selling again in or near the market with the same effect, while ingrossing involved buying up to create a monopoly.

However, like King Canute trying to hold back the waves, threats did not work, and a charter was granted to make Southwark, along with Westminster, one of the thirteen food markets permitted to trade. In time, both manorial markets in the Borough were moved further south to prevent stalls spreading onto London Bridge, with St Thomas's trading on the east side, and the Guildable, whose powers had been acquired by the City, trading on the west as far as St Margaret's Church and on the east up to the Swan Inn. Whether customers appreciated this fine distinction is a moot point. Any distinction was ended in the reign of Edward VI in 1550 when the whole market was put in the hands of the City and the number of days of trading was increased to four. The high street had become danger-ously overcrowded and the stalls represented a major impediment to traffic to and from London Bridge, so measures were put in place to try to achieve some kind of order.

Traders were supervised by bailiffs and constables, enforcing price controls, collecting fees and inspecting goods for quality. A weighing beam, known as the King's Beam, was installed so that sacks of grain could be checked in public before being put on display. Places for stall-holders were allocated from the Thames southwards: fishwives who sold from baskets; fish stall-holders; butchers; country poul-terers; grain sellers; herb wives; fruiterers; bakers; and poulterers from London. These stalls, it was ordered, should be no more than a yard from the drainage channel running down the street. Hucksters, who bought up market goods for resale, could only do so after 11 a.m.

In 1598 Hugh Alley presented to the Lord Mayor and Aldermen of the City a book of drawings, a *Caveat*, which is now in the Folger Library in Washington.[6] Alley, who lived in Westminster, described himself as a 'plaisterer', but he apparently acquired a job as an informer, determined that the regulations of the markets of London should be more stringently enforced. Busybody he may have been, but as a result we have a remarkable picture of London street life, including the market in Southwark (plate XII).

Certain features are common to the illustrations for all thirteen markets of London. One is an indication of the sources of the produce. Southwark therefore has five columns topped with flags, labelled London, Middlesex, Essex, Kent and Surrey. Stallholders, men and women, are depicted sitting with their produce at the bases of the columns. Next to them is a feature that appears only in the Southwark picture, a multiple pillory used to punish market offenders. Alley's structure shows the heads of the unfortunate prisoners, but no bodies. There are two possibilities: that there was an elevated cage; or that he forgot to draw in the lower halves.

An open market hall is shown, constructed in the sixteenth century, with a bell atop. This was rung by the bailiff at 2 p.m. in the winter and 3 p.m. in the summer to signal the closure of the market. The Southwark bell, along with the pillory, were paid for by the Bridge wardens (p. 31). The sacks of grain brought to the market hall by farmers to be weighed on the King's Beam are also shown. Alley's drawing is misleading, for in fact the market hall stood in the middle of the high street, presenting an even greater obstruction to traffic that was only resolved when it was destroyed in the Great Fire of Southwark in 1676.

The inns along Borough High Street kept illegal markets, constantly at odds with the authorities. In particular, they offered dairy produce and poultry for sale in their courtyards. A petition presented in 1618 complained that 'tradesmen in the Borough and upon London Bridge . . . have their greatest utterances of their wares

... by such as lodge and guest in the common inns'.[7] Six years later, ordinances were issued to prevent this example of forestalling, declaring that no person should buy provisions in any inn or private warehouse, but only in the open market. The ordinances identified another problem: the habit of butchers entering shops or slaughter-houses with live cattle. In his depiction of the market, Alley indicated the shops that belonged to butchers by drawing carcasses on their frontages. Butchery would have taken place in yards and enclosures adjoining, with reports of animals breaking free and running amok.

The overriding impression of Southwark Market and of the high street is of bustling chaos, and this even extended to the parish church of St Saviour. The retrochoir behind the high altar, where Bishop Stephen Gardiner had held his heresy trials during the reign of Mary Tudor (p. 75), fell into disuse at his death in 1555. The area was then let to a baker, who permitted the wintering of pigs and fowl here, while the Lady Chapel became a bakehouse furnished with ovens and a kneading trough. This was precisely the time when St Paul's Cathedral was turned into a kind of market, with commercial activities taking place in the nave against the backdrop of services held behind the screen in the choir. When the leading members of St Saviour's parish purchased their church from the Crown at the beginning of the seventeenth century, calm was restored in Southwark; but St Paul's was to suffer even greater indignities until the Restoration of Charles II in 1660.

Although the City was reduced to ashes by the Great Fire of London in 1666, it rose again in a remarkably short time, developing in wealth and importance. London Bridge thus became ever more critical as the one trade route from the south into the City. Eventually, it was decided that Southwark Market had to be abolished. In 1754, during the reign of George II, a bill went before Parliament declaring that as 'the market obstructs much trade and commerce' it should cease trading by 25 March 1756, and that thereafter 'no person shall use any stall, trussel, block, or other stand, or expose to sale upon such stands peas, beans, herbs, victuals or other commodities'.[8]

The residents of Southwark, however, were determined to retain a market, so they petitioned to be allowed to start a new one, away from the high street and independent of the City. The parishioners of St Saviour's were able to get a second act through Parliament, allowing them to acquire land, and winning the important privilege that no provisions apart from hay or straw could be sold within 1,000 yards of the new market. With this valuable monopoly they were able to raise the money from the sale of annuities, and an area of Rochester Yard known as the Triangle was duly purchased. A further sum was collected within two years so that the site could be enlarged and a market house built. Advertisements were placed in newspapers in February 1756, announcing: 'a commodious place for a market is now preparing on the backside of Three Crown Court on the west side of the high street of the borough, and will be ready by the 25th March next for the reception of all country carriages and others bringing any kind of provisions to the said market'.[9] Continuity had thus been achieved. In 1906, the year following the establishment of St Saviour's as Southwark Cathedral, the management of the market was put into the hands of twenty-one voluntary trustees, drawn from the local community.

Originally, this newly established market was limited in extent, but in the nineteenth century it developed into a significant commercial centre, concentrating on the wholesale trade in vegetables and fruit, thanks to its excellent transport links and its close proximity to riverside wharves. A new hall was designed in 1851, with a handsome domed roof in glass and iron. This can be seen in an engraving made by the French artist Gustav Doré, showing elegant cast-iron pillars rising above the bustle of the market below. The accompanying text by his friend Blanchard Jerrold describes how the market was 'a commodious structure, almost choked even now with surrounding streets, of the poor, red-tiled houses that may be reckoned by the league, from the eminence of the railway between the City and the West End'.[10] Jerrold was writing in the early 1870s, just eight years after the South Eastern Railway Company decided to

*14. Gustav Doré's engraving of Borough Market in 1872, with its fine domed roof of glass looking down upon the market carts and costers' barrows below.*

extend its lines westwards from London Bridge Station to Cannon Street and Charing Cross on the north bank of the Thames (p. 196). A railway viaduct was built that drove straight through the market, bringing huge noise and pollution, but also adding to its accessibility. The need to widen the railway line in 1897 sadly spelt the end of the handsome dome.

The character of the market at the very turn of the century was captured in an essay on London's food supply for a partwork:

Very early in the mornings all manner of burdened vehicles flock into Borough Market . . . there are country carts, driven by

185

sun-burnt, sleepy countrymen, toiling in with masses of cabbages, carrots, and turnips from the market gardens of Kent and Surrey; you may see railway and carriers' vans bringing sacks and hampers and cases of fruit and vegetables from docks and railway stations; and an hour or two later the carts of retailers will come jogging in, and the market will be a roar of buying and selling.[11]

A strong sense of community prevailed among the market traders. In 1904 a cricket match was arranged between the fruiterers and salesmen, with the fruiterers claiming a great victory. The following year a general sports day was instituted, and this became an annual event, held first in Herne Hill and then at Crystal Palace. After the First World War, William Blackman, a former trader and secretary of the Borough Market trustees, decided that the idea of the sports day should be revived, and in 1930 he wrote around to newspapers, business organisations and celebrities for their support. His enterprise paid dividends, for perhaps the most famous show-business personality in the world at that time responded favourably. Born in 1889, probably above his Irish grandfather's bootmaker's shop in East Street in Walworth, Charlie Chaplin had experienced intense hardship as a child in Lambeth and Southwark, spending periods in the local workhouses. His initial contribution of £20 to the Borough Market sports day transformed the occasion, which attracted national interest and featured on Pathé news.

The leading event of the day was the half-bushel basket-carrying handicap. Open to all comers, this brutal test involved competitors racing around the stadium at Crystal Palace with twelve wicker baskets, each weighing almost 2 kilos, balanced on their heads. Other events were added to the programme, such as cycling and all kinds of running races, including an inter-market relay. Chaplin's contribution for 1932 featured prizes for a lookalike competition. According to the *South London Press*, 'Borough Market has among its porters a number of clever amateur actors, and they were practising "making up" behind piles of potato sacks to impersonate the famous film star'. Three years later, Chaplin stipulated that as a consolation prize, £2 10s of his contribution should be presented to the wife who had endured the misfortune of being married to an unsuccessful competitor for the longest time. The sports day raised thousands of pounds for charity, with Guy's Hospital as a main recipient. However, at the beginning of September 1939, with the BBC preparing to broadcast highlights, this extraordinary annual event was cancelled as news arrived of the German invasion of Poland, marking the end of an era for the Borough Market community.[12]

Life became parlous for the market, both structurally and commercially. Although an entrance in the Art Deco style was added on Southwark Street in 1932 when the Old Crown Square was demolished, successive expansions to the railway infrastructure have made significant changes to the market buildings, including another viaduct being erected by Thameslink in the early twenty-first century. In the 1970s the growth of supermarkets was presenting a financial threat, while the move of the flower and vegetable market from Covent Garden to a new site in Vauxhall spelt the end of Borough Market as a vital wholesale hub. However, at the beginning of the twenty-first century, the south portico from Covent Garden's Floral Hall was re-erected here, bringing back some elegance.

Covent Garden's other contribution to Borough Market's future was to act as a catalyst in initiating its renaissance as a specialist market, especially for the sale of artisan food. Pioneering food businesses that had moved into the area's empty warehouses began to host special retail events for the public, and, encouraged by the response, they asked the food writer Henrietta Green to hold a three-day Food Lovers' Fair in November 1998. This attracted around fifty food producers as part of the annual Southwark Festival, opened by the TV cookery stars, the Two Fat Ladies. Clarissa Dickson Wright always described herself as the world expert on the cardoon, but, in fact, she and Jennifer Patterson were skilled at inspiring enthusiasm for traditional English cooking. With this event proving such a success, the decision was made to hold a regular retail market at the Borough, which in time opened six days each week, and now offers produce from all over the world.

The market today has echoes of both of the earlier commercial Southwark enterprises: the Lady Fair, with events reflecting the traditional year, such as St George's Day in April and Apple Day in the autumn; and the medieval market along Borough High Street, though hopefully without the mayhem that was so often part of the proceedings.

# 13

# Pathways in the Sky

Although the heart of Southwark evolved over the centuries, it retained its essential topography: the road leading southwards from London Bridge as Borough High Street, with the medieval priory turned parish church on the west side, and the churches of St Olave and St Thomas on the east. The forms of transport that gave Southwark its character were the ships and boats arriving on the quay-sides of the Thames, and the horse-drawn carts bringing goods to the inns along the high street. A new mode of transport, however, was to bring about radical changes in the early nineteenth century, profoundly affecting Southwark's character and community: the railway.

Britain's first railway was the Stockton & Darlington, operating in north-east England from 1825, but the Kentish Railway Company was not far behind with its proposal. The aim was for a service taking in all the county from London to Dover, linking places such as Greenwich, Woolwich, Chatham and Canterbury and using 'locomotive machines' and horses. However, this scheme foundered because investors could not be found to buy into such a radical technology.

One of the people involved in this first proposal was George Thomas Landmann, a former military engineer who had built forts against incursions from the United States into Canada. With an entrepreneur, George Walter, he next devised a proposal for a route of 3.5 miles to run from near the foot of the newly opened London Bridge to Deptford, and then curving north-east to Greenwich. The company, the London & Greenwich, was floated at a meeting in November 1831 (plate XIV).

The route ran through an area of London already heavily built up, so the idea was that the rails should be set on a viaduct consisting of 878 brick arches. The response of the prestigious journal the *Quarterly Review* was one of incredulity: 'Can anything be more palpably ridiculous than the prospect held out of locomotives travelling twice as fast as stage coaches ... we will back Old Father Thames against the Greenwich railway for any sum.'[1] However, many were thrilled at such a revolutionary concept, and Landmann secured parliamentary approval in May 1833. Fierce opposition was unsurprisingly offered by ferry owners, along with the operators of coaches and omnibuses.

Landmann not only dreamt up the idea of the lengthy viaduct but suggested that the land underneath could be rented out. When 500 landowners were approached to sell their land, disputes broke out. The railway company argued that they were removing insanitary and cholera-ridden streets, but as houses began to be demolished, so the disputes increased in scale, with some residents, especially in Bermondsey, refusing to move out and challenging the navvies. Some of the navvies were English, but the majority were Irish, only too pleased to have escaped the terrible conditions of hunger in their native land, the result of the potato famine. Pitched battles between the two groups ensued, so that the authorities had to segregate them into Irish and English Grounds. The Irish Ground has gone, but the English Ground is still to be found in a small street off Battle Bridge Lane.

The arches closest to London Bridge were the last to be built, so that the line, beginning in Deptford, ended at Spa Road with 1 mile to go. Spa Road Station, although a makeshift affair, had the honour of being the first terminus in London.

15. *The viaduct carrying the London & Greenwich Railway terminus*
*at London Bridge in 1836.*

Such was the novelty of the project that the construction of the
brick arches became a tourist attraction, with people coming to watch
as around 100,000 bricks were laid each day by a team of more than
600 men. And when the final part of the route was completed in
December 1836, a party was held at London Bridge, attended by the
Lord Mayor and several thousand guests, with musicians dressed as
beefeaters from the Tower of London performing perilously on the
roof of one of the railway carriages. This first London Bridge Station
was a modest affair of three tracks and two platforms, reached by a
60-yard ramp and steps. No protection from the weather was offered
to passengers until a tarred canvas was installed.

In 1830, after London Bridge had been rebuilt at a much higher
level, and St Saviour's was found to be in a dilapidated state, the idea
of a completely new church was proposed, built on a series of arches.

The vestry noted 'we should thus not only improve the comfort and appearance of the building, but possess the additional accommodation of Vaults, and save the Parish the expense of a new Burying ground which will otherwise soon be wanted'. As Gillian Tindall wryly points out, this is the Useful Railway Arch theory of architecture.[2] The startling concept for the church was never put into practice, but the railway companies were thinking along similar lines, proposing that houses should be built under their arches.

Two model dwellings were actually constructed near the station at Deptford. As the smoke from coal emanating from their chimneys would be unpleasant for passengers on the trains above, gas was installed for cooking and lighting. However, this scheme proved unworkable, for householders would be obliged to live like troglodytes, forever in the dark and with rain seeping in, while trains would be constantly trundling a few feet above bedrooms. Other schemes for the use of the land below the arches were put forward, but five years after the opening of the route, only fifty-two arches had been let out, principally for stables and small businesses. Those arches that were untenanted rapidly became a shelter for the homeless and the place where prostitutes might make their assignations.

Although this first route was not a great financial success, this did not discourage railway developers, and four other companies got permission to connect with the original route. One, the London & Croydon, used the track to Bermondsey and then branched out to Croydon. It required a new, larger station at London Bridge, 300 feet in length with a train shed 100 feet in width. Separate sets of steps were built for first and second class passengers to reach the platforms. The character of the station was to be much grander than that of its existing neighbour. As one contemporary writer noted with enthusiastic and careful detail: 'We reach the west front which is an elegant façade of stone in the Roman style of architecture. This leads immediately into a vestibule 60 feet in length, 30 feet in breadth and 22 feet high, the roof of which rests on a double range of Roman

Doric columns, coated, as are the walls of the interior and of the staircases, with a new kind of white cement, capable of a polish equal to that of marble. This is the booking office of the Croydon Railway.'[3]

The London & Croydon were innovators. The railway, described as 'atmospheric', was powered by static steam engines, creating a vacuum in a continuous pipe between tracks, into which a piston attached to the train would be pulled along. This was a similar principle to the vacuum tubes used in department stores to send money to the cashier. But when the London & Croydon amalgamated with the London & Brighton, this system was ditched. Criticism of the service ranged from delays and clocks being inaccurate to the lascivious behaviour of the railway staff. A local newspaper reported that lady passengers were experiencing distress 'because the conductors were rather lax in letting down the carriage steps to the fullest extent, thus exacting a display of the beauty of their legs and ankles'. It was thought that this was not accidental, because 'when helping the weaker sex into carriages, these officials were apt to press the ladies' fingers and stare them full in the face'.[4]

As more and more railway companies invested in routes into Southwark, so the station at London Bridge was enlarged to cater for the influx of passengers, which reached around 4,000 a day by the mid-century. Squeezed in between St Thomas' Hospital and Tooley Street was yet another Italianate building topped by a bell tower, elegantly designed by William Cubitt, complete with booking hall, parcels office, waiting rooms and a main train shed well protected from the weather. But this lasted only five years, before being rebuilt yet again, with the companies falling out with each other and a wall dividing two termini.

The proliferation of the railways coming into London Bridge was throttling the coach trade that had for centuries been bringing goods, as well as people, from the south into the capital, and also bringing the raison d'etre of the great coaching inns to an end. Not only were they being threatened financially, but part of the land that they occupied was also threatened physically, as noted in Chapter 11.

Echoing this, a similar fundamental change was taking place on the Thames. The squat sailing vessels that were the feature of the Pool of London at the beginning of the nineteenth century were by the 1840s giving way to slimmer, sleeker ships such as the tea clippers that plied the fast route from India. Hundreds of ships were moored, several deep and crowding the wet docks that had recently been built. Along with their sails, these ships carried tall smoke stacks announcing the arrival of steam power. Henry Mayhew, in his book *London Labour and the London Poor*, noted that the Thames 'is no longer the "silent highway", for its silence is continually broken by the clatter of steamboats. This change has materially affected the position and diminished the number of the London watermen'.

By the 1840s, in parallel with the expansion of the railways causing the collapse of the coach trade and of the livelihood of the inns along Borough High Street, steamers were posing a serious threat to the livelihood of the watermen who had for centuries plied their craft along the Thames. Mayhew observed: 'Since the prevalence of steam packets as a means of locomotion along the Thames, the "stairs" (if so they may be called) above bridge, are for the most part almost nominal stations for watermen.' He wrote how, at the stairs on the north bank of the river, 'there now lie but three boats, while before the steam era, or rather before the removal of the old London Bridge, ten times that number of boats were to be "hailed" there.'[5] Although he characterised the watermen as civil and honest, he found that they were very poor, and unable to afford to repair their ageing boats. The records of St Saviour's Church often noted that the watermen, and their families, were destitute, driven to pick up discarded bread crusts in gutters. This situation did not affect the lightermen, who could work with the steamboats equally well as with sailing ships.

In the 1860s the ambitions of the railway companies significantly stepped up. In 1861 a Terminus Hotel was built by the Brighton & South Coast Railway. It was 5 storeys high, with 150 bedrooms with bathrooms and water closets, lifts and restaurants. Ladies could take coffee in their own room, separated from the library by a general coffee room. Gentlemen had smoking and billiard rooms in a separate block. The facilities on offer were reminiscent of those being installed at the hotel for St Pancras Station, some of which can still be seen today. However, the London Bridge Terminus Hotel did not flourish: it was in the wrong place, surrounded by the rough streets that still housed the large working-class population. The hotel ceased trading and became railway offices, finally being extinguished by bombs in the Second World War.

Frustrated by the fact that passengers were obliged to leave the trains in Southwark and continue into the City and West End across London Bridge, companies were now looking at gaining direct access to the north bank by building rail bridges across the Thames. The South Eastern Railway, for example, found that more than half the passengers arriving at London Bridge were heading for the West End and had a slow journey by road thereafter, for there was no Underground system. Samuel Smiles, known best today as the author of *Self Help*, was the secretary of the South Eastern Railway. He proposed with great enthusiasm a central West End terminus which 'would be of much convenience to the highest classes of society – the nobility, the gentry, members of Parliament and their families, who principally reside at the West End of London – by enabling them to arrive in town during the season, and to leave it when it is over for their residences, or for sea-bathing quarters, or for the Continent'.[6]

Smiles sought potential routes, and decided that the best location on the north side of the river would be the site of the former Hungerford Market next to the Strand, and that it would be possible to make a direct connection to Waterloo Station to link up with the services of the London & South Western Railway. In 1859 the Charing Cross Railway Company was formed, on behalf of the South Eastern Railway, to build the extension and gained permission to build a 2-mile connection. Work began in 1860, with a new bridge replacing an earlier suspension bridge designed by Isambard Kingdom Brunel.

Like Samuel Smiles, the writer of a piece for *The Builder* wrote with blithe optimism and a total disregard for what the construction of the railway might mean for the inhabitants of Southwark. Anticipating the changes planned for the embankment at Lambeth, a prolongation of Bankside, the correspondent pointed out how it would render:

> that which was in the memory of some living a dreary and, in part, impassable marsh, dry and wholesome. The increased bridge and railway accommodation will also confer benefits ... the locality will become more suitable for healthy dwelling and for the purposes of various descriptions of industry ... wharfs [for] coal, stone, wood and many other materials crowd the once unprofitable land; shot and other factories ... and matters too numerous in brief space to mention give employment to thousands.[7]

In Southwark the new Charing Cross route curved to the south-west to avoid St Saviour's Church, although it passed alarmingly close. When a small parcel of land belonging to St Thomas' Hospital was required, the governors compelled them to buy the whole site for a large sum. This enabled the hospital to be relocated to Lambeth, to a site near the palace of the archbishops of Canterbury, where the embankment was being built onto the river. The foundation stone was laid by Queen Victoria on 13 May 1868, with the new hospital opening in 1871 on the principles approved by Florence Nightingale.

The railway company, however, baulked at paying compensation to Barclay Perkins, so the line skirted the Anchor Brewery. Not only did this mean building a viaduct across Borough Market (p. 185), but it also required the removal of the almshouses built in the late sixteenth century with the bequest of Thomas Cure, along with their graveyard. Thousands of bodies – it was reckoned at least 7,950 – exhumed during this operation were relocated to Brookwood Cemetery near Woking in Surrey. Following the cholera epidemic, the cemetery had been created in 1849 by the London Necropolis Company, with the intention of accommodating the capital's deceased at a time when it was becoming increasingly difficult to cope with the population of both the living and the dead. By 1854 it had become the largest cemetery in the world, with the London Necropolis Company incorporated by Act of Parliament. While the northern section was reserved for Nonconformists, the main part, for members of the Church of England, was consecrated by Charles Sumner, Bishop of Winchester, and opened in November. The first burial there was that of the stillborn twins of a couple who lived in Ewer Street in Southwark. As this was a pauper burial, they were consigned to an unmarked grave.[8]

In 1862 the bodies from the burial ground of Cure's College were packed into 220 large containers, each holding 26 adults plus children, along with some of the headstones, and shipped by the London Necropolis Railway to Brookwood. It is a nice irony that they were conveyed by train, for it was the coming of the railway that had caused this major disruption. Samuel Smiles, ever the utilitarian, wrote, 'Each body has cost us less than three shillings. It was fortunate that such reasonable terms could be made at Woking Cemetery', although he did add that 'a more horrible business you could not imagine; the men could only continue their work by the constant sprinkling of disinfectant powder'.[9]

The Necropolis Railway, possibly the most extraordinary of all British railway lines, had a special station next to Waterloo. Trains consisted of passenger carriages reserved for first, second and third class passengers, with other carriages for coffins, also divided into different classes. The route ran into the cemetery on a dedicated branch from the main line of the South West Railway at a junction just to the west of Brookwood Station. From here, passengers and coffins were then transported by horse-drawn vehicles. The line was closed in 1945.

The disruption to Southwark caused by the expansion of the railway system in the Victorian era was enormous, and it was the misfortune of the Borough's inhabitants that the railway came first to this part of London, with all lessons yet to be learnt. As one twentieth-century writer on railway history put it: 'The machinations and fallouts between a number of Victorian railway companies were the cause of more than a century's chaos at London Bridge. Decisions taken in the 1850s and 1860s have blighted its layout to this day, and London Bridge remains the most difficult station in the capital to use.'[10]

When the termini were built for the railway companies in the northern part of London, and the demolition of thousands of homes was being threatened, a Royal Commission was set up. Its remit was to consider an area of London roughly quadrilateral in shape, bounded by Park Lane in the west, Marylebone and Euston roads in the north, and the City's Square Mile. It was decided that no railways should be allowed within this area, and that the termini should be located around the periphery; hence, Liverpool Street, Kings Cross, St Pancras, Euston, Marylebone, Paddington and Victoria form such an arc.

The Admiralty expressed concern that more bridges over the Thames might pose a risk to shipping, and that therefore only one extra bridge should be built. In fact, four railway bridges were built, at Battersea, Charing Cross, Blackfriars and Cannon Street. At one stage it was also suggested that a bridge should be built across the Thames from Southwark, crossing St Paul's Churchyard close by the eastern end of the cathedral. Many buildings were allowed to deteriorate in Southwark to prepare for this, but it never materialised due to protests from the City. However, an obtrusive bridge was built across Ludgate Hill in 1863–65 for the London, Chatham & Dover Railway, blighting the famous view of St Paul's: the last vestige of this was removed only in 1990.

In the nineteenth century many were greatly excited at the new technology, describing the routes raised up on viaducts in Southwark as 'pathways in the sky', a description to be echoed a hundred years later by those who advocated high-rise housing with walkways in the sky following the Second World War. The complex of London Bridge Station was also a source of much wonder: a reporter from the *Illustrated London News* wrote in the summer of 1858 how it was 'suspended in mid-air, more wonderfully than the Hanging Gardens of Babylon, looking down from an altitude of seventy feet upon Tooley Street and sending forth its convoys along an elevated route which lifts them above the chimney pots of Bermondsey.'[11]

Others were less impressed. The physician William Rendle wrote in 1878 how 'people of this utilitarian age have made it possible to skirt with a gigantic and ugly thundering iron trough one of the loveliest of old churches, St Saviour's, Southwark. And the trough might, as I heard was intended, so easily have gone further south. Outer (or ultra) barbarians! As the Chinese might, with show of reason, call us'.[12] He was mourning the passing of the historic inns along Borough High Street, but as Medical Surgeon to the Poor he was also lamenting the condition into which so many of the poor of Southwark were cast. As two modern historians have put it: 'These seemingly subterranean, Stygian and even threatening streets are stark evidence of how the railway viaducts penetrated, dominated and then destroyed the cohesiveness of the communities over which they passed, creating new divisions as they did so and establishing this gloomy and depressing no man's land.'[13]

This lamentable condition is illustrated by some of the wood engravings made by the artist Gustav Doré and published in *London: A Pilgrimage*. One in particular has become iconic, with the title 'Over London – by Rail'. In a scene that is the stuff of nightmares, it shows two stretches of the brick-arched aqueducts with a steam train chugging over the one in the distance, belching smoke. Below are

OVER LONDON—BY RAIL.

*16. Gustav Doré's arresting engraving, 'Over London – by Rail', with trains running on viaducts above the terraces of houses.*

closely packed terraces of houses, their backyards full of people, and some with washing hanging on lines despite the grime and soot.[14]

In contrast to the viaducts, a very different railway once operated in Southwark, this time underground. In 1884 parliamentary powers were obtained for the City of London & Southwark Subway, the world's first deep-level tube line and the first major electric railway. Work began in October 1886 for a cable-operated railway that was to run between the Monument at the north end of London Bridge to the Elephant and Castle, a distance of around 1.5 miles. The following year permission was given to extend the line southwards to Stockwell via Kennington, making it around 3 miles in length, which brought into question the viability of the cable traction. It was decided to use electricity, with a third rail laid alongside the lines to supply power and to employ locomotives. The tunnels were only 10 feet 6 inches in diameter, so the rolling stock was much smaller. The line was opened in November 1890 by the Prince of Wales, who spoke of how this would be a solution to the severe traffic congestion bedevilling London. The average speed of the trains, including stops, was 11 mph, which was certainly faster than any road vehicles could normally achieve.

Despite this, there were many drawbacks. The carriages had no windows – the company justified this by pointing out that there was nothing to see, anyway – and given the narrowness of the stock and the high-backed seats, they soon acquired the nickname of padded cells. Standing passengers were flung about, since there were no straps to hang on to. The steep incline up to King William Street proved problematic, with the electric supply insufficient, so that sometimes the lights dimmed and the train ran backwards before stopping and trying again. Passengers got down to the trains by large hydraulic lifts and were accompanied on board by conductors riding on the platforms of each carriage. In contrast to that other eccentric railway, the London Necropolis, the class system did not operate; instead, there was a flat fare of 2 pence. Each train had a smoking carriage, to which female passengers were not allowed access. There was a station in Borough High Street, but not one at London Bridge, which would have generated much more traffic.

The many teething problems accompanying this new style of transport did not deter imitators, and in 1891 the Central London Line was given parliamentary approval. It was decided that the City & South London, as it was now known, should extend northwards to the Angel, Islington, and that the section between just north of Borough to King William Street should be abandoned, and new tunnels driven under the Thames. An underground station was built at London Bridge, linked across the river to the Bank, with the first part opened in February 1900. This line now forms the City branch of the Northern Line.

The effect of the coming of these different railways on London's population was to impel those who could afford it to move out of the inner city to the suburbs, and to travel in to work or to visit. Camberwell, along with Islington and Hackney north of the Thames, was a 'walking suburb', accommodating clerks who were able to make their way to their offices on foot in the early nineteenth century. Their arrival and departure was to be commemorated in 1922 by T.S. Eliot in *The Waste Land*, where he described a mass of city clerks flowing over London Bridge at dawn on a winter's day, amid the smog that was such a horrible feature of the time.

By the end of the nineteenth century the commuter suburbs were located still further out but accessible by train. A description of this phenomenon is provided by the writer V.S. Pritchett. Born in 1900, he travelled into London Bridge daily as a teenager to work in a leather factory. In his autobiography of his early life, *A Cab at the Door*, he creates a remarkable evocation of the station:

> The distinction of London Bridge Station, on the Chatham side, is that it is not a terminus but a junction where lives begin to fade and then blossom again as they swap trains in the rush hours and make for all the regions of South London and the towns of Kent. The trains come in and go out over those miles of rolling brick arches that run across South London like a massive Roman wall. There were no indicators on the platforms in my day and the confusion had to be sorted out by stentorian porters who called out the long litanies of stations in a hoarse London bawl and with a style of their own.

With his novelist's ear, he savoured the sounds:

> They stood on the crowded platform edge, detected the identifying lights on the incoming engine and then sang out. To myself, at that age, all places I did not know, seemed romantic and the

lists of names were, if not Miltonic, at any rate as evocative as those names with which the Georgian poets filled up their lines. I would stare admiringly, even enviously at the porters who have to chant the long line to Bexley Heath; or the man who, beginning with the blunt and challenging football names of Charlton and Woolwich, would go on to comic Plumstead and then flow forward over his long list till his voice fell to the finality of Greenhythe, Northfleet and Blackheath.[15]

Pritchett also provided a description of the scene half a century later, in 1974: 'The southern side of London is crossed by miles of high, bowling, blackened railway arches, solid on Roman walls, deeply tunnelled and cellared, never penetrated, I believe, by bombs. If London were totally devastated, this would, very likely, be the only surviving architecture of the city, outlasting all, as the Roman aqueducts have done in Spain and Italy.'[16]

In recent years the station at London Bridge has undergone huge refurbishment, so that the failings mentioned earlier have been redressed. But one of the unnerving experiences for those not accustomed to using the station is how passengers have to take steep escalators up to the platforms, and thus set off along the Victorian viaducts to descend from chimney pot level several miles to the south and east. A visit to the upper floors of the Shard reveals this extraordinary urban landscape. This domination of Southwark by the railway has been further reinforced in modern times by the building of Thameslink to marry up with services to Gatwick Airport and northwards to Bedford, Luton and St Albans. A viaduct was built between 2009 and 2011 to add extra tracks, driven over the top of Borough Market to pass over the lines from London Bridge to Charing Cross and Cannon Street. Now visitors to the market and to the precinct of Southwark Cathedral are met with the constant sound of groaning and grinding as trains pass overhead.

# 14

## A Tale of Two Boroughs

Perhaps the most famous descriptions of nineteenth-century life in Southwark come from the pen of Charles Dickens. He lived for a time in the Borough after his father John was committed to the Marshalsea Prison in 1824.

At the beginning of the nineteenth century, Southwark was home to no fewer than five prisons, compared to eighteen in the rest of London. The Clink, the private prison of the Bishops of Winchester, has given its name in slang to all prisons. The White Lion, sounding comfortingly like an inn, was the Surrey Gaol. The Borough Compter was the prison of the City Corporation, the authority from across the river, originally at St Margaret's Hill, then in Tooley Street. The King's Bench took its name from the court which originally travelled from town to town. By the eighteenth century the King's Bench was located permanently on a site to the east of Borough High Street, and a large proportion of the inmates were debtors. The Marshalsea has a watery name, appropriate for an area that is built over marshy ground, but is in fact derived from the office of the Knight Marshal of the Royal Household. Like the King's Bench, it originally travelled around the country, dealing with trespass, contempt, debt and, later, issues connected with the Admiralty. The Marshalsea was always a much smaller prison than the King's Bench.

In Tudor times the Knight Marshal was Charles Brandon, whose London house, Suffolk Place, faced the two prisons, the King's Bench and the Marshalsea, across Borough High Street (p. 36). When Brandon exchanged Suffolk Place for another residence in the capital, the house became a royal residence, and part was used as a Mint. After most of it was demolished in 1557, the area became a notorious rookery, adopting some of the pre-Reformation concepts of sanctuary, beyond the rule of law.

Southwark came to have four of these 'sanctuaries': in addition to the Mint, these were Montague Place, Deadman's Place and the Liberty of the Clink, an ironic example of a term of contradiction. Prisoners from the King's Bench, for example, might live outside the gaol in the Mint for a price, immune from arrest, and by the end of the seventeenth century this privilege was claimed by all those residing within the area. In 1697 a Southwark resident, Thomas Lant, was able to buy up some of the empty land of the park of old Suffolk Place, and he built a warren of courts and tenements which carried suggestive names, such as Rebel Row and Robin Hood's Court.

As Jerry White points out in his history of the Marshalsea, *Mansions of Misery*, for centuries almost everybody in London had some form of debt.[1] Indeed, this is true today, with mortgages and credit mechanisms from banks and building societies. The Elizabethan theatre manager Philip Henslowe ran a lucrative sideline in pawnbroking, and brokers are still with us, as are, more seriously, loan sharks. But the difference between today and the situation up to the nineteenth century is that debt was then a personal relationship, with the lender being able to secure the arrest and imprisonment of the borrower, and once in prison, it could often be impossible to escape from the web of the system. The stories of debtors caught up in this web in the Marshalsea are particularly well documented because some of the inmates were professional and literate men and women.

One such was Jean-Baptiste Grano, whose journal of his time in the gaol covering the years 1728 and 1729 is now in the Bodleian Library in Oxford. Grano followed in his Sicilian father's profession as a musician, performing in all the major London venues as both a flautist and a trumpeter, as well as composing pieces. Socially ambitious and tempted into purchasing the genteel lifestyle with money that he did not have, in the spring of 1726 Grano fell into debt and was committed to the Marshalsea. The prison that he entered had two sides. The first was the Master's, with about eighty prisoners, men and women, accommodated in five houses, with a coffee room, a chandlers' shop and a separate alehouse. The second was the Common side, with over 300 prisoners crowded together in wards. The conditions here were dire, with scarcely enough to eat, sickness rife and some perishing in the stifling conditions in summer. Grano, with his notions of gentility, was determined to remain on the Master's side, which involved finding the wherewithal for a bed in a room shared with a 'chum', paying a woman to clean, to cook, and on occasion to take to bed.

The prisoners were locked up at night, but during the day they could walk around the open ground within the prison, known as 'the Park', again divided between the two 'sides'. Here Grano was able to play at battledores and shuttlecocks with other prisoners. Hearty meals are recorded in his diary, some cooked on the premises, others brought in from the Royal Oak Inn: the smell of the food must have been a torture to the unfortunates on the Common side. Grano took advantage of a room known as the Parlour for drinking with other prisoners and performing on his flute. When the Southwark Fair was held, he was able to enjoy the entertainments on offer, including a performance of John Gay's *Beggar's Opera* at a booth just outside the prison gate (p. 206). At other times of the year, he was allowed out to attend meetings such as that of the Freemasons' lodge at Thurtle's coffee house near Bankside.

But this all came at a price. The staff of the prison were not salaried, depending rather on making a living from their prisoners. The Governor of the Marshalsea at this time was William Acton, and Grano ensured that he ingratiated himself by volunteering all kinds of payments. Acton was to become notorious for 'skinning the flint'. A series of charities sent money into the prison for the neediest inmates, but these were diverted into the pockets of Acton and his turnkeys. Highly capricious, Acton could be charmingly social, but also very cruel, not flinching from using torture as punishment, and allowing inmates to starve to death. Although he was charged in 1729 with the responsibility for the death of four prisoners, Acton was acquitted on each occasion. He did not return to the Marshalsea but became publican of the Greyhound across the road.

A committee was set up the same year at the behest of an MP and soldier, James Oglethorpe, to look into the conditions in all the prisons in which debtors were incarcerated. As a result, torture was forbidden, money found to rescue the starving, and hundreds of prisoners released. Oglethorpe founded the North American colony of Georgia, and many ex-prisoners were settled there.

Attempts to improve conditions were made through the rest of the century, including an act in 1779 increasing the limit for arrest for debt from £2 to £10. The awful conditions continued, however, providing dramatic fare for writers, many of whom had themselves experienced debt. Tobias Smollett, for example, in his first novel published in 1748, *Roderick Random*, has his hero imprisoned for debt in the Marshalsea. Although Smollett was never himself imprisoned, he was all too familiar with the effects of debt. Of Roderick Random, he wrote: 'I, seeing my money melt away, without any certainty of deliverance, and in short, all my hopes frustrated; grew negligent of life, lost all appetite, and degenerated into such a sloven, that during the space of two months, I was neither washed, shifted, nor shaved; so that my face, rendered meagre with abstinence, was obscured with dirt, and overshadowed with hair, and my whole appearance squalid and even frightful'.[2] The novelist was later to apply the phrase 'mansions of misery' to debtors' prisons.

In 1780 Gordon rioters attacked the various London prisons as symbolic institutions of injustice (p. 164). While John Perkins was able to save the Anchor Brewery from destruction, the Marshalsea was badly damaged by fire, and many prisoners escaped because the old buildings were like a sieve. Seven years later, a new Marshalsea Prison was built just 130 yards further to the south, opening on Christmas Eve 1811, with fifty debtor prisoners and eleven Admiralty inmates. Although the living conditions were better than in the old prison, the accommodation was much more cramped. On a long narrow site, the central block was surrounded by an exercise yard. Again, there were two sides, the Master's and the Common, but now, importantly, the keeper and his turnkeys were salaried, and thus not constantly finding ways to extract money. Nevertheless, there were still opportunities for small profits to be gained from inmates.

This was the prison that John Dickens entered in February 1824. He was the educated son of upper servants and, like Jean-Baptiste Grano, had notions of gentility and expensive tastes. Becoming a clerk in the Navy Pay Office, John frequently moved his growing family, with debts mounting up until his arrest. His son Charles visited him in the Marshalsea soon after. He described the scene many years later to his biographer, John Forster: 'My father was waiting for me in the lodge, and we went up to his room (on the top story but one), and cried very much. And he told me, I remember, to take warning by the Marshalsea, and to observe that if a man had twenty pounds a-year, and spent nineteen pounds, nineteen shillings and sixpence, he would be happy; but that a shilling spent the other way would make him wretched.' John Dickens' comment on financial improvidence was to be used by his son Charles in his portrayal of Wilkins Micawber in *David Copperfield*, delivered in characteristically grandiloquent tones. He continued:

I see the fire we sat before, now; with two bricks inside the rusted grate, one on each side, to prevent its burning too many coals. Some other debtor shared the room with him, who came in by-and-by; and as the dinner was a joint-stock repast, I was sent up to "Captain Porter" in the room overhead, with Mr. Dickens's compliments, and I was his son, and could he, Captain P, lend me a knife and fork?

Captain Porter lent the knife and fork, with his compliments in return. There was a very dirty lady in his little room and two wan girls, his daughters, with shock heads of hair. I thought I should not have liked to borrow Captain Porter's comb ... I saw his bed rolled up in a corner; and I knew (God knows how) that the two girls with the shock heads were Captain Porter's natural children, and that the dirty lady was not married to Captain P.[3]

John's wife and family moved into the prison, taking the place of the 'chum' mentioned in Charles's account, with a workhouse servant coming in daily. However, his two eldest children did not join them. Money was found to send Fanny to the Royal Academy of Music. Charles was not so lucky: a family friend got him employment in a blacking factory at Hungerford Stairs, on the north bank of the Thames off the Strand. The humiliation of this was to haunt him for the rest of his life. At first, he was found lodgings in Camden Town, but when the inconvenience of this was pointed out to his father, he was moved to Lant Street, named after the developer of the Mint site, just across from the Marshalsea. Thus, Charles, at just twelve years of age, came to know Southwark in all its extraordinary variety, and, as his biographer, John Forster, observed, his response to the grimness and squalor that he encountered was a 'profound attraction of repulsion'.[4]

Dickens gives a description of Lant Street in *The Pickwick Papers*:

In this happy street are colonised a few clear-starchers, a sprin- kling of journeymen bookbinders, one or two prison agents for the Insolvent Court, several small housekeepers who are employed in the Docks, a handful of mantua-makers, and a seasoning of jobbing tailors. The majority of the inhabitants either direct their energies to the letting of furnished apartments, or devote themselves to the healthful and invigorating pursuit of mangling. The chief features in the still life of the street are green shutters, lodging-bills, brass door-plates, and bell handles; the principal specimens of animated nature, the pot-boy, the muffin youth, and the baked-potato man. The population is migratory, usually disappearing on the verge of quarter-day, and generally by night. His Majesty's revenues are seldom collected in this happy valley, the rents are dubious, and the water communication is frequently cut off.[5]

A much more squalid scene is presented in *Oliver Twist*, published in 1837–38. Here Dickens presented the traumatic childhood of the eponymous hero as he escaped the cruelty of the workhouse and an unhappy apprenticeship, only, when he arrived in London, to fall into the hands of a gang of thieves headed by the old Jew, Fagin, and the burglar, Bill Sikes. Dickens chose to locate Sikes's house, where he lived with his mistress, Nancy, in Folly Ditch on Jacob's Island, a notorious slum in Bermondsey. His description of the dwellings to be found here is horrific:

crazy wooden galleries common to the backs of half a dozen houses, with holes from which to look upon the slime beneath; windows, broken and patched, with poles thrust out, on which to dry the linen that is never there; rooms so small, so filthy, so confined, that the air would seem to be too tainted even for the dirt and squalor which they shelter; wooden chambers thrusting themselves out above the mud and threatening to fall in it – as some have done; dirt besmeared walls and decaying foundations, every repulsive lineament of poverty, every loathsome indication of filth, rot and garbage; all these ornament the banks of Folly Ditch.[6]

It was in this unsavoury place that Dickens had Nancy violently done to death by Sikes. Her fate was sealed when she arranged to meet two people who had rescued Oliver from the gang and was overheard telling them how he was in great danger of being seized by Fagin and a sinister character, Monks. Although Nancy did not implicate Sikes, he assumed that she had betrayed him. The meeting with Oliver's rescuers took place on London Bridge, the handsome structure designed by John Rennie to replace the medieval bridge. This in turn was demolished in the 1960s, but a small section survives just by Southwark Cathedral, and the steep steps up to the roadway have been named Nancy's Steps.

Twenty years later Southwark featured large in another of Dickens' novels. The profound effect on Charles of his father's imprisonment in the Marshalsea, along with his own humiliation of working in the blacking factory, led to him to write *Little Dorrit*, the first instalment of which appeared in 1855. The misfortune of an incomplete contract with the wonderfully named Circumlocution Office had led to William Dorrit's imprisonment in the Marshalsea. He had been there so long that he was known as 'the Father', while his youngest daughter, Amy, 'Little Dorrit', had been born there and was thus known as the 'Child of the Marshalsea'. Dickens' descriptions of life in the prison reflect both the straitened circumstances and the extraordinary social life of the inmates. Ultimately, an unexpected discovery of a generous inheritance enabled the Dorrit family to leave.

Unlike that of William Dorrit, John Dickens' stay in the Marshalsea was not protracted. A new Insolvent Debtor's Act passed in the spring of 1824 allowed him to walk free at the end of May. Even so, as a sociable man, he had quickly adapted to the prison's way of life. There was a Marshalsea debtors' constitution known as 'College Regulations', and John was elected the chairman of the college, getting up a petition to the king, George IV, for a gift to drink his health on his forthcoming birthday. Charles took time off work in the blacking factory to witness the occasion, later giving Forster an amusing account of the reading of the petition by John's friend, Captain Porter. There is a hint here that John rather enjoyed the life in the Marshalsea, free from fear of being dunned by his creditors, and this is echoed in *Little Dorrit*, where the family did not always find life outside the prison following their departure easy to deal with.

Although John Dickens obtained work reporting parliamentary debates, his finances were ever precarious, and he became a shameless borrower from Charles's friends. He narrowly escaped arrest in 1834, when Charles was possibly also in danger, and his debts were to follow John to the grave. In 1838, however, an important piece of legislation was passed, known as Lord Cottenham's Act. Cottenham, from the family of the diarist Samuel Pepys, secured the enactment of a statute abolishing imprisonment for debt on mesne process so that thereafter a person could not be arrested on the mere affidavit of another that he was owed £20. The effect of the act was greatly to reduce the number of debtor prisoners, so that when the Marshalsea was closed in November 1842, only three people were left there.

When Dickens wrote *Little Dorrit*, the prison was already a past memory, although one that continued to haunt him. Having completed the book, he returned to the site and wrote: 'Whosoever goes into Marshalsea Place, turning out of Angel Court, leading to Bermondsey, will find his feet on the very paving-stones of the extinct Marshalsea jail; will see its narrow yard to the right and to the left, very little altered if at all, except that the walls were lowered when the place got free; will look upon the rooms in which the debtors lived; will stand among the crowding ghosts of many miserable years.'[7]

Charles Dickens was to revisit Southwark in 1869. Now rich and famous, he had returned from a triumphant reading tour of the United States. In January of that year he attended a meeting of the

Ancient Society of College Youths, with a bell-ringing practice at St Saviour's, which he subsequently wrote up in *All the Year Round*. St Saviour's church bells were particularly fine: the seventeenth-century playwright Thomas Dekker likened them to the jingle of gold coins. The society was formed in 1637 and played a leading role in the development of change-ringing. Dickens' son, also Charles, wrote in 1879 how St Saviour's had become their headquarters, attracting an increasing number of members from the working classes because the rules were few and the subscription low. Dickens Senior climbed up to the tower with them on his 1869 visit and described how it rocked as the bells clashed with the tenor booming at intervals. Below, the organist was trying to practise, no competition against the clamour of the bells, so Dickens ends his account: 'pursued by a triumphant burst of sound from the organ, as if the organist were glad to get rid of us, we troop off to the meeting place of the Society at the King's Head'.[8]

In fact, Dickens was suffering increasingly from ill health, exacerbated by the exhausting schedule that he maintained. The previous autumn he had added to his repertoire of public readings the terrible account from *Oliver Twist* of the death of Nancy at the hands of Bill Sikes on Jacob Island. Including it in his programme became such an obsession that his doctors tried to persuade him not to do so because his pulse rate rose so rapidly. One doctor monitoring it noted that the rate rose from 72 to 95, and subsequent readings hit 124. In acting out the murder of Nancy, he was murdering himself. Dickens insisted that he present a final series of readings in London, ending the last of these in March 1870 with the dramatic flourish: 'From these garish lights I vanish now for evermore with a heartfelt, grateful, respectful and affectionate farewell.'[9] He died that summer. Strangely, unlike the characters portrayed by William Shakespeare and Geoffrey Chaucer, there is no memorial to those of Dickens in the cathedral of Southwark.

Dickens' account in *All the Year Round* of his visit to St Saviour's makes scant mention of the environment of the church but suggests he did not encounter the utter deprivation that he so vividly described in his novels. Despite the impact the arrival of the railway had on the Borough, as described in the previous chapter, there is evidence that the Southwark community still displayed a mixture of the comparatively well-to-do and the poor that was so clearly manifest in the sixteenth century. For example, the site of the Marshalsea Prison was developed into a drapery emporium. From 1838 through to the 1840s, a Clerkenwell printer, John Tallis, published 'a complete stranger's guide through London', with double pages engraved with perspectives of principal streets. For a fee, Tallis would include the names of the proprietors and the nature of their businesses. Three of these elevations are from Southwark: of Borough High Street and its southern extension, Blackman Street, and further south still, Newington Causeway.

The shops named on the perspectives are purveyors of consumer goods enjoyed by a middle-class clientele: silk mercer, tailor and draper, glove-maker, jeweller and watchmaker, confectioner, wine and spirit seller, dealer in foreign fruit and tea, cheesemonger, seedsman and florist. Although not named, the entrances to the yards of the great inns that offered all kinds of goods and services as well as accommodation punctuate the elevations. One shopkeeper paid extra to have his shop illustrated in an engraving: the Borough Cloth Market, which dealt in Manchester goods, usually of cotton cloth. This may be the shop that occupied the former site of the Marshalsea Prison.

This mixture of middle class and poverty side by side continued into the twentieth century, according to one commentator looking at the various high streets of London. Introducing Borough High Street, he describes how:

from numberless obscure by-ways a teeming people congregate in a raucous glare of shop-lights. Day in this neighbourhood discloses everywhere, trickling into the main road, a very plague of squalid alleys, eloquent of poverty most abject. The High Street itself is lively and exhilarating; St George's Church, standing out boldly at its southern end amid low-growing trees, lends a touch of grace to the scene. Such roads as this you will find traversing a score of similar districts round about – in Walworth, Bermondsey, and over the water, from Whitehapel to Silvertown. They are like mighty rivers in a wilderness of misery and want. The horrid streets lie cheek by jowl in serried rows between them, dark, dirty, forbidding, differing from one another in no particular save the depth of their degradation.[10]

There had been a growing chorus of condemnation that such abject poverty should be allowed to exist in the capital of one of the richest nations of the world. Charles Dickens in his novels wrote graphically of the conditions in some of the most deprived areas, and the theme was taken up by journalists such as Henry Mayhew, who began a series of articles in the *Morning Post* in 1849 when he visited Bermondsey, which had been hit by a grave outbreak of cholera. In 1861 he gathered the articles in a book, *London Labour and the London Poor*. In that same year, John Hollingshead, who frequently contributed to Dickens' journals, published *Ragged London*. The germ of his book came from ten letters that he had written to the *Morning Post* at the beginning of that year 'in an attempt to beat the bounds of metropolitan dirt and misery'. His chapter on Southwark is entitled 'Over the Water', and he pulls no punches in his graphic description of the grimness of the scenes he had personally witnessed.

Beginning with Jacob's Island in Bermondsey, which he described in very much the same terms as had Dickens, he moved westwards: 'Going towards London Bridge, you can branch off on either side. And visit numerous small courts and alleys, more or less dirty, neglected and degraded.' Although he talks of old housing that had fallen into intense dilapidation, such as 'old black, rotten wooden dwellings chiefly rented by river thieves' in White Hind Alley, when he moves on to the courts around the Skin Market on Bankside, he finds some examples that had recently been constructed. New they may have been, but they were mean in their dimensions:

> There is Pleasant Place, where the rooms are only about three yards wide, the back-yard about three feet square, and the windows not more than two feet and a half square. The court or passage in front is in exact proportion with these dimensions, and the houses stand in three parallel rows with their faces to each other's backs. I stood at the side of one of the end houses, and it seemed to me that I could almost span it with my arms. Each house lets for about four shillings a week, and contains two of these confined rooms.[11]

Thirty years later, the dire state of London's poor was taken up by Charles Booth. A successful businessman, he used some of his wealth to devise and organise one of the most comprehensive social surveys of London life, which appeared in a series of publications. These included poverty maps dating from 1898–99. In these, Booth employed a colour-coding system to indicate the economic composition of streets, running from gold through to black. Gold, reserved for the wealthiest streets of London, does not feature in Southwark, but the next level down, red, representing well-to-do and middle class, delineates Borough High Street and the other principal Southwark highways, along with residential squares such as that of Trinity Church. Behind the main streets the colour turns to pink, fairly comfortable on good ordinary earnings, and light blue, poor, with an income of 18 to 21 shillings per week. Immediately behind one section of the High Street, the alleys and courts of the Mint are shown in dark blue, in chronic want, and black, vicious and semi-criminal.[12] The information for the maps was acquired not by house-to-house surveys, as with the government censuses, but by investigators speaking to experts, such as school board visitors, and local knowledge.

In 1891 Booth published the second volume of his *Life and Labour of the People in London*, in which he looked at the borough of Southwark, among other parts of the capital. In his statistics of poverty, he divided South London into four parts, Central, Eastern, Southern and Western. Central is in essence 'Old Southwark', the parishes of St Saviour's and St Olave's, with a population of approximately 300,000 inhabitants, of whom he estimated 60 per cent were living in poverty, on a par with the East End of London. This contrasted with the outer areas, with places like Lewisham in the Eastern part at 32 per cent, Dulwich in the Southern at 21 per cent and Battersea in the Western at 27 per cent. While the Elephant and Castle is described by Booth as a middle-class hub with a handsome area of shops, the part of Southwark close to the river is depicted as largely industrial. Montague Close, for example, is described as having had in the past 'indifferent good and well inhabited houses' but as having had these superseded by wharves and huge warehouses where 'rats are the only inhabitants'. The men and women working in the riverside industries needed to live nearby because they could not afford to travel, so they were crammed into the courts and alleys, with the overcrowded situation exacerbated by demolitions, along with the influx of poverty-stricken refugees.[13]

Booth also published a series looking at religious influences and assessing various philanthropic enterprises. Southwark had always had charities seeking to alleviate poverty, such as the foundations established by Thomas Cure and Edward Alleyn (p. 93). Their almshouses have not survived, but those built in 1752 as a result of a bequest from Charles Hopton are still to be seen in a street named after him just behind Tate Modern. Hopton was a wealthy fishmonger who never married, so he left money for the building of twenty-six almshouses for 'poor decayed men'. Just as Thomas Cure left detailed instructions on how the recipients of his charity should conduct themselves, so Hopton specified rules, including the banning of the drinking of gin, which had become such a problem in the eighteenth century. The year after Hopton's almshouses were opened, money left by Edward Edwards, a stonemason who had prospered in the building boom as London expanded, was used to help the poor of the parish of Christ Church.

Recognising that one of the best ways out of such poverty was to provide education, Elizabeth Newcomen, a wealthy widow of the parish of St Saviour's, in 1674 had endowed charity schools for boys and girls: her memorial to that effect is to be seen in the transept of the cathedral. More recent projects included that of the Quaker Joseph Lancaster, who at the beginning of the nineteenth century established his first school at a room in Borough Road, open to all faiths and none, and introducing the monitor system. After a shaky start, his venture was reconstituted as the British and Foreign School Society, with its headquarters in the Borough Road.

The concept of providing decent housing for the poor began in the 1840s, but the philanthropic organisations then formed failed to have a lasting impact on the problem, partly because of the lack of legislation at both local and government level. By the 1860s, the housing consisted of a large number of tenements, many dating from more than half a century earlier, along with a smaller number of cottages, again often old. Lodging houses provided accommodation for the lowest paid and casual labourers. However, in that decade two philanthropic organisations began to construct and manage working-class housing for Southwark: the Improved Industrial Dwellings Company (IIDC) and the Peabody Trust.[14]

The philanthropist Sydney Waterlow, who had built up a highly successful printing and stationery business, was particularly interested in the provision of clean water and good housing for London's poor. In 1862 he built at his own expense a block of working-class dwellings in Finsbury. Although these were designed for comfort and let at moderate rents, he managed a good return on his outlay, so he began the IIDC and lobbied for state loans to the company, urging compulsory purchase of land for housing development. In 1864 the

IIDC built the first block of tenements in Southwark, in Red Cross Street. The *South London Press* duly reported:

> a building, which although plain in design, has a deal of interest attached to it, being the improved industrial dwellings for the working classes ... and is now fully occupied by mechanics and their families. Each floor is almost like a house itself, and is furnished with every convenience. It is hoped, while ground remains to be disposed of in this street, that more of these dwellings will be established, giving, as they do, so great a boon to the working classes, hundreds of whom through the improvements in Southwark, and the requirements of the various railway schemes, were forced to leave their dwellings[15]

One such block, with its open stairs and iron balconies, has survived near Cross Bones Graveyard.

George Peabody, a wealthy American banker, began in 1862 to donate funds to be used to improve the lives of the working classes at the discretion of a trust, which decided to concentrate on building houses. To contain building and maintenance costs, and to ensure high density, the design of these dwellings was much plainer than that of those built by IIDC. All designed by Henry Darbishire, they followed a pattern of five to six storeys, with toilet and washing facilities shared between one to four dwellings. According to the rules drawn up by the trust, tenants had to earn less than a set weekly wage, usually 30 shillings. There was to be no sub-letting, washing to be taken in or drunken behaviour, and any sick children had to be sent to a hospital. Peabody Trust dwellings were built in Southwark Street when the new roadway was cut as a direct route from Borough High Street to Blackfriars Road in 1876.

As Martin Stilwell points out in his study of Victorian philanthropists, 'in the case of both Peabody and the IIDC, the target tenant would have been those earning over 20s a week, which left some of the lowest classes to look elsewhere ... the only person seemingly interested in their plight was Octavia Hill'.[16] Hill, a champion of the Open Space movement who was to become one of the founders of the National Trust, purchased her first London property in 1884 in Marylebone. Her work among the poor there inspired the Ecclesiastical Commissioners to ask her to manage their property lying around Redcross Street, now Redcross Way. First, she developed a garden, funded by the Kyrle Society and laid out by gardeners from the Metropolitan Public Gardens Association. Next, a row of houses, Redcross Cottages, was built in the Tudor Revival style, with a community hall, followed by Whitecross Cottages in the Arts and Crafts style in Ayres Street. These represented the embodiment of her belief that the working classes deserved a civilised environment rather than the tenements that were so often their lot. Both rows of cottages have survived, and the garden, all but lost during the Second World War, has now been restored to its Victorian layout.

Charles Booth greatly admired Octavia Hill's work on housing, and she went on to work with him on his great survey. However, he recognised the limitations of philanthropy and of conditional charity and argued that a more coordinated approach was required, including state intervention. He was, for example, one of the proponents of pensions to provide a practical way of alleviating destitution in old age, something to which Octavia Hill was strongly opposed, feeling that a universal application was unjust.

Another man who believed in a coordinated approach to tackling poverty was Anthony Thorold, appointed Bishop of Rochester in 1877. The episcopal map of London was being redrafted, so that he, rather than the Bishop of Winchester, was responsible for the diocese. A great organiser, he encouraged initiatives such as the settlements of public-school missions. Charterhouse, for example, established a mission at Colliers Rents on Great Dover Street, described as 'the belly of the beast' because of its extreme poverty.[17] Interestingly, the first Missioner lived nearby, in the much more salubrious Trinity

Church Square, marked red on Booth's map. Many of the Oxbridge colleges also established settlements in Southwark, including women's colleges such as Lady Margaret Hall. The settlement for Pembroke College Cambridge still operates, offering a wide range of social services.

Thorold also created organisations such as the order of deaconesses, led by Isabella Gilmore, who then went out into the community (p. 154), and began the much-needed restoration of St Saviour's Church, projecting its elevation to a quasi-cathedral. In 1905, ten years after Thorold's death, it became London's second Anglican cathedral, opening a new chapter in Southwark's history.

# 15

# A New Diocese

In 1905, St Saviour's, with the additional dedication of St Mary Overie, became Southwark Cathedral. Anthony Thorold, as noted in the last chapter, had prepared for this transition in his role as Bishop of Rochester.

The survival of the church had been in jeopardy in the early nineteenth century, with those in favour of demolition calling it a folly and a damp old monastery. The conservationists prevailed, however, thanks to the determination of local activist Thomas Saunders, although the Bishop's Chapel to the east of the retrochoir was pulled down for the road to be widened, along with the church of St Mary Magdalene. The Southwark architect George Gwilt, who was particularly interested in the antiquities of the Borough, restored the tower and the choir in the 1820s and created at the east end of the church an elevation of his own invention with lancet windows and a circular window in the gable above. Public subscription enabled the Lady Chapel to be restored, with Gwilt giving his services as an architect 'gratuitously', as Pevsner puts it. In 1841 a makeshift nave was constructed by Henry Rose that caused the architect A.W. Pugin to protest that it was 'as vile a preaching place as ever disgraced the 19th century'.[1]

By the end of the century the church fabric was again badly in need of restoration, so the present nave was built to the designs of Sir Arthur William Blomfield. His father, Charles, as Bishop of London had begun a programme of new ecclesiastical construction in the capital, and Arthur Blomfield was responsible for the design of a considerable list of churches. For St Saviour's he chose appropriately the Gothic Revival style, with the foundation stone laid by the Prince of Wales in 1890. Thorold described Rochester as the Cinderella diocese: history does not record what he thought of the fledgling diocese of Southwark. In 1897 the church became the pro-cathedral of South London, and eight years later Edward Talbot was enthroned as the first Bishop of Southwark.

A reorganisation of the local government of London had taken place in 1889, with the creation of twenty-eight metropolitan boroughs. That of Southwark took in the Borough, Bankside, the Elephant and Castle, Walworth and Newington. This arrangement was to last until 1965, when Southwark was amalgamated with Camberwell and Bermondsey to make the London Borough of Southwark.

In 1905 there was, in fact, already a cathedral in Southwark. To the south, on the Lambeth Road, St George's had been established in 1852 as a cathedral for the Irish community, rapidly rising in numbers with the arrival of navvies to help with the building of the railways. It became one of the first of the returning Roman Catholic dioceses created in England and Wales. Both of the Southwark cathedrals had widely mixed communities, with immigration from all parts of the world that was to continue to increase in the twentieth century.

Although the new diocese of St Saviour and St Mary Overie contained some very leafy areas, such as Dulwich, Blackheath and Lewisham, its immediate precinct was not the gracious close of cathedrals such as Lincoln or Salisbury. Rather, it was quintessentially an inner-city area in the immediate vicinity of the Thames.

It was all too convenient for the City, and later the West End, to consign the smells and discomforts of industry to Southwark. Many of the industries were centuries old, and some were largely small-scale, such as hat-making, for example. In the sixteenth and seventeenth centuries, fashionable hats were made from beaver fur: the top hat worn by one of Richard Humble's wives on the tomb in the cathedral is probably an example (plate VI). Later, silk became the principal material. The bowler hat, which came to be the ubiquitous symbol of the city clerk, was named after Thomas and William Bowler, whose business was located in Southwark Bridge Road. In 1841 it was estimated that there were 3,500 hat-making factories trading in Southwark, many employing women brought down from the Midlands industrial towns. The process in the manufacture involved the use of poisonous mercury that not only endangered the health of workers – 'as mad as a hatter' was not a conceit of Lewis Carroll's – but also threatened the whole community when it was discharged into local watercourses. In his biography of Charles Dickens, John Forster described as unforgettable the smell that emanated from these hat manufactories.

Large-scale businesses included glassworks, soap manufacturers, flour mills and, of course, breweries. The range became even more diverse in the nineteenth century, very often involving noxious elements. Enterprises included Potts and Sarsens vinegar works, taking advantage of the by-product of brewing, Epps Steam Cocoa Mills and the shoe polish factory of Day & Martin. Numerous iron founders provided the items eagerly demanded by the Victorians, from railway equipment to kitchen ranges.

Many businesses were involved in manufacture of foods, such as Pearce Duff, custard makers, Crosse & Blackwell's pickle factory and Hartley's jams. The raw materials for these would be landed at wharves along the south bank, becoming in essence London's larder. Several of the tea and spice warehouses at Cotton Wharf just to the east of London Bridge were destroyed in 1861 in what has been described as the Great Fire of Tooley Street. A massive amount of cotton bales, barrels of tallow and oil also went up in flames, creating a fire that lasted for two weeks. While battling the blaze, the super-intendent of the London Fire Establishment, James Braidwood, lost his life. A memorial to him and to the fire is located on the corner of Tooley Street and Battle Bridge Lane.

At the western edge of Bermondsey was one of the largest manu-factories in South London, the biscuit makers Peek Frean. Their records have survived, giving us a detailed picture of the life of the local community, especially in the twentieth century. The original premises of the tea merchant, James Peek, were located at Dockhead by St Saviour's Dock, which had been developed centuries earlier by the monks of Bermondsey Abbey. Peek had been joined in business by George Hender Frean, a miller and ship's biscuit maker who had married his niece. Yet another serious fire broke out here in 1873, destroying the premises, so the business moved south to an area of 11 acres of former market gardens on Clements and Drummond Roads. The factory developed was so large in scale that it became known as Biscuit Town, with 4,000 employed at the height of the business. Peek Frean was particularly adept at advertising and producing decorative tins of biscuits. Their famous Christmas puddings were stored in the nearby railway arches to achieve an even temperature – a novel use of the railway system that dominated the skyline.

Peek Frean was paternalist in outlook, offering their employees facilities for athletics and drama, a library, and the services of a doctor, dentist and chiropodist were on hand well before the establishment of the National Health Service. Unsurprisingly, there were long-lasting dynasties among the employees, although women were obliged to leave when they got married. By the 1960s, however, the number of employees was in decline, and the factory eventually closed in 1989, with the rabbit warren of buildings eventually rede-veloped into the Tower Bridge Business complex. A rich collection of records, photographs and Peak Frean products can be seen in the Biscuit Museum in a building on the site.[2]

Of vital importance to Peek Frean, along with many other businesses in Bermondsey and Southwark, was access from the docks, provided by the workforce that was employed there. A description of the south bank of the Thames at the beginning of the twentieth century is given in a compilation of life in the capital, *Living London*, published in 1902–3 when the elevation of St Saviour's Church to cathedral status was already in motion. Looking at the working and residential communities, the writer takes his walk 'on a fine morning in June . . . We are standing on London Bridge at a very early hour . . . our route lies along the bank of the Thames towards Blackfriars.' He continues:

> We walk down the stone steps into the Borough Market, which is alive with human beings working hard in the early hours of the morning to supply the vegetable wants of Londoners. We glide off to our right, by the side of St Saviour's Cathedral, through Clink Street, and we find ourselves on Bankside. Here, for a while, we watch the wayside labourers at work. We see them loading a barge with grain. Some of the younger men are of Herculean proportions and have almost the strength of a Samson. The sacks they carry on their backs weigh, on average, two hundredweight and a half. These men heave them with perfect ease, and run along a narrow wooden plank that bends under their weight. The older men, who have to keep pace with the younger ones in life's terrible struggle, groan and grasp under their heavy burdens, but still stagger bravely on. They know only too well from painful experience that once they fail there is no further employment for them in that branch of the labour market.

Our commentator reminds us that this is the land of Shakespeare and the Globe Theatre, but now the site accommodates:

> Poor, dilapidated dwellings . . . Moss Alley, Ladd's Court, Bear Gardens, and White Hind Alley – which abut on the banks of the

river. Hard, indeed, are the lives of the poor families that dwell therein .... The waterside labourer earns a precarious income. Half of the year he is without work. The great struggle for existence presses heavily upon him. When he gets any money he often spends it with absolute recklessness.

Many of the wives have to help the waterside labourer in getting the living, some of them by charing [sic], others by fur-pulling – that is, pulling the fur off rabbit skins – which until recently they did in their own homes, but, now that the ubiquitous sanitary inspector has vetoed it as a home occupation, the women have to perform this work in the factory, where they are unable to get the assistance of the girls of their family.

This factory was located near the centuries-old Skin Market on Bankside, on the site now occupied by the modern Globe Theatre. Here, the rabbit fur would be spun into a fine wool, while the skin went to the hatters.

The precarious nature of their lives is made clear: 'In the winter months many of these poor families are on the verge of starvation, and it is a blessing to them that their children are supplied with free meals through the agency of various funds. But for these meals many of the waterside labourers' children would starve.'[3]

Today, mudlarking on the Thames has become a popular pastime, seeking archaeological remains. For earlier generations, it was a way of supplementing a family's income. Henry Mayhew described how, along with pure-finders who scoured the pavements for the droppings of dogs to be used in leather tanning, young mudlarks gathered lumps of coal or fragments of old iron from the slimy riverside. Half a century later, the commentator for *Living London* noted: 'Along Bankside on a summer's day there are always to be seen a number of boys wading in the mud, and trying to find such treasure as may have fallen into the river during the day or night. Here are a party of lads making their first attempt to swim. Every season a number of them terminate their youthful career in a muddy and watery grave.'

From the people of this world, the commentator turned to the various craft on the Thames, 'from the great iron vessel that is being laden with cargo for a long voyage, to the small skiff in which the waterman plies for hire between the stairs on one side of the river to the other'. As noted earlier, watermen were facing a very uncertain future. The commentator notes, 'Our song writers have told us of the "jolly life of the waterman"', but he makes it clear that they found it difficult to achieve even a bare subsistence:

> At Horsleydown Stairs the men are busy. They are rowing whar-fingers across the stream, and seamen to their ships. A waterman's life is a busy one for a few months of the year. He commences his work early in the morning and ceases late at night. He runs many risks. At times he is in danger of being run down by a passing steamer, or he is run into by a barge and capsized; yet compara-tively few among them can swim. Scarcely a week passes without an inquest on the body of a waterman or lighterman who was drowned while engaged in his daily task.[4]

There was some light relief from this grim existence. At the end of July the Doggett's Coat and Badge Race was held, a competition named after the actor manager Thomas Doggett, who provided in his will at his death in 1715 for a race rowed by young watermen. The competitors were drawn from the Waterman's Company (p. 128) and raced between London Bridge and Cadogan Pier in Chelsea, a gruelling distance of 4.5 miles, for a silver badge. The race continues to this day. Regattas were also held each year at locations along the banks of the Thames from Greenwich through to Bankside. A skiff was offered as first prize, with the winner hoisted into it and drawn along by a wagon in a triumphal procession.

One of the longest-established industries of the area was the tanning of leather, with references made to its manufacture in Bermondsey from the Middle Ages. Charles Knight in his magisterial survey of London, published in 1842, explained: 'Until within the last few years, there were two places used as skin-markets on the Southwark side of the water, one near Blackfriars Road, and the other near the Southwark Bridge Road [on Bankside]: but the tanners and leather-dressers, deeming it desirable to concentrate the whole routine of operations, made arrangement for building the present Leather and Skin Market.'[5] This was the Leather Exchange in Weston Street in Bermondsey, consisting of two rows of buildings, with a central courtyard incorporating some older warehouses. Behind them was a trading area where tanners, curriers and leather-sellers came together in fifty bays or sales stalls.

The Exchange closed in 1912, just three years before the novelist and journalist V.S. Pritchett began to work as an office boy for a firm of leather factors. On his first day, accompanied by his father, he arrived at London Bridge Station from their home in Dulwich, to find:

a yellow fog was coating the rain as we went down the long flights of sour stone stairs into the malodorous yet lively air peculiar to the river of Bermondsey. We passed the long road tunnels under the rail tracks, tunnels which are used as vaults and warehouses convenient to the Pool of London. There was always fog hanging like sour breath in these tunnels .... One breathed the heavy, drugging, beer smell of hops and there was another smell of boots and dog dung: this came from the leather which had been steeped a month in puer or dog dung before the process of tanning. There was also – I seem to be haunted by it at the critical moments of my childhood – the stinging smell of vinegar from a pickle factory; and smoke blew down from an emery mill. Weston Street was a street of leather and hide merchants, leather dressers and

fell-mongers. Out of each brass-plated doorway came either that
oppressive odour of new boots; or, from the occasional little slum
house, the sharp stink of London poverty. It was impossible to
talk for the noise of dray horses striking the cobbles.

Pritchett described how the industry had developed by the early
twentieth century:

The firm was one of the most important factors in the trade . . . .
We – it turned out – were the agents of a very large number of
English tanners and fell-mongers, also of large sheepskin tanners
in Australia, of hide merchants in general and also in dry-salted
South American hides. More rarely, and reluctantly 'we' dealt in
Moroccan and India dressed leather and woolled sheepskins.
There was more money in the raw material. A large part of this
stock was stored in the warehouse attached to the office, but also
in the docks, in the wharves of the Pool of London and in the
cold storages.

He was fascinated by the varied character of the area:

The thing I liked best was being sent on errands in Bermondsey.
They became explorations, and I made every excuse to lengthen
them. I pushed down south to the Dun Cow in the Old Kent
Road, eastward by side streets and alleyways to Tower Bridge. I
had a special pleasure in the rank places like those tunnels and
vaults under the railway: the smells above all made me feel importantly a part of this working London. Names like Wilde's Rents,
Cherry Garden Street, Jamaica Road, Dockhead and Pickle
Herring Street excited and my journeys were not simply street
journeys to me: they were like crossing the desert, finding the
source of the Niger. London was not a city; it was a foreign
country as strange as India and even though I knew the Thames

is a small river compared with the great ones of the world, I would patriotically make it wider and wider in my mind. I liked the Hide Market, where groups of old women and children hung about the hide men who would occasionally flick off a bit of flesh from the hides: the children like little vultures snatched at these bits and put them in their mothers' bags. We thought the children were going to eat these scraps, but in fact it is more likely – money being urgent to all Londoners – they were going to sell them to the glue merchants.[6]

Another vivid picture of Southwark, this time in the 1930s, is provided by the author and artist Grace Golden in her book *Old Bankside*. Grace was born in the East End of London in 1904, but her working-class family moved to the City end of Southwark Bridge Road five years later, and from the top of the house she watched life across the river. As she grew older, she began to make forays at week-ends to Bankside and 'tried my childish pencil on drawings of barges clustered amid stream; barges with furled reddish brown sails; a brightly painted houseboat with lace curtains coquettishly draped back to reveal the potted fern standing in the tiny window; the cranes with complicated lattice work'.[7]

The alleys around the Skin Market fascinated her, although she was horrified at the deprivation:

On one side, a row of two-storied, jerry-built houses; on the other, the crumbling brickwork of half-demolished dwellings. Skeleton roofless rooms are filled with rubbish, old tin baths, bits of broken crockery, soleless boots; a scrap of clothing, caught on the remaining cross-beam of the vanished ceiling flaps in the wind but refuses to be dislodged from its vantage point. A child with bare feet and matted hair crawls out of the open doorway up to the level of the alley. The gas-lit interior – there is no daylight except from the doorway – shows a broken brass bedstead and tumbled bedding. A woman pushes aside the torn lace curtain and rubs a broken window pane. The paleness of her face is repeated by the glimmer of the Sunday morning fire. Down a tributary alleyway there are the pathetic remains of a few square years of fenced-in garden. A shabby bassinet stands in front of the door which leads straight into the living-room. Under and beside the window, fruit and vegetables are stacked against the wall – ready for selling the next day. A wheelbarrow almost closes the passageway.[8]

Southwark had survived the First World War comparatively lightly as far as the built environment was concerned. The one notable air raid on the north part of Southwark came in 1917 when three people were killed at a tea warehouse in Southwark Street. V.S. Pritchett, working in the leather factory in Bermondsey, talks of a Zeppelin raid on Bromley in 1915 and even expresses excitement in seeing maroons going off in an air-raid warning during a packed train journey. However, it came as a shock to him when German aircraft began to be seen over Southwark during daytime. Their bombs in fact hit the area around Billingsgate on the north bank, but this was a warning of what was to come. It was the great number of local men dead and injured from the trenches that hit Southwark. A war memorial in Borough High Street erected in 1924 commemorates the men of St Saviour's, while a bronze memorial mounted on a wall nearby is a reminder of the hopmen of London who gave their lives.

The situation was rather different in the Second World War, for the area of docklands and the railway system presented particular targets for the Luftwaffe. St Peter's Church, which had been built in the mid-nineteenth century on ground in Sumner Street leased from the Bishop of Winchester to the vinegar distiller Potts, was completely destroyed by German bombs in 1940. A particularly devastating night occurred the following February, when a high explosive bomb

burst into a medical aid shelter in one of the railway arches in Stainer
Street near London Bridge Station. A great number of people had
taken refuge here, and 68 died, with 175 injured, many crushed by
the steel doors. The incident is remembered in a plaque at the St
Thomas end of Stainer Street. A bomb hitting Borough Market
destroyed the stained-glass windows commemorating Elizabethan
playwrights in the south aisle of the cathedral. Southwark was to be
one of the most heavily bombed areas in the capital.

Even before the war had ended, the town planner Sir Patrick
Abercrombie was already creating plans for the future of London.
His 1943 London County Plan, which he drew up with J.H. Forshaw,
architect to the London County Council (LCC), proposed that
Southwark's population should be half what it was before the
outbreak of the war, through zoning schemes. Those people who
remained in this inner-city area would be rehoused in blocks of flats.
Along Bankside he envisaged a fringe of trees lining the riverside,
behind which would be a wall of offices and flats, concrete blocks of
medium height set at right angles to each other.[9]

Before any of this could be implemented, it was decided that a
power station should be built on Bankside, in the area that in the
nineteenth century had been earmarked for a railway line and a
bridge to be built across to St Paul's Churchyard (p. 198). Although
that scheme never materialised and was eventually shelved at the
outbreak of the First World War, the buildings in the area had been
allowed to deteriorate. In the 1920s the City of London Electric
Lighting Company built a station with six chimneys, taking in the
Bankside Gas Works that had been erected here in the early nineteenth century. By the 1940s, this needed to be replaced by a more
up-to-date version to provide even greater capacity. As Gillian
Tindall points out, 'You might have supposed, given Abercombie,
the new post-war concern for "zoning" and for the removal of noxious
industries from central London, that plans would be made to site the
new plant anywhere rather than opposite St Paul's .... It was as if the

City were a house and Bankside was its unregarded back door, necessary but beneath attention – or as if the watery space that separated
London from its Surrey side was perceived to be much wider than it
was in reality.'[10]

The architect chosen to design the new Bankside Power Station
was Sir Giles Gilbert Scott, who had already designed the coal-fired
Battersea Power Station and the Anglican cathedral for Liverpool.
His vision for Bankside was very modern, with a soaring chimney,
99 metres in height, described as a brick cathedral. The chimney
could have been even higher but for the fact that it would have
dwarfed Wren's Baroque cathedral across the river. The *Illustrated
London News* sought to calm the storm of protests that arose when
the scheme was published: 'The new power station would have only
one chimney, designed as a "campanile".... Oil-fuel would be used,
delivered by underground pipe-lines from barges discharging at a
small jetty off-shore. Thus there would be no derricks or coal dumps,
nor smoke from the "campanile", which would emit only exhaust
fumes which had been cleaned, washed, and purified prior to reaching
the upper air.'[11]

Construction on Bankside Power Station began in 1948 and
continued until 1963. After all the alarums and excursions, it was
already taking on the character of a white elephant, and it was in
operation only until 1981, when it was abandoned. Its construction,
however, had completely dominated the character of the area. Gone
was Abercrombie's plan for offices and flats, replaced instead by
wharfs and warehouses. Remarkably, four of the original early eighteenth-century houses that once graced the riverside here survived.
One, 49 Bankside, next to Cardinal Cap's Alley, became in 1945 the
home of Malcolm Munthe. When old houses were being demolished along the riverside west at Falcon Stairs, Munthe found in a
skip a plaque that stated that Sir Christopher Wren had lived there
during the construction of St Paul's. He put it up on his own house,
giving birth to the legend that 49 Bankside was once the home of the

great architect: it is the subject of Gillian Tindall's fine book *The House by the Thames*.

In Grace Golden's book, published in 1951, the author expressed a sadness about Abercrombie's plans for new housing on Bankside: 'Braving the frown of the progressive town planner, I admit that I shall regret the loss of alleyways and wharfs whose names and situations have been familiar to Londoners for hundreds of years. But that is the obvious destiny of this strip of river front'. She went on, however, to look at the plans that had been developed for the Festival of Britain: 'Already immediately to its west are gigantic upheavals. The newest ideas in building construction are being used to raise the great concert and exhibition halls for the 1951 Exhibition: and shall we soon gaze from London Bridge at a wide embankment gardens and streamlined blocks of offices and flats?'[12]

When Abercrombie published his plan for the future of London, despite his rather disappointing scheme for tackling the housing problem in the boroughs on the south side of the river, he also included an imaginative proposal that had first been mooted by Herbert Morrison when he was the leader of the LCC in 1935. This was to develop the squalid, run-down area between Westminster and Waterloo Bridge. 'The South Bank should be regenerated as part of London's civic centre and full use made of the river front', Abercrombie announced. He suggested new theatres, a concert hall, an assembly hall, sports facilities, such as a swimming pool, hotels, cafés and restaurants, offices and shops. Further east, in Southwark, there was to be a Shakespearean quarter, with a new Globe Theatre on the site of the original. Southwark Cathedral would be provided with a more worthy setting by the removal of the railway viaducts and the construction of a new railway service underground.[13]

This was an extraordinarily ambitious proposal – rather too ambitious, it transpired, for the time – but a beginning was made by the creation of the Festival of Britain of 1951 and the establishment of the concept of the South Bank. An open letter was sent in September

1945 by Gerald Barry, the editor of the *News Chronicle*, to Sir Stafford Cripps, then President of the Board of Trade. In this, Barry argued for 'a great Trade and Cultural Exhibition to be held in the centenary year of 1851 [the Great Exhibition]'.[14] The Second World War was at an end, but intense austerity gripped the country, and the *Daily Express*, for one, declared it a waste of public money. The Cabinet, however, agreed to the proposal in 1947, and a budget was agreed. Even then, there was opposition, but Herbert Morrison, who had been appointed minister for the festival, refused to countenance postponement.

The site chosen for the festival was derelict land lying partly in the metropolitan borough of Lambeth and partly in that of Southwark. The shallow bank and mud flats had made it suitable for industrial use, rather than residential, but in 1917 the Red Lion Brewery was demolished and the site chosen for the new County Hall to house the LCC. Now an area of 27 acres was to be dedicated to an ambitious exhibition that looked at all aspects of British life, including a Dome of Discovery, an area on the Land and its People, and a reminder of the industrial history of the locality, incorporating the tower of a lead-shot factory. Similar exhibitions were held countrywide, and Battersea Park was transformed into a pleasure garden recalling Vauxhall Gardens from the eighteenth century.

The festival proved a huge success, visited by millions delighted to be informed and entertained, putting aside the years of the war. However, once the Exhibition closed, the festival buildings were demolished, including the Dome of Discovery, the spectacular Skylon obelisk and the venerable shot tower, to make way for the Jubilee Gardens. The concert hall, the Royal Festival Hall, built by the LCC, remained to be part of the South Bank Centre, which grew eventually into the arts and entertainment complex imagined by Abercrombie. Eventually is the key word, for in 1974 the catalogue to an architectural exhibition was to express disappointment that the Festival of Britain did not 'as Morrison and others had hoped it would, help bring the South Bank into London: the South Bank, in spite of its potential, has always been a desolate spot, an industrial slum before the Festival, a car park and the Shell Centre after it ... It has never really succeeded in merging with the West End.'[15]

The Queen Elizabeth Hall and the Purcell Room were built in the 1960s, followed by the Hayward Gallery and the National Theatre in the 1970s, and although great patience had to be exercised, the 'South Bank' concept was firmly established. The term also came to be applied to theology. In 1959 Mervyn Stockwood was made Bishop of Southwark. When he arrived in his diocese, he characterised it as 'hundreds and hundreds of drab streets housing a working class to whom the Church of England means next to nothing, to whom a bishop is as relevant as an Ethiopian ambassador, to whom our liturgy and our gospel are meaningless'. A flamboyant figure both in dress and in speech, Stockwood would frequently refer to the ambassador from Ethiopia without ever having met him. Despite this gloomy assessment, under him the diocese became one of the best known in the Church of England. He embraced the radical wing, for example, encouraging marches against racism and favouring homosexual law reform. He took care to draw Evangelicals into the life of the diocese, sometimes teasing by referring to them as 'Tyndalle men'.[16]

In the same year that he arrived in Southwark, Mervyn Stockwood appointed John Robinson as suffragan Bishop of Woolwich. Together they introduced the idea of the training of worker-priests, described as a theological college without walls, that proved a great success. In 1963 John Robinson published *Honest to God*, drawing upon the work of apparently opposed theologians. Arguing that secular man needs to recognise that the idea of 'God out there' is an outdated simplification of divine nature, he urged that Christians should take as their cue the theology of Paul Tillich and consider God to be 'the ground of our being'. From Deitrich Bonhoeffer he derived his argument that secular man requires a secular theology. These ideas at the time roused enormous interest and controversy, with the book selling over a million copies and translated into seventeen languages. The media coined the phrase 'South Bank religion'.

Stockwood, although liberal in his theological views, was basically orthodox, and according to Robinson's wife, Ruth, he didn't really understand the arguments put forward in *Honest to God*. He was, moreover, drawn to the practices of High Church Anglo-Catholicism, being the first Church of England diocesan bishop to preach at the National Pilgrimage to the shrine of Our Lady of Walsingham. While not being accorded a palace in Southwark, like the medieval Bishops of Winchester, he nevertheless presided with panache over parties at his comparatively modest house in Streatham, with Princess Margaret among his guests. When he retired from Southwark in 1980, the South Bank was now firmly on the map, both artistically and ecclesiastically.

By this time, life on the Thames on both banks was undergoing a radical revolution. At Tilbury in Essex on the estuary of the river, a port was being built for huge container ships that did not require the unloading that had been the traditional way for centuries. As a result, the docks along the Thames and the Pool of London were affected. Ironically, considering the domination that roads and railways had played in the history of Southwark, there was not an adequate transport system to link the container port with the docks, and so they began to close, starting with the East India Dock in 1967, followed by St Katharine's Dock by the Tower of London, the London Dock at Wapping and the Surrey Docks just east of London Bridge in the 1970s. The final closure was the Millwall Dock in 1983.

Much of the trade went to Tilbury, the rest to other coastal ports in Britain and to Rotterdam in the Netherlands, marking the end of London's long history as a major world port. The tradition of the lightermen, dependent on the river wharf trade, also drew to a close. Before the Second World War, there had been around 9,000 lighters on the Thames, a familiar sight moored in the centre of the river awaiting the tugs. Within thirty years this number had halved, and was going down rapidly, so that when a journalist on the *Evening Standard* interviewed a group of lightermen in 1974, he quoted one of them as saying 'now this great God-given east-west highway has been allowed to die'. Southwark and its people were about to enter a new phase of life.

# 16

## Modern Times in Old Southwark

If Wenceslaus Hollar were to set up a topographical glass today in the tower of Southwark Cathedral, what perspective might he choose to depict? He could take in the north bank of the Thames, with the dome of St Paul's Cathedral still just about dominating the skyline, and the several bridges, rail, road and pedestrian, that now link Southwark with the City and the West End. In 2016, in celebration of the 400th anniversary of the publication of Visscher's view (p. 13), the artist Robin Reynolds published just such a perspective.

However, the twenty-first-century Hollar might choose to focus instead on the remarkable riverside life of the south bank of the Thames, stretching along Bankside in one direction and north of Tooley Street on the other, with Borough High Street setting out southwards.

A remarkably prescient observation about this area was made half a century ago, by the writer V.S. Pritchett, in what might be described as a brief biography of the River Thames. He published it in 1974, at a key moment in the history of riverside London when the docks were in the process of being closed. He wrote: 'The river men have always quarrelled with the City, and nowadays the quarrel is with the roads, for road transport is killing the coastwise traffic. Some say that

17. *Robin Reynolds' perspective of the Thames, drawn in 2016 to celebrate the 400th anniversary of a view published by Visscher.*

in fifty years half the area will revert to what it once was: a pleasure ground.'[1]

Redevelopment of the areas formerly occupied by docks was undertaken at a pace. Nicholas Ridley, as Minister for the Environment in Margaret Thatcher's government, was able to write in 1987: 'Take a trip around London's Docklands and see what has happened. In five years it has been transformed from a desert of dereliction to a showpiece of British building design, architecture and business. It has created thousands of jobs by stimulating private enterprise. Homes have been built and refurbished.'[2]

Ridley was, of course, *parti pris*, and this wonderful renaissance was not for all. A quango agency, the London Docklands Development Corporation (LDDC), had been set up in 1980 to tackle the regeneration of the riverside to the south and south-east of London. It was established by Michael Heseltine, Ridley's predecessor as the Minister, financed by a grant from central government and the proceeds from the disposal of land for development. One of its features was that its powers were separate from those of local, democratically elected councils, which in this case was Southwark, with Lewisham and Greenwich on the south bank and Newham and Tower Hamlets on the north. Its undemocratic nature was justified by one of the corporation's executives as 'an extraordinary arrangement for an extraordinary situation, defensible if at all, as a temporary expedient to achieve something special in a short period of time'.[3]

From June 1981 to March 1988, regeneration was achieved by compulsory purchase and by the transfer of land from local authorities for sale to developers at knock-down prices. Thus, as Ridley was to note, the developments often included regeneration of buildings rather than wholesale rebuilding. One such project was to redevelop the area between Tooley Street and the Thames. In 1983 the Government duly gave approval to a scheme proposed by the LDDC for the building of a series of office blocks that provided for the retention of some of the old warehouses, including those of Hay's Wharf.

The founding of Hay's Wharf had come in 1651 when Alexander Hay acquired a former brewhouse alongside a small inlet from the Thames. Warehousing became its business in the following century, when customs authorities allowed goods such as tobacco to be stored here on payment of a percentage of the import duty. If the product was then exported, the duty was repaid, a scheme known as sufferance. Hay's was just one of a number of such warehouses that lined this part of the south bank of the river. In the nineteenth century it became the leading wharf for the reception of tea from China, with the clippers able to moor in the inlet. Although Hay's Wharf was damaged in the Great Fire of Tooley Street in 1861 (pp. 224–5) and suffered bomb damage in the Second World War, the imposing Victorian buildings were converted into loft-style apartments and shops, with the inlet filled in, and opened as Hay's Galleria in 1987.

Another example of regeneration was the transformation of Hartley's Jam Factory on Green Walk, off Tower Bridge Road. The factory was built by the wonderfully named philanthropist Sir William Pickles Hartley and opened in 1901. The site had previously been a tannery, a reminder of which is provided by the local public house, the Jolly Tanners, and a linoleum factory. Hartley's factory was built to the most modern standards of health, safety and convenience, while the workers were paid more than those of his competitors. Remarkably, female employees were particularly well paid. The factory closed in 1975, but the buildings were reconstituted as a complex of offices, restaurants and modern apartments, with the top floor of the blocks, where women used to sort and grade the summer fruits, now transformed into penthouses. The one striking reminder of the factory's previous existence is a high chimney stack declaring 'Hartleys' in bold white letters.[4]

Some of the new apartments created by the LDDC initiatives became the residences of 'yuppies', the term coined for young and fashionable middle-class professionals with well-paid jobs, often in offices rising at Canary Wharf across the river on the Isle of Dogs. Their living conditions in Southwark stood in marked contrast to local residents in the social housing blocks of flats that had been provided by the former London County Council. Many tenement blocks were built during the late nineteenth century, and there was a rapid public housing programme after the First World War, but this largely took place in the southern part of the borough, in Camberwell, Eltham, Lewisham and Merton. In the 'inner city' part of the borough the social housing was provided, in the words of the architectural historian Nikolaus Pevsner, as 'lumpy' flats of no more than five storeys, solidly built, although not as austere as the nineteenth-century tenements.

A survey conducted in 1996 found that at least half of the population of Southwark had not reaped any benefits from the millions poured into regeneration by the LDDC. The houses and shops that had featured in the street perspectives produced in the early Victorian period by John Tallis (p. 214) along Borough High Street were now turned into office developments. No council housing was built in Southwark during the 1990s because the council was stymied by lack of finance as a result of the Tories' Right to Buy policy for council houses, which prevented local authorities from using the money thus accrued to build further properties.

The political composition of Southwark Borough Council in the last four decades of the twentieth century experienced a series of twists and turns. Old Labour in the 1960s was followed by Militant Labour in the 1970s and 1980s and a significant shift to very New Labour in the 1990s, actively encouraging gentrification.

These years inevitably witnessed conflicts of interest in Southwark between the council and some of the schemes for regeneration. Sir Patrick Abercrombie's radical proposal back in 1943 that Southwark Cathedral should be accorded a more worthy setting by the removal of the railway viaducts (p. 235) proved an ideal that could not be achieved, and indeed the railway was to tighten its coil over Borough

Market. However, his suggestion that the south bank 'extending on the front as far as London Bridge and inland to York Road, Stamford Street and Southwark Street might well include a great cultural centre, embracing amongst other features, a modern theatre, a large concert hall and the headquarters of various organisations' offering a major potential amenity for all of London had fired the imagination of the American actor and director, Sam Wanamaker. In his report, Abercrombie had specifically made the connection with Shakespeare and the Globe by reproducing a detail of the Elizabethan theatres on Bankside from Hollar's *Long View* of 1647.[5]

It has been suggested that Wanamaker's stage debut as a teenager playing in a replica in plywood and paper of the Globe Theatre at the Chicago World Fair in 1934 provided the damascene moment for his devotion to Shakespeare and his theatre. In 1952, putting the Atlantic Ocean between himself and the political witch hunt being conducted by Senator Joe McCarthy, he arrived in London as a jobbing actor. He soon sought out the site of the Elizabethan Globe, expecting it to be fittingly commemorated, only to find a blackened plaque in the wall of the bottling plant of the Anchor Brewery. Two decades later he created the Globe Playhouse Trust, which became the Shakespeare Globe Trust, and determined that he would recreate the theatre. It was not to be a primrose path. He faced opposition from members of his own profession, who considered him 'an upstart crow', in the words applied by the Elizabethan dramatist Robert Greene to William Shakespeare. There was also an element of academic snobbery, with *The Times* dubbing his vision as 'Falstaffland' and, as an American, recreating a world of Walt Disney.

Wanamaker's most difficult relationship, however, was with the local council. Initially, it seemed that Southwark Council would approve his scheme, and an agreement was reached for the trust to buy a site on Bankside: a disused Georgian warehouse in Bear Gardens along with two properties in Rose Alley. A development company became involved and plans were drawn up. But in 1982 the

Old Left councillors who had been in control for many years were being superseded by a younger generation with more militant views. A body calling itself the North Southwark Community Group decided that a new Globe would be contrary to the needs of the traditional working-class community. As Gillian Tindall points out, 'they had apparently failed to notice that two-thirds of the working population had already moved out to places further south such as Eltham, Penge and Merton, and that any further threat to the borough would not come from history-lovers but from private property developers with their eyes on waterfront sites'.[6] One claim from the group was that the site was wanted for low-income housing – all well and good, but impractical both physically, because of the proximity of the river, and financially, because the council lacked funds. Another objection advanced rather weakly argued that the site could not be developed because it was currently in use as a yard and store for the barrows and brooms of the street sweepers.

The Globe Trust took the council to court for reneging on their agreement, and in June 1986 the case reached the High Court, who found in favour of Wanamaker. Although the council threatened a further appeal, the case was already proving very costly, at more than £9 million. Moreover, a local poll recorded substantial support for rebuilding the Globe. Remains of the original Elizabethan theatre were found three years later on the former site of the Anchor Brewery, and those of Alleyn and Henslowe's Rose further west, by Southwark Bridge, kindling great interest in the subject.

In 1969 Wanamaker had met Theo Crosby, the South African-born designer and architect, and together they worked on the plan to reconstruct the Globe. Is it just coincidence that two men from distant parts of the world should be the initiators of such an ambitious project concerning Shakespeare? Wanamaker's original concept of the modern Globe was that it should be a drum-like structure. It was Crosby who convinced Wanamaker that the new theatre should be as exact a replica as possible, and that only authentic materials should be used in its construction. Thatch for roofing, which had of course caused the demise of the Elizabethan theatre (p. 118), was to be used for the first time in London since the Great Fire of 1666. The type of reeds chosen were based upon samples found during the excavation of the Elizabethan Globe. Green oak was cut and fashioned using sixteenth-century methods, while the laths and staves supporting the lime plaster were covered with the lime wash made up from a contemporary recipe. When the remains of the original theatre and of the Rose began to be uncovered, it was discovered that these buildings were polygonal, and Crosby eventually decided that the new Globe should be twenty-sided (plate XVI).

Wanamaker had his detractors, but his charisma enabled him to secure the interest and support of the great and the good of the theatrical world: Judi Dench, John Gielgud and Anthony Hopkins, to name but three. A truly memorable occasion came in 1974 when a service in Southwark Cathedral was held to open a week of events to celebrate Shakespeare's birthday. The oration, 'In Honour of Shakespeare', was delivered by Alf Garnett, the ranting right-wing bigot from Johnny Speight's television series, *Till Death Us Do Part*, as performed by Warren Mitchell. From the pulpit he declared, 'Old Shakespeare would turn in his grave if he knew what they was doing with his theatre. Hot bed of Communism. Innit?'[7]

The Duke of Edinburgh had early declared himself a supporter of Wanamaker's project, and once credibility had been demonstrated, he played a public role. The theatre was opened for 'workshop' and 'prologue' seasons in 1995 and 1996, and then finally formally by Queen Elizabeth II in 1997. As was pointed out at the time, it was an irony worthy of Shakespeare's tragedies that Sam Wanamaker died in December 1993 before he could enjoy the fulfilment of his dream. Theo Crosby likewise did not see its completion, passing away the following autumn.

Sam Wanamaker's contribution to the theatrical life of Southwark is remembered by a memorial tablet just to the right of the Shakespeare

Window in the south aisle of the cathedral, and in the name of the playhouse next to the Globe. Based on early seventeenth-century plans for an indoor theatre, the Sam Wanamaker Playhouse gives the audience the experience that would have been enjoyed at the Burbages' Blackfriars and at Jacobean court entertainments lit by candlelight. The project, begun in 2012, was completed two years later, compared to the long gestation that had dogged the Globe, an indication of how attitudes to Bankside entertainment had changed.

To the west of the Globe complex stands the soaring modernist building that now houses Tate Modern. Its transformation from a power station into a gallery devoted to art was not an entirely easy one, however. As noted earlier, Giles Gilbert Scott's grandiloquent Bankside Power Station, completed in 1963, was all too soon an anachronism and closed in 1981. Discussion about the development of the prime site included the building of an opera house, proposed by Theo Crosby: his design resembled a *schloss* on the Rhine. Crosby also proposed that a footbridge should be built across the Thames, linking the south bank to the area around St Paul's Cathedral.

The *schloss* remained a pipe dream, because the conservation movement was gathering momentum, with the Twentieth Century Society campaigning against the idea of demolishing the power station. Francis Carnwath, then the Deputy Director at the Tate, went in 1993 to see Bankside in his position as Chairman of the London Advisory Committee for English Heritage. By chance, his visit coincided with a BBC television crew making a programme for the *One Foot in the Past* series. As Carnwath left the building, he was asked for his view on its architectural merit by the architectural historian Gavin Stamp, who then suggested it would make a wonderfully appropriate gallery to house the modern art of the Tate.

On his return to Millbank, Carnwath described the Bankside to Nicholas Serota, the Curator of the Tate, whose first reaction was that the building would prove impossibly large. However, on his way home, he visited Bankside and estimated by counting his steps as he walked round the power station just how big it was, reckoning that it was just about on a par with the gallery on Millbank. As a result, the Trustees of the Tate opened negotiations with the station's owners, Nuclear Electric, and with Southwark Council. Visiting Bankside in July of that year, the Trustees were bowled over not only by the potential of the space but also by its position, immediately across the river from St Paul's Cathedral. Perhaps they were aware of Theo Crosby's vision of a footbridge linking the two banks, for they real- ised that a Bankside Tate could be reached within minutes from the City of London.

Southwark Council was also excited by the idea, well aware of the high unemployment within Borough and the over-provision of offices, estimated at 20 per cent. A survey taken in 1992, when a new broom had swept through the council, discovered that the majority of 3,000 households that were interviewed supported the idea of a major educational or exhibition space. The council agreed to put funding towards the initial development.

However, there was also local opposition. The director of the Southwark Environment Trust did not mince his words when he wrote to the *Independent* in November 1993: '[The power station] presents a vertical acre of the ugliest-ever bricks to the City and to the river, unredeemed by any masterful detailing. Despite some art deco styling, previously associated with high spirits, the building still casts a miasma of depression.' He went on to declare, 'Its construc- tion was a disaster in urban planning, which its retention perpetu- ates', before ending with a flourish: 'How backward-looking, how necrophiliac; how very Britain of the Nineties.'

Among those who responded was a correspondent who begged to differ: 'Refurbished, cleaned and lit in the same dramatic manner as the Lloyds building, Bankside would make a stunning beacon of culture among the commercial dross of that part of the Thames . . . Let the Tate have Bankside, and rejuvenate an awe-inspiring building to provide some much-needed refinement to the Southwark desert.'[8] The local community, once more being consulted, also supported the idea of the new Tate, and Southwark duly offered substantial financial help.

It was decided that the original Millbank gallery would become Tate Britain, showing British art from the 1500 to the present, while the Bankside site would house a new gallery of international modern and contemporary art as Tate Modern. Nicholas Serota succeeded in securing funds from a range of private sources to make up a shortfall of the final cost of £135 million, and the conversion on Bankside began in June 1995. All the power station machinery was removed, along with the roofs of the boiler house and turbine hall. The work was completed five years later, with the former boiler house becoming the Tate Modern galleries and the turbine hall, a dramatic space 500 feet long and 100 feet high, giving a home for specially commissioned pieces by contemporary artists. For the inaugural exhibition, Louise Bourgeois provided a giant bronze spider. To link Tate Modern on the south bank with St Paul's Cathedral on the north, the Millennium Bridge was designed by Norman Foster, Anthony Caro and Ove Arup.

The two renowned cultural venues, the Globe Theatre and Tate Modern, have provided Southwark's riverside with an immense draw for residents of London and visitors from all over the world, forming part of a 'necklace' of attractions that can be accessed by the Jubilee Walk. This was created to celebrate Queen Elizabeth II's Silver Jubilee in 1977 to connect many of London's major tourist attractions in a series of loops.

The eastern loop starts at Tate Modern and moves east along the Thames to Tower Bridge. A short diversion leads to Southwark Cathedral and Borough Market, while a replica of the *Golden Hinde* is berthed in St Mary Overie Dock. This is a fully working copy of Sir Francis Drake's famous ship, in which he circumnavigated the globe in three years from 1577. When Drake returned to Plymouth in triumph in September 1580, Queen Elizabeth I knighted him on deck, and the *Golden Hinde* became the first museum ship when she decreed that it should be preserved at Deptford to enable the public to visit. Remarkably, the ship survived for nearly a century before rotting and being broken up.

As the Jubilee Walk passes under London Bridge, visitors can take more short diversions to enjoy the mixed pleasures of the Clink Prison Museum and the London Bridge Experience, reminders of the harshness of authority here in past centuries. To the east of the bridge, public houses, restaurants and shops are to be found around Hay's Galleria, along with HMS *Belfast*, a Town Class light cruiser that was launched in 1938 and supported the Normandy landings during the Second World War. It is now part of the Imperial War Museum.

Resonances of 'Old Southwark' are everywhere along the riverside bank, and more are to be found to the south along Borough High Street, still an important exit from central London, although the inns have, with the sole exception of the George, been replaced by shops and offices. These include, on the east side, the campus of King's College London, supporting the medical expertise of Guy's Hospital. A reminder that this area was the theatrical heartland of Elizabethan London are the Bridge Theatre in Potter's Field by Tower Bridge, the Menier Chocolate Factory in Southwark Street and the Southwark Playhouse, which is located near to Newington Butts, where the first playhouse was opened south of the river. Another reminder are the performances given by the Lions part (*sic*), a group of professional actors, in a range of venues, including the Globe Theatre and Borough Market (plate X).

Inevitably, for an inner-city area, not all the resonances are entirely happy. As ever, Old Southwark has a mixed community. The many immigrants echo the groups who came here over the centuries to find religious liberty and for employment. While the apartments that look out over the Thames are mainly occupied by the comfortably off, social housing is not in great supply in the northern part of the borough, despite the fact that Southwark has the greatest proportion in England.[9] The dearth in Old Southwark is due to a variety of factors, from railway development in the nineteenth century to zoning policies in the twentieth. The majority of such properties are now located further south, such as the Heygate and Aylesbury estates at the Elephant and Castle.

The dire poverty that beset many in the community from the late eighteenth century onwards, as eloquently described by Dickens and Mayhew, among others, is thankfully no longer with us in quite the same squalid and desperate form. However, the rise in demand for foodbanks, the inadequacy of housing provision and the growth in low-paid, insecure employment are potent reminders that these problems have not yet been solved. There is still a demand to provide accommodation and help for the old, the needy and those in distress. The St Saviour's Charity established at the Reformation with generous donations from men like Thomas Cure and Edward Alleyn continues to operate, now as United St Saviour's after taking in Hopton's almshouses, and is building a new almshouse in Bermondsey. The bequest of the early eighteenth-century stone mason, Edward Edwards, is run by the Trustees of Southwark Charities based near to Blackfriars Road, with plans to redevelop the site to more than double the number of homes including communal space for both residents and neighbours. The Clerk of the Trustees, Chris Wilson, points out that while the original benefactors of charity in Southwark lived side by side with those in need, there is a degree of separation today. The need for such provision nevertheless is still very much with us.[10]

The annual service of regret, remembrance and restoration held at Cross Bones Graveyard by the Dean of Southwark is a reminder of the members of the community who were outcasts (p. 69). Coming into the twenty-first century, there is one outcast who has achieved extraordinary celebrity: a cat. Doorkins was a stray on the streets of Southwark when she sought shelter within the cathedral, and was given her name as she could be found waiting every morning by the entrance.

Doorkins the Magnificat duly gained sanctuary, but in June 2017 a terrorist attack took place in Borough Market. Three occupants of a van driven over London Bridge began to stab people in and around the restaurants and public houses. They were what were described as radical terrorists, and ISIS subsequently claimed responsibility. In all, eleven people were killed, including the terrorists, shot dead by the police. Amid the horror and panic of the situation, the area was closed down, and Doorkins found the doors of the cathedral shut. When she eventually gained entrance, she never left, eventually suffering a decline in health and dying in 2020.

The tragedy of the Borough Market attack is reminiscent of the darker side of Southwark's history: a reminder of the religious conflicts and violence of previous centuries. This is part of the story, but the broader, wider story tells us of tales of ambition, imagination and great achievements culturally and socially. One major difference, however, between modern 'Old Southwark' and that of past centuries is that it is no longer the disregarded back door of the City, but rather an integral part of the vibrant heartland of London. Today, as visitors from all over the world make their way across the Thames, we can celebrate this fundamental change and look forward to the story continuing to evolve, to intrigue and to fascinate.

# ENDNOTES

## Chapter 1 Setting the Scene

1. Richard Coates in Richard Coates and Andrew Breeze, *Celtic Voices, English Places: Studies of the Celtic Impact on Place Names in England*, Shaun Tyas, 2006, pp. 22 and ff.
2. Jack Blackburn, *The Times*, 14 June 2023.
3. John Stow, *Survey of London*, vol. 2, reproduced from the 1603 text and edited by Charles Lethbridge Kingsford, Clarendon Press, 1971, p. 56.
4. 'The True History of the Life and Sudden Death of Old John Overs, the Rich Ferry-Man of London, Shewing How he Lost his Life by his own Covetousness. And of his Daughter Mary, Who Caused the Church of St Mary Overs in Southwark to be Built; and of the Building of the London Bridge', first published in 1637.
5. Stow, *Survey of London*, vol. 2, p. 56.
6. Martha Carlin, *Medieval Southwark*, Amberley, 1996, p. xxiii.
7. David J. Johnson, *Southwark and the City*, OUP, 1969, p. 42.
8. An engraved stone plaque in the south aisle of the cathedral was installed in 1977 by Czech exiles to celebrate the anniversary of Hollar's death in 1677, and the reinstatement of their nationhood, first from the Austro-Hungarian Empire, and then from the Soviet Union. It is accompanied by a verse written in the eighteenth century by George Vertue, a great admirer of Hollar's art:

> The works of Nature and of Man,
> By thee perceived, take Life again;
> And ev'n thy PRAGUE serenely shines,
> Secure from Ravage by thy Lines,
> In just Return this Marble Frame
> Would add some Agest to thy Name:
> Too frail, alas! 'tis forced to own,
> Thy SHADOWS will outlast the STONE

## Chapter 2  London Bridge is Falling Down

1. Bede, *A History of the English Church and People*, trans. Leo Sherley-Price, Penguin Classics, 1955, p. 103.
2. See Marc Morris, *The Anglo-Saxons: A History of the Beginnings of England*, Penguin, 2021, pp. 224 and ff.
3. Morris, *The Anglo-Saxons*, p. 353.
4. Snorre Sturlason, *Heimskringla*, ed. E. Monsen and A.H. Smith, W. Heffer & Sons, 1932, pp. 223–5, quoted in David J. Johnson, *Southwark and the City*, OUP, 1969, p. 6.
5. See Jan Ragnar Hagland and Bruce Watson, 'Fact or Folklore: the Viking attack on London Bridge', *London Archaeologist*, spring 2005.
6. Quoted by Rachel Holdsworth, 'How the King of Norway pulled down London Bridge', *The Londonist*, 19 February 2013.
7. Frank Barlow (ed. and trans.), *The Life of King Edward Who Rests at Westminster*, 2nd edn, OUP, 1992, pp. lxxiii–lxxvii.
8. Hagland and Watson, 'Fact or Folklore', p. 331.
9. Charles Dickens, *Oliver Twist*, Chapter XLVI.

## Chapter 3  Mansions of Southwark

1. Johnson, *Southwark and the City*, p. 19.
2. Quoted in C. Paul Christianson, *The Riverside Gardens of Thomas More's London*, Yale University Press, 2005, p. 42.
3. Martha Carlin, 'The Urban Development of Southwark, c. 1200 to 1550', unpublished PhD dissertation, University of Toronto, 1983, p. 355.
4. The accounts are kept in the Corporation of London's Records Office. Details of these are given in Christianson, *The Riverside Gardens of Thomas More's London*, p. 202, footnote 7.
5. MS BHA, vol. 6 (1525–41), fol. 93v.
6. MS BHA, vol. 6 (1525–41), fol. 93v.
7. Other 'Midsummer Men' included mugwort and plantain. See Margaret Willes, *The Domestic Herbal: Plants for the Home in the Seventeenth Century*, Bodleian Library, 2020.
8. Stow, *Survey of London*, vol. 1, p. 101; John Parkinson, *Theatrum Botanicum*, 1640, p. 729.
9. The sketch is in the Ashmolean Museum in Oxford.

## Chapter 4  On the Road to Canterbury

1. The analysis of *Speculum Meditantis*, along with *Vox Clamantis* and *Confessio Amantis*, is principally drawn from the entry on John Gower by Douglas Gray in the *Oxford Dictionary of National Biography*, 2004.
2. See John H. Fisher, *John Gower, Moral Philosopher and Friend of Chaucer*, Methuen, 1965, p. 171.
3. G.C. Macaulay (ed.), *The Complete Works of John Gower*, 4 vols, 1899–1902, Clarendon Press, vol. 1, p. 2.
4. Details of Gower's will are translated by Martha Carlin in Chapter 1 of Stephen Rigby (ed.), *Historians on John Gower*, Boydell & Brewer, 2019.

5. Caroline Spurgeon, *Five Hundred Years of Chaucer Criticism and Allusion*, 3 vols, CUP, 1925, vol. 1, pp. 16 and 34.
6. Harvard's Geoffrey Chaucer website, General Prologue.
7. The identification of the Knight with Sir John Hawkwood is proposed by Terry Jones in *Chaucer's Knight: The Portrait of a Medieval Mercenary*, Methuen, 1985.
8. See Melvin Bragg, *The Adventure of English: The Biography of a Language*, Hodder & Stoughton, 2003, Chapter 6.
9. Translation in Fisher, *John Gower*, p. 281.
10. I am grateful to Mary Chisholm and her website, 'Exploring Building History'.
11. F.J. Furnivall and W.G. Stone (eds), *The Tale of Beryn*, London, 1887.
12. Julian Munby, 'Zacharias's: A 14th-century Oxford New Inn', *Oxoniensia*, 57, 1992, pp. 305–6.
13. N.F. Blake, *William Caxton and English Literary Culture*, The Hambledon Press, 1991, p. 121 (Spurgeon, *Five Hundred Years of Chaucer*, vol. 1, p. 37); Fisher, *John Gower*, p. 8.

## Chapter 5  The Bishop's Geese

1. St Augustine, *De Ordine*, Book 2, Chapter 4; St Thomas Aquinas, *Summa theologica*, translated in Gamini Salgado, *The Elizabethan Underworld*, Sutton, 2005, p. 36.
2. Carlin, *Medieval Southwark*, pp. 215 and ff.
3. Stow, *Survey of London*, vol. 2, pp. 54–5.
4. Gillian Tindall, *The House by the Thames: And the People Who Lived There*, Chatto & Windus, 2006, p. 24.
5. Charles Wriothesley, *A Chronicle of England during the Reign of the Tudors from AD 1485 to 1559*, ed. W.D. Hamilton, vol. 2, Camden Society, 1875, p. 4.
6. J.M. Cowper (ed.), *Selected Works of Robert Crowley*, pp. 13–14, quoted in Carlin, *Medieval Southwark*, p. 227, footnote 80.
7. PRO SP12/125, fol. 42.
8. Donald Lupton, *London and the Countrey Carbonadoed*, 1632.
9. Ben Jonson, *Epigrammes*, CXXXIII, 'The Famous Voyage'.
10. Quoted in Jessica A. Browner, 'Wrong Side of the River: London's Disreputable South Bank in the Sixteenth and Seventeenth Century', *Essays in History*, vol. 36 (1994), p. 20.
11. Ben Jonson, 'An Execration Upon Vulcan'.
12. Shakerley Marmion, *Holland's Leaguer*, Act IV, Scene 3.
13. R.C. Latham and W. Matthews (eds), *The Diary of Samuel Pepys*, Bell & Hyman, 1974, vol. 9, 25 March 1668, p. 132.
14. Stephen Gosson, 'The School of Abuse', quoted in Browner, 'Wrong Side of the River', p. 21.
15. Samuel Pepys, *The Diary of Samuel Pepys*, vol. 4, 3 August 1663, pp. 262–2.
16. Stow, Survey of London, vol. 2, p. 55.
17. My thanks to Lucy Coleman Talbot for pointing this out.
18. John Constable's *Southwark Mysteries* was published in 1999 by Oberon Books.

## Chapter 6  Spreading the Word

1. Quoted by David Daniell, *The Bible in English*, Yale University Press, 2003, p. 75.
2. John Foxe, *Foxe's Book of Martyrs*, 1563, vol. 2, p. 366.
3. Details of Nicolson's career and of his Coverdale Bible are given by Peter W.M. Blayney in *The Stationers' Company and the Printers of London, 1501–1557*, vol. 1, CUP, 2013, pp. 348–51.
4. Another Southwark glazier, Francis Williamson, seems to have worked with Nicolson at his printshop and to have imported books.
5. Quoted by J.F. Mozley, *Coverdale and his Bibles*, Lutterworth Press, 1953, pp. 122–3.
6. Foxe, *Foxe's Book of Martyrs*, vol. 6, p. 611.
7. Daniell, *The Bible in English*, p. 439.
8. Marianne Dorman (ed.), *The Liturgical Sermons of Lancelot Andrewes*, vol. 1, Pentland, 1992, Gonville & Caius website.
9. P.E. McCullough, *Oxford Dictionary of National Biography*, 2008.
10. House of Lords Record Office, main papers, June 1641.
11. Quoted in T.P. Stevens, *The Story of Southwark Cathedral*, Sampson Low, n.d., p. 18.
12. William Bisset, *The Modern Fanatick: With a Large and True Account of the Life, Actions, Endeavours . . . of the Famous Dr Sach—l*, 1710, p. 1.
13. Henry Sacheverell, *The Perils of False Brethren, both in Church and State: Set Forth in a Sermon Preach'd before the Right Honourable the Lord-Mayor, Aldermen, and Citizens of London, at the Cathedral-Church of St Paul, on 5 November 1709*, 1709, A2, 8–9, 23. Ironically, Henry Sacheverell's maternal grandfather was reputedly a signatory of the death warrant of Charles I.

## Chapter 7  A Mixed Community

1. Browner, 'Wrong Side of the River', p. 1.
2. Translated in *Schools Inquiry Commission*, vol. 2, Misc Papers (1868) 73–6. It has been adapted by Alan H. Nelson, the University of California, Berkeley.
3. Cited in Jeremy Boulton, *Neighbourhood & Society: A London Suburb in the 17th Century*, CUP, 1987, p. 93.
4. The token books are now in the LMA archives, P92/SAV/1314–7. An interim search site is at tokenbooks.folger.edu, ed. William Ingram and Alan H. Nelson.
5. C.H. Sneyd (ed.), *A Relation of the Island of England about the year 1500*, Camden Society XXXVII, 1847, p. 43. This was probably written by the secretary to the Venetian Ambassador, Francesco Capello.
6. Details from Carlin, *Medieval Southwark*, pp. 165–6.
7. Carola Hicks, *The King's Glass: A Story of Tudor Power and Secret Art*, Chatto & Windus, 2007, opposite p. 87.
8. Blayney, *The Stationer's Company and the Printers of London*, vol. 1, p. 348.
9. Kieron Taylor, Ian Betts and Roy Stephenson (eds), *London's Delftware Industry: The Tin-Glazed Pottery Industries of Southwark and Lambeth*, Museum of London Archaeology Service, 2008, Section 8.

10. Philip Stubbes, *Anatomy of Abuses*, 1583, p. 10.
11. Miranda Kaufmann, *Black Tudors: The Untold Story*, OneWorld, 2017, Chapter 5.
12. Thomas Dekker, *The Wonderfull Yeare*, 1603, sig. D1r. Quoted in Kaufmann, p. 128. It was used as the model for Daniel Defoe's *Journal of the Plague Year*.
13. James Balmford, *A Short Dialogue Concerning the Plagues Infection*, 1603, A2r.
14. Boulton, *Neighbourhood & Society*, pp. 111 and ff.

### Chapter 8 Entertaining London

1. *Calendar of Patent Rolls*, 1547–48, p. 249.
2. Details from R.A. Foakes and R.T. Rickert (eds), *Henslowe's Diary*, CUP, 1961, f. 74v (p. 146) and f. 59 (p. 115). The original diary, discovered in the late eighteenth century, is in Dulwich College Library.
3. Edward Guilpin, *England's Parnassus*, 1600, Sig B.2b.
4. The National Archives, PRO, SP12/285, fol. 149v.
5. Quoted by Edmund Malone in *The Plays and Poems of William Shakespeare*, 1821, p. 49.
6. Platter and Weever quoted in James Shapiro, *A Year in the Life of William Shakespeare, 1599*, Faber & Faber, 2005, pp. 169–70. Weever was the author of *Epigrammes in the Oldest Cut and Newest Fashion, ad Gulielmum Shakespear*.
7. William Shakespeare, *The Winter's Tale*, Act IV, Scene 3.
8. L. Grenade, *The Singularities of London, 1578*, ed. Derek Keene and Ian W. Archer, London Topographical Society, 2014, pp. 89–90. A splendid model of the bridge is to be seen in the church of St Magnus the Martyr.
9. Margaret Spufford, *Small Books and Pleasant Histories*, CUP, 1985, pp. 114–5.
10. These examples are taken from Dorian Gerhold, *London Bridge and its Houses, c.1209–1761*, London Topographical Society, 2019.
11. Quoted in Shapiro, *A Year in the Life of William Shakespeare*, p. 170.
12. Nicholas Rowe, *Works I*, J. Darby, 1728, pp. viii–ix.
13. A letter from Sir Henry Wotton, 2 July 1613, in Logan Pearsall Smith (ed.), *The Life and Letters of Sir Henry Wotton*, vol. 2, Clarendon Press, 1907, pp. 32–3.
14. Latham and Matthews, *The Diary of Samuel Pepys*, vol. 7, 14 August 1666, pp. 245–6. E.S. de Beer (ed.), *The Diary of John Evelyn*, Clarendon Press, 1955, 16 June 1670, vol. 3, p. 549.
15. Latham and Matthews, *The Diary of Samuel Pepys*, vol. 8, 27 May 1667.
16. William Shakespeare, *The Tempest*, Act IV, Scene 1.

### Chapter 9 Brave New World

1. Shakespeare, *The Tempest*, Act V, Scene 1.
2. The Second Virginian Charter, 1609, from the website 'American History from Revolution to Reconstruction and Beyond', http://www.let.rug.nl.
3. Anon, 'Londons Lotterie', 1612, English Broadside Ballad Archive, 20085.
4. The details of Margaret Dauson and other maids who went to America are taken from Jennifer Potter, *The Jamestown Brides: The Bartered Wives of the New World*, Atlantic Books, 2018.

5. Martin Parker, 'The wiving age, Or A great complaint of the Maidens of London', 1627?, English Broadside Ballad Archive, 20178.
6. Lawrence Price, 'The Maydens of Londons brave adventures, Or A Boon Voyage intended for the Sea', London, printed for Francis Grove on Snow-hill, 1623–61, English Broadside Ballad Archive, 30869.
7. The Southwark members of the Brownist church are identified in Graham Taylor, *The Mayflower in Britain: How an Icon was Made in London*, Amberley, 2020, pp. 48–57.
8. William Shakespeare, *Twelfth Night*, Act 3, Scene II.
9. Taylor, *The Mayflower in Britain*, pp. 177–82.
10. From Thomas Fuller, *History of Cambridge*, 1655.

## Chapter 10 Medical Matters

1. Quoted in 'The Old Operating Theatre Museum - The History of St Thomas' Hospital', Part 1, Medieval, p. 1, www.thegarret.org.uk.
2. 'The Old Operating Theatre Museum', p.4.
3. BL Egerton MS 1995, fol. 86v.
4. *Calendar of Patent Rolls*, 1550–53, pp. 130–1.
5. While St Thomas's Hospital and Christ's Hospital have retained their names, Bridewell eventually evolved into a school and is now called King Edward's School, Witley. I am grateful to Susan Mitchell for this information. For details of Francis Barnham's role as governor of St Thomas's Hospital, see Lena Cowen Orlin, *Locating Privacy in Tudor London*, OUP, 2007, pp. 30–1.
6. James Boswell's *The Life of Samuel Johnson*, 1791, vol. 4, p. 222.
7. Ann Windsor, Nottingham Record Office, Saville Ms 221/97/7.
8. In the Wellcome Collection, London.
9. Hyder Edward Rollins (ed.), *The Letters of John Keats, 1814–1821*, 2 vols, Harvard University Press, 1958, vol. 1, p. 114.
10. Quoted in George Worley, *Southwark Cathedral: The Cathedral and the See*, Bell, 1905, p. 127.

## Chapter 11 Yards of Ale

1. Thomas Dekker, *Lanthorne and Candle-light*, 1608.
2. Andrew Boorde, *Introduction of Knowledge and Dyetary of Helth*, ed. F.J. Furnivall, Early English Text Society, 1893, p. 256.
3. For more gruiting herbs, see Margaret Willes, *The Domestic Herbal: Plants for the Home in the Seventeenth Century*, Bodleian Library, 2020.
4. John Taylor, *Ale-vated into the Ale-titude, A learned Oration before a Civill Assembly of Ale Drinkers*, 1653, p. 11.
5. Geoffrey Chaucer, 'The Miller's Tale, Words between the Host and the Miller', *The Canterbury Tales*, Penguin Classics, 1958, p. 103.
6. Quoted in Pete Brown, *Shakespeare's Local*, Pan, 2013, p. 215.
7. Christopher Hudson is quoted in Browner, *Wrong Side of the River*, p. 14.
8. Ben Jonson, *Every Man in his Humour*, Act 2, Scene 1.
9. Latham and Matthews, *The Diary of Samuel Pepys*, vol. 7, pp. 271–2, 2 September 1666.

10. John Taylor, *The Carrier's Cosmographie; or, a Brief Relation, of the Innes, Ordinaries, Hostelries, and other lodgings in, and neere London*, 1637. Pete Brown provides details particularly for the George Inn in *Shakespeare's Local*, Pan, 2013, pp. 190–1.
11. Brown, *Shakespeare's Local*, p. 230.
12. The plan of their location in 1807 is reproduced in Thomas Almeroth-Williams, *City of Beasts: How Animals Shaped Georgian London*, Manchester University Press, 2019, p. 83.
13. K.C. Balderston (ed.), *Thraliana, the diary of Mrs Hester Lynch Thrale 1776–1809*, 2nd edn, Clarendon Press, 1951, vol. 1, p. 437.
14. Boswell, *The Life of Samuel Johnson*, 1791, entry for 6 April 1781.
15. Charles Dickens, *The Pickwick Papers*, Chapter X.
16. Brown, *Shakespeare's Local*, p. 248.
17. Grace Golden, *Old Bankside*, Williams & Norgate, 1951, pp. 66–7.

### Chapter 12  A Centre of Commerce

1. Carlin, *Medieval Southwark*, p. xix.
2. See Appendix (d), extract from the Charter of Edward IV, 9 November 1462, in Johnson, *Southwark and the City*.
3. De Beer (ed.), *Diary of John Evelyn*, vol. 3, pp. 255–6, 13 September 1660.
4. Latham and Matthews (eds), *The Diary of Samuel Pepys*, vol. 9, 21 September 1668, p. 313.
5. Quoted in 'London Rebel History', http://past=tense.org.uk/calendar2017.html.
6. Folger MS V.a.318. See Ian Archer, Caroline Barron and Vanessa Harding (eds), *Hugh Alley's Caveat: The Markets of London in 1598*, London Topographical Society, 1988.
7. Quoted in Brown, *Shakespeare's Local*, p. 135.
8. Mark Riddaway, 'Borough Market Began with a Bridge', www.boroughmarket.org.uk.
9. Riddaway, 'Borough Market Began with a Bridge'.
10. Blanchard Jerrold and Gustav Doré, *London: A Pilgrimage*, London 1873, p. 154.
11. Arthur St John Adcock, 'London's Food Supply', in George Sims (ed.), *Living London*, vol. 3, 1903, p. 295.
12. Charlie Chaplin's contributions to the Borough Market sports days are given in 'Market Life History', www.boroughmarket.org.uk. I am particularly grateful to Kate Howell and Mark Riddaway for this information.

### Chapter 13  Pathways in the Sky

1. Quoted in Frank Ferneyhough, *Liverpool and Manchester Railway, 1830–1930*, Robert Hale, 1980, p. 73.
2. Tindall, *The House by the Thames*, p. 125.
3. R. Tyas, *The Croydon Railway and its Adjacent Scenery*, 1839, quoted in R.H.G. Thomas, *London's First Railways: The London & Greenwich*, Batsford, 1972, p. 150.

4. *Kentish Mercury*, 31 March 1838.
5. Henry Mayhew, *London Labour and the London Poor*, Frank Cass, 1967 reprint, vol. 3, pp. 327, 330.
6. Quoted in Chris Heather, *London's Railway Stations*, Crowood Press, 2018, p. 95.
7. Quoted in Tindall, *The House by the Thames*, p. 164. She adds as an aside that 'One senses that the writer had no real idea what he was talking about'.
8. Another major consignment of bodies from Southwark was made in 2000 but this time to Sidcup, as Brookwood is now a private cemetery.
9. Quoted in David Brandon and Alan Brooke, *Bankside: London's Original District of Sin*, Amberley, 2013, p. 237.
10. Oliver Green, *Discovering London's Railway Stations*, Shire, 2010, p. 72.
11. Quoted in Brandon and Brooke, *Bankside*, p. 235.
12. William Rendle, *Old Southwark and its People*, W. Drewett, 1878, p. vi.
13. Brandon and Brooke, *Bankside*, p. 236.
14. Jerrold and Doré, *London: A Pilgrimage*, 1872, p. 121.
15. V.S. Pritchett, *A Cab at the Door, An Autobiography: Early Years*, Chatto & Windus, 1968, p. 183.
16. V.S. Pritchett, *London Perceived*, Chatto & Windus, 1974, p. 80.

## Chapter 14  A Tale of Two Boroughs

1. Jerry White, *Mansions of Misery: A Biography of the Marshalsea Debtors' Prison*, The Bodley Head, 2016, p. 1.
2. Tobias Smollett, *The Adventures of Roderick Random*, 1748, Chapter LXIV.
3. John Forster, *The Life of Charles Dickens*, 1872–74, vol. 1, pp. 24–5.
4. Forster, *The Life of Charles Dickens*, p. 11.
5. Charles Dickens, *The Posthumous Papers of the Pickwick Club*, 1836–37, Chapter XXXII.
6. Charles Dickens, *Oliver Twist*, Chapter L.
7. Charles Dickens, preface to *Little Dorrit*, 1857.
8. Charles Dickens, *All the Year Round*, 27 February 1869.
9. K.J. Fielding (ed.), *The Speeches of Charles Dickens*, Clarendon Press, 1960, p. 413.
10. Edwin Pugh, 'Representative London Streets', in George Sims (ed.), *Living London*, Cassell & Co. (see 15/3), vol. 1, 1902, p. 368.
11. John Hollingshead, *Ragged London in 1861*, Smith, Elder & Co., 1861, pp. 172–4.
12. The maps, along with Booth's notebooks, are in the library of the London School of Economics, www.booth.lse.ac.uk.
13. Charles Booth, *Life and Labour of the People in London*, vol. 2, Williams & Norgate, 1891, pp. 28–9, 391–5, 401.
14. See Martin Stilwell, 'Victorian Heroes: Peabody, Waterlow & Hartnoll', Part I, 'Southwark and its Housing Problem', MA dissertation, Kingston University, published online in 2015.
15. Quoted in Tindall, *The House by the Thames*, p. 165.
16. Stilwell, 'Victorian Heroes', p. 15.

17. Quoted in Alan Parkinson and Chris Wilson, *A Helping Hand: Improving the Lives of South London's Victorian and Edwardian Poor*, p. 31.

### Chapter 15  A New Diocese

1. Quoted in the guidebook to Southwark Cathedral, Scala Arts, 2012, p. 6.
2. Visitors can visit the Biscuit Museum if they email gary.maygold@btinternet.com.
3. Arthur Moss, 'Waterside London', in George Sims (ed.), *Living London*, Cassell & Co., vol. 1, 1902, pp. 68 and ff.
4. Moss, 'Waterside London'.
5. Charles Knight, *London*, 1844, vol. 3, p. 26.
6. Pritchett, *A Cab at the Door*, pp. 175-7, 183-5.
7. Grace Golden, *Old Bankside*, Williams & Norgate, 1951, p. 11.
8. Golden, *Old Bankside*, pp. 169-71.
9. Sir Patrick Abercrombie and J.H. Forshaw, *County of London Plan*, Macmillan & Co., 1943, Plate XLVIII.
10. Tindall, *The House by the Thames*, p. 209.
11. Quoted in Tindall, pp. 209-10.
12. Golden, *Old Bankside*, p. 14.
13. Abercrombie and Forshaw, *County of London Plan*, p. 132, Plate XLIX.
14. Quoted in the *News Chronicle's* souvenir of the Festival.
15. 'It's Another World', an exhibition of the buildings of the South Bank Festival of Britain, 1974.
16. Michael De-la-Noy, *Mervyn Stockwood*, Mowbray, 1996, p. 144.

### Chapter 16  Modern Times in Old Southwark

1. V.S. Pritchett, *London Perceived*, Chatto & Windus, 1974, pp. 63-4.
2. Writing in the *Listener*, 3 December 1987.
3. Eddie Oliver, writing in *The Times*, 19 April 1985, quoted in Tim Brindley, Yvonne Rydin and Gerry Stoker, *Remaking Planning: The Politics of Urban Change*, Routledge, 1996, p. 117.
4. Information taken from Jennie Howells' backstory in bermondseystreet.london/jam-yesterday-the-hartleys-jam-factory.
5. Abercrombie and Forshaw, *County of London Plan*, p. 131 and Plate L.
6. Tindall, *The House by the Thames*, p. 227.
7. Quoted in Barry Day, *This Wooden 'O': Shakespeare's Globe Reborn*, Oberon Books, 1996, p. 111.
8. The letters are quoted by Frances Spalding in *The Tate: A History*, Tate Publishing, 1998, pp. 279-80.
9. Recent figures record a total of 43.7 per cent, of which 31.2 per cent is council housing and the rest in the hands of housing associations.
10. See Alan F. Parkinson and Chris Wilson, *A Helping Hand*.

# SELECT BIBLIOGRAPHY

**Primary Sources**

Ingram, William and Alan H. Nelson (eds), *The Token Books of St Saviour Southwark*, tokenbooks.folger.edu

**Primary Printed Sources**

Abercrombie, Sir Patrick and J.H. Forshaw, *County of London Plan*, Macmillan & Co., 1943

Archer, Ian, Caroline Barron and Vanessa Harding (eds), *Hugh Alley's Caveat: The Markets of London in 1598*, London Topographical Society, 1998

Beer, E.S. de (ed.), *The Diary of John Evelyn*, Clarendon Press, 1955

Booth, Charles, *Life and Labour of the People in London*, vol. 2, Williams & Norgate, 1891

Concanen, Matthew and A. Morgan. *The History and Antiquities of the Parish of St Saviour's, Southwark*, Gale Ecco Editions, n.d.

Foakes, R.A. and R.T. Rickert (eds), *Henslowe's Diary*, CUP, 1961

Golden, Grace, *Old Bankside*, Williams & Norgate, 1951

Grenade, L. *The Singularities of London, 1578*, ed. Derek Keene and Ian Archer, London Topographical Society, 2014

Hollingshead, John, *Ragged London in 1861*, Smith, Elder & Co., 1861

Howes, John, *Contemporaneous Account in Dialogue-Form of the Foundation and Early History of Christs' Hospital and of Bridewell and St Thomas' Hospital, 1582, 1587*

Jerrold, Blanchard and Gustav Doré, *London: A Pilgrimage*, London Grant & Co., 1872

Latham, R.C. and W. Matthews (eds), *The Diary of Samuel Pepys*, Bell & Hyman, 1974

Mayhew, Henry, *London Labour and the London Poor*, Frank Cass, 1967 reprint

Mayhew, Henry, *Mayhew's London*, ed. Peter Quennell, Bracken Books, 1974

Pritchett, V.S., *A Cab at the Door, An Autobiography: Early Years*, Chatto & Windus, 1968

Pritchett, V.S., *London Perceived*, Chatto & Windus, 1974

Sims, George R. (ed.), *Living London*, 3 vols, Cassell and Co., 1902–3

Stow, John, *Survey of London*, reproduced from 1603 text, ed. Charles Lethbridge Kingsford, 2 vols, Clarendon Press, 1971

Tallis, John, *London Street Views*, London Topographical Society, 2002

Wriothesley, Charles, *A Chronicle of England During the Reign of the Tudors from AD 1485 to 1559*, ed. W.D. Hamilton, 2 vols, Camden Society, 1875

## Secondary Sources

Barlow, Frank (ed. and trans.), *The Life of King Edward Who Rests at Westminster*, 2nd edn, OUP, 1992

Blayney, Peter W.M., *The Stationers' Company and the Printers of London, 1501–1557*, vol. I, CUP, 2013

Boulton, Jeremy, *Neighbourhood & Society: A London Suburb in the 17th Century*, CUP, 1987

Bragg, Melvin, *The Adventure of English: The Biography of a Language*, Hodder & Stoughton, 2003

Brandon, David and Alan Brooke, *Bankside: London's Original District of Sin*, Amberley, 2013

Brown, Pete, *Shakespeare's Local*, Pan, 2012

Browner, Jessica A., 'Wrong Side of the River: London's Disreputable South Bank in the Sixteenth and Seventeenth century', *Essays in History*, vol. 36 (1994)

Carlin, Martha, *Medieval Southwark*, Amberley, 1996

Carlin, Martha, 'The Urban Development of Southwark, *c.* 1200 to 1550', unpublished PhD dissertation, University of Toronto, 1983

Chivers, Tom, *London Clay: Journeys in the Deep City*, Transworld, 2021

Coates, Richard and Andrew Breeze, *Celtic Voices, English Places: Studies of the Celtic Impact on Place Names in England*, Shaun Tyas, 2000

Day, Barry, *This Wooden 'O': Shakespeare's Globe Reborn*, Oberon Books, 1996

De-la-Noy, Michael, *Mervyn Stockwood*, Mowbray, 1996

Fisher, John H., *John Gower, Moral Philosopher and Friend of Chaucer*, Methuen, 1965

Gerhold, Dorian, *London Bridge and its Houses, c.1209–1761*, London Topographical Society, 2019

Godley, Robert, *Southwark: A History of Bankside*, Southwark Historical Association, nd

Hibbert, Christopher and Ben Weinreb, *London Encyclopedia*, Macmillan, 1983 edn

Hicks, Carola, *The King's Glass: A Story of Tudor Power and Secret Art*, Chatto & Windus, 2007

Johnson, David J., *Southwark and the City*, OUP, 1969

Kaufmann, Miranda, *Black Tudors: The Untold Story*, Oneworld, 2017

Lindley, Keith, *Popular Politics and Religion in Civil War London*, Scolar Press, 1997

Morris, Marc, *The Anglo-Saxons: A History of the Beginnings of England*, Penguin, 2021

Naismith, Rory, *Citadel of the Saxons: The Rise of Early London*, IB Tauris, 2019

Payne, David et al., *Southwark Cathedral*, Scala Arts & Heritage, 2012

Potter, Jennifer, *The Jamestown Brides: The Bartered Wives of the New World*, Atlantic Books, 2018

Rendle, William, *Old Southwark and its People*, W. Drewett, 1878

Rendle, William and Philip Norman, *Inns of Old Southwark and their Associations*, Longmans, 1888

Roe, Nicholas, *John Keats*, Yale University Press, 2012

Spalding, Frances, *The Tate: A History*, Tate Gallery, 1998

Spufford, Margaret, *Small Books and Pleasant Histories*, CUP, 1985

Stilwell, Martin, 'Victorian Heroes: Peabody, Waterlow and Hartnoll', MA dissertation, Kingston University, 2005

Taylor, Graham, *The Mayflower in Britain: How an Icon was Made in London*, Amberley, 2020

Tindall, Gillian, *The House by the Thames: And the People Who Lived There*, Chatto & Windus, 2006

Tindall, Gillian, *The Man Who Drew London: Wenceslaus Hollar in Reality and Imagination*, Pimlico, 2003

Uglow, Jenny, *Hogarth: A Life and a World*, Faber & Faber, 1998

Waller, Maureen, *London 1945: Life in the Debris of War*, John Murray, 2004

Whinney, Margaret, *Sculpture in Britain 1530–1830*, Pelican History of Art, Penguin Books, 1988

White, Jerry, *Mansions of Misery: A Biography of the Marshalsea Debtors' Prison*, The Bodley Head, 2016

Wilson, Chris, *A Great Boon and Blessing: A History of Edward Edwards Charity, 1717–2017*, available via chriswilson@wilson.tf

Wilson, Chris and Alan Parkinson, *A Helping Hand: Improving the Lives of South London's Victorian and Edwardian Poor*, available via chriswilson@wilson.tf

Wolmar, Christian, *Cathedrals of Steam*, Atlantic Books, 2020

Worley, George, *Southwark Cathedral: The Cathedral and the See*, Bell, 1905

### Maps

A Map of Medieval London, the City, Westminster & Southwark, 1270 to 1300, The Historic Towns Trust

A Map of Tudor London, England's Greatest City in 1520, *British Historic Towns Atlas*, in association with the London Topographical Society

### Online Sources

'The Bishop's Profitable Sex Workers', wellcomecollection.org/articles

'The George Inn, Norton St Philip: Wine, Wool and Worship', www.exploring-buildinghistory.co.uk

Hagland, Jan Ragnar and Bruce Wilson, 'Fact or Folklore: The Viking attack on London Bridge', *London Archaeologist*, Spring 2005, https://www.medievalists.net/2010/08/fact-or-folklore-the-viking-attack-on-london-bridge/

'The Old Operating Theatre', www.thegarret.org.uk

'Remembering the Winchester Geese on Bankside', pastinthepresent.net/2012/11/22

Riddaway, Mark, 'Borough Market Began with a Bridge', www.boroughmarket.org.uk

Sweetland, David, 'A London Inheritance' blog, alondoninheritance.com

'Today in London Festival History: Illegal Attempt to Hold Southwark Fair, 1763', pasttenseblog.wordpress.com/2017/09/19

United St Saviour's Charity, www.ustc.org.uk

# INDEX

*Illustrative material is entered in italics*